THE PUNISHED PEOPLES

Aleksandr M. Nekrich

THE PUNISHED PEOPLES

The deportation and fate of Soviet minorities at the end of the Second World War

Translated from the Russian
by George Saunders

W · W · NORTON & COMPANY · INC · NEW YORK

Copyright © 1978 by W. W. Norton & Company, Inc.
Published simultaneously in Canada by George J. McLeod Limited, Toronto.
All Rights Reserved
First Edition

Library of Congress Cataloging in Publication Data

Nekrich, Aleksandr Moiseevich.
  The punished peoples.

  Includes index.
  1. Minorities—Russia.   2. Population transfers.
3. Russia—Political government—1936–1953.   I. Title.
DK33.N44 1978   940.53′150694   77–26201
ISBN 13: 978-0-393-00068-9

Designed by Paula Wiener
Printed in the United States of America.
1 2 3 4 5 6 7 8 9 0

To those of my countrymen who still believe in justice

Contents

Author's Note

THIS BOOK was completed in the spring of 1975. In the summer of that year the first copy of the manuscript was sent to the West. I sent it out because there was no chance of this work being published in the Soviet Union. Nor was there for any of my other principal works.

For the last ten years an unstated quota has been set for me—one article per year in an academic publication of limited circulation. Wider publication was refused even for research that I carried out in accordance with the projects of the Institute of General History of the USSR Academy of Sciences, where, for all practical purposes, I worked throughout the postwar period, research that had been approved for publication by the academic council of the Institute. The fact is, I received the salary of senior research scholar and doctor of historical sciences (by Western standards this corresponds to the position of full professor) in return for my silence.

I was ostracized because of my book *June 22, 1941,* published in Moscow in 1965 by Nauka (Science) Press, and subsequently translated and published in the United States and many European countries.

In June 1967, for my refusal to acknowledge my "errors," the

Party Control Commission of the CPSU Central Committee, presided over by Politburo member A. Pelshe, expelled me from the party. In August 1967, by order of the authorities, my book was removed from most libraries in the Soviet Union and destroyed—the exception being those libraries which have a "special collection." Since then the professional opportunities available to me as a historian have been limited in the extreme. My attempts to break out of this charmed circle and still remain in the Soviet Union ended in failure. Therefore I made the decision to leave my country and did so in June 1976.

I wish to work, and to have the results of my labors visible. I hope that in the West I shall be able to publish my works freely and—no less important—to write freely, shaking off the inner policeman of self-censorship once and for all, and no longer being inhibited by fear of official censorship.

Aleksandr M. Nekrich
London, July 1976

Acknowledgments

The Punished Peoples could hardly have been written without the help of some people of good will, my countrymen. They have provided me with documentary materials and recollections, read my manuscript, and expressed their opinions. To my regret, it is impossible to name these courageous people now because it would be damaging to them. But they can be sure of my sincere gratitude.

I am indebted to my first reader in the West, Dr. Nils Morten Udgaard, a Norwegian historian and journalist, who has given me his invaluable help. My English colleague, Professor Leonard Schapiro, has read my manuscript and supported the idea of its publication.

The subject of my manuscript was discussed at the London School of Economics, at Glasgow University, and at Harvard University, by courtesy of Professors Leonard Schapiro, Peter Reddaway, Alec Nove, and Edward L. Keenan.

All the work in the last stage of preparation of this manuscript was done during a fellowship at the Russian Research Center of Harvard University. The director of the Center, Professor Edward L. Keenan, and the staff created favorable conditions for finishing the manuscript.

The manuscript was translated from Russian into English by George Saunders with great care and attention to details.

Active support to *The Punished Peoples* was given by Professor Robert C. Tucker of Princeton University, who recommended the manuscript to W. W. Norton & Company, Inc., where James L. Mairs and Emily Garlin edited and prepared it for publication.

Christine P. Balm and Mary Christopher of the Russian Research Center of Harvard University typed the text with exceptional accuracy.

I wish to express my sincere gratitude to all the people who have given their encouragement and support to my work.

Aleksandr M. Nekrich
Cambridge, Massachusetts
September, 1977

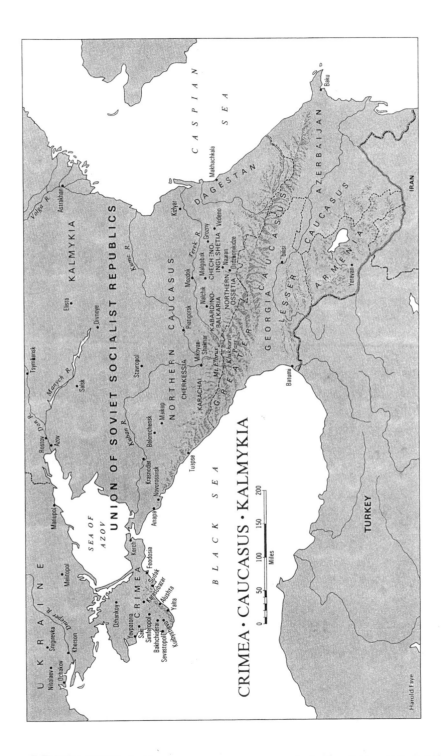

CRIMEA · CAUCASUS · KALMYKIA

THE PUNISHED PEOPLES

Introduction

I⊤ WAS May 1944 and I was twenty-four years old. I was serving in the political department of the Second Guards Army. Our troops were liberating the Crimea. In the aftermath of the heavy fighting at Sevastopol I found myself in Yevpatoria, a small resort city on the Black Sea coast.

Waiting for someone I needed to see, I was standing outside a theater building where a meeting of the town's active party membership was in session. I had instructions from my superiors to set up a town commission to investigate the crimes of the German fascist occupation forces and make sure it was running smoothly.

The theater doors opened and the slim, dark-haired chairman of the town Soviet, K., appeared. "How are things?" I asked him— that ordinary question to which no reply is expected. But a reply was forthcoming, and it was a puzzling one to me. "We're getting ready for the big day." I nodded, simply to be polite. In fact I couldn't imagine what he meant. But this book should have been started at that very moment.

Our conversation had barely begun when an unfamiliar colonel-general came out the doors of the theater. "Who is that?" "That's Kobulov, Beria's deputy," my interlocutor replied, for some reason lowering his voice. K. drove off. I found the person I wanted and we went about our business.

The next day, or perhaps two days later, I was returning from Yevpatoria to the political department headquarters in the town of Saki. An unusual air of tension prevailed everywhere. A friend told me: "Tonight they are going to ship off the Tatars, every last one. The men have been locked up for the time being in the registration and enlistment building." I walked past that building, pausing for a moment. Through the closed doors someone's voice carried, a rapid, fiery speech in an unfamiliar language.

Today I must return to that past in my thoughts. After all, the study of the past is my profession.

No one—neither the people nor the government leaders—ever imagined that the war would start out so unfavorably for the USSR. The psychological preparations for the war caused people to expect not only that we would be victorious from the beginning but also that the war would be fought on enemy territory. A reflection of that attitude could be seen in the widespread rumors in Moscow on the first evening of the war that Soviet troops were storming Koenigsberg.

How much more bitter and hard to bear the truth turned out to be. After heavy fighting along the border, beginning at dawn on June 22, 1941, the Soviet front line was broken, and Hitler's troops, driving deep wedges and leaving behind them thoroughly defeated Soviet armies lacking any strategic leadership, moved rapidly ahead into the heart of the country. On June 28 Minsk was taken, in September the battle for Kiev was fought, in October the fascist armies stood on the outskirts of Moscow and Leningrad, Tauria had fallen, and the enemy was knocking at the gates of the Crimea.

In three months of war the Soviet armed forces had lost at least three million persons.

The courageous struggle of the soldiers and commanders of the Red Army, of individual units, and even of large formations could not contain the enemy onslaught.

The population of the abandoned Soviet territories watched the retreating Red Army units with tears in their eyes and, soon after, gazed with horror at the endless columns of Soviet soldiers being marched off as prisoners-of-war. The Nazis took between three and four million prisoners in 1941. They were driven into hastily constructed camps where, denied food and water and subjected to insults and humiliations by their guards, they soon began to die off. Tens of thousands of prisoners-of-war were simply shot by the Nazis.

Alexander Dallin reports that by May 1944, 1,918,000 prisoners of war had died in Hitler's camps. In addition, about 1,248,000 were exterminated.[1]

The confusion and disarray of the Soviet military and political leadership were intensified by the de facto desertion of Stalin, who hid himself in his country home at Kuntsevo, abandoning his post for an entire week. Fortunately the people didn't know that Stalin was the first deserter of the war.

Because of the circumstances, a new psychological atmosphere began to develop during the very first days and weeks of the war in the enemy-occupied republics and regions of the Soviet Union. The farther east the war moved, the more hopeless the situation seemed to the population that found itself under the enemy's boot in 1941. As yet there was no partisan movement; here and there it was being created from scattered groups that had broken out of encirclement and were stranded deep in the enemy's rear. Moreover, diversionary and underground groups had not yet undertaken decisive action. The enemy arrived. The *Einsatzkommandos* * were already on the prowl, hunting down Jews and Communists and their families for extermination. In the marketplaces, on the walls of buildings, and on fences white leaflets gleamed, bearing the commands of the new Germany authorities. And, here and there, black-and-crimson posters appeared depicting a man with plastered-down hair and a Charlie Chaplin mustache, with the caption "Hitler the Liberator."

---

* A special branch of the German army devoted to seeking out and destroying "enemies of the Third Reich."

From the earliest days of the occupation the Germans began to set up their own administrative apparatus, which in each town consisted of a *Burgomeister* (German-appointed mayor), his deputies, a chief of *Polizei* (police), and local police officers. In the villages, *starosty* (elders) were appointed. In a number of localities recruiting went on among the local inhabitants to form "self-defense" detachments. Later on, *Hilfswillige* (volunteers) also began to be recruited for service in the rear echelons of the German army and, later still, for participation in punitive actions against the partisans, as well as in front-line operations.

No historian has yet succeeded in gaining access to the archive materials that would make it possible to piece together an accurate picture of who the Soviet citizens were who entered the service of the Nazi occupation apparatus, to clarify their social make-up. From the scanty information published in connection with local trials of war criminals held in the USSR it is possible to isolate certain categories. First of all, there were individuals who had been convicted by the Soviet authorities at one time or another, hardened criminals, and deserters. A second category consisted of people hostile to Soviet rule because of their political convictions. Prominent among them were advocates of secession from the USSR for the Ukraine, Byelorussia, the southern and eastern borderlands, and the Baltic states. They hoped to achieve their aims with the help of Hitler and Germany. Third, there apparently was a substantial layer of people without political convictions, conformists willing to serve any regime. Besides these, there were people who simply lost their bearings, demoralized by the defeats of the Red Army and lacking any hope of victory.

It was with such people that the local apparatuses were staffed, including the local police.

Separate mention should be made of the prisoners-of-war. They were placed under horrifying and inhuman conditions, next to which the conditions provided for prisoners of war from the Western countries, especially the Americans and British, could be called quite satisfactory. The captured Soviet soldiers' situation was complicated further by the fact that their own government in fact repudiated them, leaving them to the mercies of fate. The prisoners-of-war had this dinned into their heads incessantly by their own tormentors, the guards, and by those seeking to recruit them to serve the Germans.

Many prisoners had to face the problem of choosing whether to perish behind barbed wire in a German camp or to betray their oath, their own people, and their entire past life by signing up as "volunteers." Many of those who took the latter course planned to seize the first favorable occasion and return to their own people, to the Red Army. But few succeeded in doing so.

On the Manych in the winter of 1943 I first saw former Soviet soldiers dressed in German uniforms. I asked one, then another, "How could you have done this, fellows?" I felt sorry for them but at the same time I could scarcely bear to look at them. They remained silent, staring at the ground or looking off to the side, but after a while one of them looked directly at me, and with an expression of such unconcealed despair that my heart shrank. And this is what he told me. In the summer of 1941 he was taken prisoner. They were herded off to a camp at Ovruch. And there it began: German guards and Ukrainian *Polizei* (it is hard to say who brutalized the prisoners worse); hunger and beatings, beatings and hunger; and all the while the recruiters—not Germans, but our own people, Russians and Ukrainians—insistently repeating the promises of a soft and comfortable life. "But if you stay here, there's no way around it, you'll die like a dog." For a long time he remained firm, but in the summer of 1942 he could hold out no longer. He put on the German uniform, hoping to escape at the first opportunity. But no such occasion presented itself. The German command kept his battalion of "volunteers" in the rear, and only during the retreat was the battalion compelled to cover the withdrawal of the German units. As soon as the German soldiers had gone, many of the Russian "volunteers" threw down their guns. And that was how he came to be back among his own. I do not know what became of him. But his look of despair, of no hope and no future, engraved itself in my memory forever.

Hitler was categorically opposed to the formation of auxiliary or front-line units composed of Russians. He distrusted, hated, and feared them. Tens of millions of Russians were slated for annihilation, and the remainder were to become the slaves of the Reich. The Fuehrer was also opposed to giving any support to the Ukrainian nationalists, and in general he took a negative view of the nationalism of the conquered peoples, regarding nationalists as potential enemies of the Reich. However, in practice the Nazi command made use of the nationalists for its own purposes. For example, in the Ukraine, the nationalist leaders Stepan Bandera and Andrei Melnyk were used to help form local "self-defense" detachments. The concentration-camp guard force was similarly staffed, as were the town police, the *Einsatzkommandos*, etc. At the same time the Nazis decisively cut short any attempt by the Ukrainian separatists to establish their own governmental forms. The rival "governments" of Bandera in Lvov and Melnyk in Kiev were dispersed by the Germans and the leaders placed under arrest. Later, one section of the Banderists engaged in armed struggle against both the Red Army and the Soviet partisans, on the one hand, and the German army, on the other. According to German data, the "self-defense" forces in the Ukraine reached the impressive figure of 180,000 by mid-1942.[2]

In August 1941 a Major Kononov of the Soviet army went over to the enemy, taking with him part of the personnel of the 436th Infantry Regiment. Kononov, a Don Cossack, was given permission to form a Cossack cavalry regiment, which reached a strength of seventy-seven officers and 1,799 enlisted men. Hitler consented to the formation of Cossack units because he had been told that the Cossacks were descendants not of the Slavs but of the Ostrogoths![3]

The formation of "self-defense" forces coincided with the period of the Wehrmacht's greatest successes (the summer of 1941 and the summer of 1942).

The Cossack formations were made a part of the Wehrmacht. In the summer of 1942, the general staff of the German ground forces established a special department to handle the formation of

military, auxiliary, and police forces from the ranks of former Soviet citizens. By early 1943 there were 176 battalions and thirty-
eight companies in this category, with a total of 130,000 to
150,000 men. The overwhelming majority of them made up the
so-called Russian Liberation Army, under the command of former
Lieutenant General of the Soviet Army A. A. Vlasov. By the end
of the war Vlasov had 300,000 men.

The non-Russian military formations in the Wehrmacht at the
end of the war numbered 700,000. Thus the total number of
former Soviet citizens who took up arms on the enemy side was
approximately one million. An impressive figure, it might seem.
But this represented only 1/194th, or 0.5 percent, of the total population of the Soviet Union at the end of 1939, and only 1.75 percent of the able-bodied male population of sixteen or older. The
vast majority opposed the enemy.

The military units made up of "Oriental peoples" included the
Turkestan legions and battalions (i.e., people of Central Asian origin), as well as Georgian, Armenian, Turk, Volga Tatar, Crimean Tatar, Mountaineer (i.e., people from the Northern Caucasus), Kalmyk, and some other legions and battalions.

But can we really equate such "legionnaires" with the populations of the republics from which they came? Of course not.
Those who took up arms against their homeland, who stood in the
same ranks with the Nazis, were renegades and traitors to their
own peoples.

Since August–September 1941, when special trains full of
Volga Germans proceeded eastward and their national state structure, the Volga German Autonomous Soviet Socialist Republic,
was dismantled; since the period in 1943–44 when the same road
of sorrow was traveled by freight trains loaded with Kalmyks,
Karachai, Chechens, Ingush, Crimean Tatars, and Balkars likewise deprived of their native homes and hearths, their property,
and their autonomy—since those times and those events more
than thirty years have passed.

Quite a few lies have been spread about these unfortunate peoples who were forced to pay, one and all, for the treason of a small number of their countrymen.

In the second half of the 1950s the Kalmyks and the deported peoples of the Northern Caucasus were completely rehabilitated by the government authorities. They returned to the lands which their ancestors had inhabited for centuries and their autonomy was restored.

But the chariot of justice travels slowly in the USSR; it barely pokes along. Far from their traditional lands, the Volga Germans, now numbering some two million, and the Crimean Tatars, half a million in number, still live as before. Yet the sanctions against them have formally been lifted; under the law, they are allowed to live in any part of the Soviet Union, and consequently in the Crimea as well.

Yet even today falsehoods still circulate, especially among the population of the Crimea, to the effect that the entire Crimean Tatar population collaborated with the German occupation. These lies are spread and encouraged by groups and individuals who have an interest in preventing the return of the Tatars to the Crimea.

Similar fairy tales were spread at one time about the Volga Germans, who were said to have hidden Nazi spies and saboteurs at the beginning of the war; and about the Chechens, Ingush, and Karachai, who were said to have served, every man, woman, and child, as guides for the Nazis during their offensive against the Caucasus in 1942; as well as about the Balkars, all of whom were said to have gone over to the enemy. As proof of this last assertion, a great deal was made for many years of the fact that a white horse had been sent as a gift to Hitler from Balkaria. This fact was blown up and magnified with incredible zeal by functionaries in every possible government office at every level, so that there came to be not just one white horse but entire herds of Caucasian racers grazing and cavorting on the slopes beneath Hitler's Berghof retreat. This legend is already half-forgotten, and the wounds inflicted upon the peoples of the Caucasus are healed somewhat. But how do things stand in the case of the Volga Germans and the Crimean Tatars? Where is the healing remedy that will close up the deep wounds inflicted by the many years of exile? And when will this exile be ended?

Rude attacks against the Crimean Tatar people continue to this day. In December 1973 in Simferopol three Crimean Tatars were placed on trial—not traitors, not butchers who served the Germans, not even criminals who had been amnestied in 1955, but simply three grown persons who had returned to their historic homeland and wished to remain there. The ''people's judge'' who presided at the trial, a certain Mironova, in her remarks demanded that the Tatars ''get out of the Crimea'' and go live in the region to which they had been deported, or else ''the harshest possible measures'' would be employed against them.[4] And this was said by a representative of the judiciary six years after the decree of the Presidium of the Supreme Soviet which restored to the Tatars all their civil rights—including the right to live in their own homeland.

And why were Turks, Kurds, and Khemshils* deported to the east? Why were Greeks living on the Black Sea coast deported in 1944? Why were several tens of thousands of Armenians deported from Armenia soon after the end of the war? After all, none of them had presented Hitler with the gift of a white horse!

Can we today answer the questions: By what mechanism were these decisions, affecting the fate of entire peoples, made? By what government body, on the basis of whose reports or memorandums? What part did the local authorities, military bodies, and state security agencies play in these decisions? Who bore the personal responsibility for these crimes? Stalin himself? Beria? Or X, Y, and Z? In my opinion, we can arrive at only approximate answers to these questions at this time.

Let us note parenthetically that the decision-making mecha-

---

* ''Khemshils'' is a corruption of ''Khemshins''—the name used by Armenian Muslims from Turkish Armenia who lived along the Black Sea coast in Adzharia. They numbered about twenty thousand altogether, with some seven to eight thousand living on Soviet territory.

nisms are nowhere surrounded with such impenetrable secrecy as in the Soviet government, and nowhere has the invisible system of mutual cover-up and tacit understanding and the prevalence of code words and conventional formulations acquired such a sophisticated character. The unwritten laws by which the apparatus functions and under whose cover orders and instructions are drafted and issued, the anonymity of their authors in relation to the public at large, reliably conceal not only blunders and mistakes but also, when necessary, crimes. And all this serves as a tremendous obstacle to any objective study or investigation.

There is a need, long overdue, for this unhappy and shameful part of our recent past to be examined with the eyes of the historian. Not surprisingly, this subject does not appear in any of the plans for scientific research work of the USSR Academy of Sciences. I have carried it out at my own risk, because in the USSR there is an unspoken ban on discussion of matters involving official lawlessness or arbitrary acts.

I

The Crimea under Nazi Occupation, and the Crimean Tatars

THE CRIMEAN AUTONOMOUS SOVIET SOCIALIST REPUBLIC* was under German occupation for quite a long time, from late October 1941 to April–May 1944.

The Crimea had first been annexed to Russia in 1783. The Tatars were the most numerous of the old, pre-Russian population there, the next most numerous being the Karaites and Krymchaks. In the Crimea the Tatars had evolved their own unique culture, built towns and villages, cultivated the soil, tended vineyards and orchards, and constructed roads. Under Russian rule the Tatar population, despite persecution from time to time by chauvinist-minded tsarist administrators, displayed complete loyalty to the Russian state. After the revolution and during the civil war the bulk of the Crimean Tatar population supported the Soviet side.

On the eve of World War II, in 1939, the inhabitants of the Crimea numbered approximately 1,127,000.[1] The dominant national group was Russian, constituting about half the population of the peninsula; 25 percent of the population were Tatars, 10 percent Ukrainians, and the remaining 15 percent Germans, Jews, Greeks, Bulgarians, Czechs, Estonians, Karaites, Krymchaks,

---

* The Crimean ASSR was established on October 18, 1921, as part of the Russian Socialist Federative Soviet Republic (RSFSR) [*translator's note*].

and others—an international community that lived together fairly harmoniously in this favored part of the world, with its mountains, vineyards, and maritime cities. Conflicts between national groups broke out only rarely. Some did occur around the time of the establishment of several colonies of Jewish settlers in the Crimea, a development that angered a section of the Crimean Tatar population, who saw this as a threat to lands they considered their own.*

Hitler's armies marched into the Crimea on October 24, 1941. The entire peninsula—with the exception of Sevastopol, which held out until July 1942, and Kerch, which fell in May of that year—came under German occupation.

Even before the attack on the USSR the future of the Crimea was frequently discussed by the top German leaders. There were two basic points of view: that of Alfred Rosenberg, the chief Nazi theoretician on the "Eastern question," who in 1941 held the post of *Reichsminister* of the occupied Eastern territories and who thought it expedient to join the Crimea with the Ukraine to create a puppet government centered in Kiev; and that of the Fuehrer himself (and of Himmler), who favored the total elimination of any kind of state structure in the conquered territory of the USSR. Encouragement of nationalism, whether Ukrainian or any other, conflicted with plans for the creation of "the Greater German Reich." As for the Crimea, at a conference on July 16, 1941, at Hitler's headquarters, with Rosenberg, Keitel, Goering, Lammers, and Bormann in attendance, the decision was made to treat the Crimea as an "imperial territory," to annex it directly to the Reich and germanize it. The deportation of all "national elements" from the Crimea—Russians, Ukrainians, and Tatars—was planned.[2]

In August 1941 and July 1942 Hitler insisted on the evacuation

---

* In tsarist Russia, Jews were forbidden to own or rent land. These and other restrictions were lifted after the revolution of 1917. In the nineteen-twenties a committee was formed to promote Jewish land settlements, the first of which were begun in 1923 in the Crimea. Some Crimean Tatars opposed these settlements.

of the entire Russian population from the Crimea and the immediate colonization of the peninsula by Germans. However, at the insistence of Goering, who feared an economic collapse in the Crimea and the unfavorable effect that would have on the functioning of the German army, the implementation of this deportation plan was postponed. All the different Nazi agencies continued to work out possible variants for the germanization of the Crimea. For example, Himmler's office had the intention of converting the Crimea into a resort area for "deserving SS-men." To improve travel connections the construction of an *Autobahn* (highway) from Krakow to the Crimea was proposed.[3] There was also a plan to resettle the Germans of the southern Tyrol in the Crimea and thereby to finally settle longstanding disputes with Italy.[4] At the very beginning of the occupation, in December 1941, Rosenberg proposed that Simferopol be renamed "Gotheburg" and Sevastopol "Theodorichshaven."[5]

After the occupation of the Crimea and of Melitopol region the occupation forces established a General Commissariat of Tauria, with A. Frauenfeld, a Nazi from Austria, in charge. He began an intensive search for proofs of a German historical claim to the Crimea.

The General Commissariat was under the "Reichskommissariat of the Ukraine," i.e., Gauleiter Erich Koch. However, as long as the Crimea was considered a front-line zone, operational control remained in the hands of the military authorities, assisted by the SD and SS, in particular by Einsatzgruppe D, commanded by Ohlendorf.*

The first act of the occupation regime was the registration of the population followed by the elimination of "hostile" and "racially impure" elements. Included among these were Jews, Gypsies, Communists, and their families.

According to German documentary records, 91,678 persons were liquidated in the Crimea between October 1941 and April

---

* After the war Ohlendorf was brought before the Allied court and in April 1948 was sentenced to death by hanging.

1942, i.e., nearly one-tenth of the population. The annihilation of the numerically small Karaite population began but was brought to a halt by the courageous intervention of the spiritual and secular head of the world Karaite community, the *khokhan* Hajji-Serai Shapshal (Sergei Markovich Shapshal), whose seat of office was then in Lithuania.*

The Germans had to keep in mind the complicated situation in which their army found itself. They also wished to bring Turkey over to their side, but the Turkish government had expressed its concern about the future of Soviet territories inhabited by Muslim peoples, including the Crimea. Consequently the German occupation forces followed a policy of dividing up the nationalities.

Appointments to the administrative apparatus from among the local population were made according to national criteria. Where the majority was Russian, Russians were appointed; where it was Ukrainian, Ukrainians were appointed; and where Tatar, Tatars were appointed.[6] Thus, approximately three-fourths of the appointments went to Russians and Ukrainians, and one-fourth to Crimean Tatars.

Events here followed the same pattern as they did wherever German fascist rule was imposed on Soviet territory—the mass arrest and shooting of "racially impure" and "hostile" elements, deportation of slave laborers to the Reich, economic exploitation, destruction of scientific and cultural institutions, plundering of cultural treasures, and fanning of racial hatred. In the Crimea the occupation authorities closed down all institutions of higher education and teachers' institutes, and the public schools were di-

---

* This story has a certain broader interest. An SS colonel in the Ostland administration, a specialist in Eastern cultures, warned Shapshal that the Karaites were about to be exterminated. On this colonel's advice, Shapshal appealed to Rosenberg in a memorandum outlining the history of his people. He explained the ethnic origins of the Karaites and their religious ties with the Jews. Shapshal had the courage to write, in conclusion: "The Ten Commandments of Moses stand even today at the basis of world civilization. This world-historical service of the Jewish people can never be forgotten or erased." Shapshal succeeded in persuading Rosenberg that the relation between the Jews and the Karaites was purely religious and not ethnic.

vided along national lines. In the schools, as in a number of vocational institutes that the German authorities allowed to continue in operation, the subjects offered were limited to those serving the needs of German industry. At the same time, the occupation authorities permitted the opening of fifty mosques and a number of Orthodox churches, counting on support for their policies from the clergy and, through them, from the various congregations.

Compared to the Russian population, the Crimean Tatars enjoyed certain advantages. However, as the German documents show, the policy pursued toward the Tatars was purely utilitarian and served the purposes of German propaganda.

In April 1942, at a conference on questions of propaganda among the Crimean Tatars attended by representatives of the German Foreign Ministry and the High Command of the Ground Forces, it was stressed that the aim of all measures taken was to win over at least twenty thousand Tatar "volunteers" to serve in the German army. For this purpose it was proposed that the occupation regime be relaxed in relation to the Tatars. Especially emphasized at the conference was the propagandistic nature of all concessions. These promises and concessions, it was pointed out, were not an anticipation of the decisions that would be taken concerning the Crimean Tatars after the Germany victory.[7]

One question debated by the German leadership was whether to grant the Crimean Tatars self-government in any form. By July 1942 this question had been answered in the negative.[8]

The special policies in relation to the Crimean Tatars had the foreign-policy aim, as we have mentioned, of winning Turkey over to an actively pro-German policy. And the interest expressed by the Turkish leaders "in the fate of the Muslim peoples living in the territory of the USSR" was used to advance Germany's most pressing strategic war aims in the Near East.

The person who transmitted and in part inspired this policy was the German ambassador in Ankara, von Papen.* On the Turkish

---

* In a political report to the German Foreign Ministry dated November 1, 1941—i.e., before German troops had entered the Crimea—von Papen once again proposed (having made his first proposal earlier) that an administration including

side the same role was played by generals F. Erden and H. Erkilet, leaders of the pan-Turkist movement.* In the fall of 1941 they visited the Crimea on an official mission to study the German tactics on the southern front. They obtained permission from the German authorities for a delegation of Crimean Tatar émigrés in Turkey to go to Berlin.[9]

In April 1942 the Turkish premier, Saracoglu, informed von Papen that the Turkish government could not officially support the pan-Turkist movement, but he gave permission for persons not holding official positions to establish contact with the German government on this matter.[10]

The Turkish leaders, in their subsequent talks with Hitler's diplomats, frequently emphasized their interest in the defeat of the USSR and, correspondingly, in "the fate of the Turkic peoples."[11]

The Soviet government later used this expression of "interest" against the peoples of the Northern Caucasus whom it accused of treason. These unfortunate peoples learned to their surprise that they were agents of a foreign power.

The German flirtation with Turkey concerning "the fate of the Turkic peoples" ended as soon as Hitler concluded that the Turks were not going to let his troops pass through Turkish territory to reach the Near East but would continue to balance between the Axis and the anti-German bloc. In response to Premier Saracoglu's expression of concern over Germany's reluctance to grant independence to the territories inhabited by Turkic peoples,[12] Hitler suggested that von Papen show "greater restraint" and not get into "untimely discussions."[13] The playing with pan-Turkism came to an end.

But many months before this decision the Crimean Tatar émi-

Crimean Tatars be established in the Crimea. "This," he wrote, "would have a strong political effect in Turkey" (*Dokumenty,* no. 12, p. 44).

* The pan-Turkist (or pan-Turanian) movement, unofficially supported by the Turkish government, advocated the unification of all Turkic peoples living on Soviet territory into a state that, while nominally remaining independent, would in fact be in the orbit of Turkey.

gré delegation had been admitted to Berlin at the request of Erkilet and Erden and had also been allowed to visit the Crimea. Although these émigrés did not conceal from the Germans their wish to see an "independent Tatar state" established in the Crimea, the exact opposite of the German plans, the Nazis did not decline to make use of the émigrés. They needed them to help recruit volunteer units among the Crimean Tatars.

In the interwar period there were several Crimean Tatar émigré centers—in Poland, Romania, and Turkey. Some of the émigré Tatars who lived in Poland and Romania were active in the Prometheus organization—founded by émigrés from the Caucasus who in the 1920s had a pro-English or pro-French orientation. The most active figures were Seydahmet and Kirimal. Seydahmet, a former teacher from Bakhchiserai, collaborated on a Tatar journal published in Romania. Kirimal was a lawyer active in a Crimean Tatar émigré group in Poland. Before the war they had been oriented toward France and England, as had all the elements in the Prometheus group. With the outbreak of war, they emigrated to Turkey. There Tatars from the Crimea had lived for centuries (half a million strong) without being assimilated or abandoning their own language and culture, much to the Turks' surprise. After the Crimean War a section of the Crimean Tatar population had been forcibly expelled from the Crimea by the tsarist government and many, then too, had gone to Turkey. Seydahmet and Kirimal quickly found common ground with the leaders of the "pan-Turanian movement," Erkilet and Erden, and at their recommendation made contact with the German authorities. It was Kirimal, together with the other émigrés who went to Germany and then to the fascist-occupied Crimea, who put the term "Crimean Turks"* into circulation, a term that did much harm to the Crimean Tatars in the fateful year of 1944.

The émigrés arrived in the Crimea after "Muslim committees" had been set up by permission of the occupation authorities. These committees were granted regulatory functions in the sphere

* Kirimal even titled his memoirs *The National Struggle of the Crimean Turks.*

of Tatar cultural and religious life, but they remained under strict German control, including in religious matters. When the Tatars wished to elect someone as *mufti* of the Crimea (i.e., their highest religious office), the German authorities not only prevented the election of a candidate who did not have their confidence but also forced him to flee to Romania. The "Muslim committees" were played up in Tatar nationalist propaganda as the direct descendants of the "Mohammedan committees" of the time of the civil war and German occupation in 1918, when Tatar nationalists representing the interests of the upper strata of Crimean Tatar society had tried to proclaim their own independent state (though in fact it was dependent on the troops of the Kaiser).

From the Simferopol Muslim committee, which was actually the central Muslim committee, the émigré representatives obtained recognition for themselves as delegates to the German Ministry for the Occupied Eastern Territories (Ostministerium), and with that they left for Berlin. In 1943 the Ostministerium established a department to deal with this area.

But having permitted the formation of the Muslim committees, the publication of a newspaper and a magazine, and the opening of a theater and of schools with instruction in Tatar, the German authorities began to put pressure on the Crimean Tatar population to join "self-defense" detachments and other formations to combat Soviet partisans. The organization of Tatar units began in January 1942. By February 15, only 1,632 persons had been enrolled (fourteen companies and six battalions).[14] In addition, in camps for Soviet prisoners of war in Simferopol, Nikolaev, Kherson, and Dzhankoy, thanks to considerable help by the émigrés, the occupation authorities managed to recruit several thousand more as "volunteers" (*Hilfswillige*) for the Wehrmacht's auxiliary units. The statistics on the total number of Crimean Tatars in German formations are eloquent. Kirimal, for example, gives a figure of between eight thousand and twenty thousand for the period 1941–44.[15] It should be kept in mind that battalions which are sometimes referred to in the literature as "Tatar" were in fact made up of many different nationalities.[16]

The overwhelming majority of "volunteers" were recruited among Soviet prisoners of war. They often "volunteered" under compulsion. Although some perhaps had political reasons, personal considerations were decisive in most cases. They wanted to live—to last out the war rather than die under the impossible conditions in the camps. Where there were political motivations, in the opinion of several historians, these were in reaction to the excesses of collectivization and the anti-religious measures of the Soviet authorities.* The majority of Crimean Tatars recruited for service as *Polizei* or for anti-partisan combat duty generally demonstrated passivity, resigning themselves to the vicissitudes of fate wholly in the spirit of the Koran. One of the German documents of the time notes that among the "self-defense" formations there was "neither enthusiasm nor violent hostility." †

The establishment of the Muslim committees gave a boost not so much to collaboration with the occupation forces as to Tatar nationalism. Just as the Nazis wished to use the Tatar nationalists for their purposes, the nationalists in turn hoped to utilize the situation to advance their own purely Tatar interests, as they saw them.

The Muslim committees were to a considerable extent used as a cover for underground activity by the Tatar nationalist organization Milli Firka (National Party), which advocated the formation of a Muslim state in the Crimea. This organization was banned under Soviet rule and was also persecuted by the German occupation.

With a network of Muslim committees functioning legally and with some of the Crimean Tatars organized in armed "self-defense" units, the occupation regime began to feel rather uneasy. The German High Command (Oberkommando der Wehr-

---

* Kirimal, p. 305. According to Robert Conquest (*The Soviet Deportation of Nationalities* [London, 1960], p. 87) thirty to forty thousand Crimean Tatars were deported during collectivization.

† Dalin, p. 259. It should be kept in mind that part of the population joined local "self-defense" units only to protect their villages from the attacks of "evildoers," whoever they might be.

macht) issued secret instructions that in no case was cooperation or joint action by the Muslim committees and "self-defense" units to be permitted. Both types of organizations were constantly checked and kept under strict surveillance by the German authorities.[17] One of the orders issued by the German High Command called for the "prevention at all costs of the formation of a central Tatar leadership and the pursuit of Tatar political interests."[18]

It seems that the Nazis were afraid they might not win at this game of supporting the "non-Russian peoples" in the Soviet territories they occupied. The "self-defense" units were commanded by German officers, as were analogous formations within the Wehrmacht.

Most of the Crimean Tatars did not collaborate with the occupation. It should be remembered that the men of draft age were in the Red Army. Some of them fell into Nazi hands as prisoners-of-war and later served in German units, but many others continued to fight in the ranks of the Red Army and in partisan units. In 1942 and 1943 thousands of Tatars were shipped off to Germany as "Eastern workers" (*Ostarbeiter*)—that is, they were subjected to the same pitiless exploitation as Soviet citizens of other nationalities herded off to serve the Reich. Only in 1944, when the approach of disaster became increasingly obvious within Germany itself, did the Hitler regime take a series of measures aimed at neutralizing, as much as possible, the dangerously explosive element of foreign workers. One of the maneuvers intended to divide these workers against one another was to grant non-Russian workers—the Crimean Tatars among them—the status of "Western workers," with better food and better working and living conditions.

The landing of Soviet troops at Kerch, Yevpatoria, and Feodosia in early January 1942, although it ended in failure, spurred the population of the Crimea to renewed activity. The people assisted the landing forces in any way they could, and some took part in the fighting. The reprisals for this were savage. Thousands of people were shot. Among them, of course, were Tatars.

The difficult economic situation, especially in the cities; hunger; severe food rationing; and the export of almost all agricultural products intensified the dissatisfaction of the Crimeans.

The occupation authorities in the Crimea maintained the *kolkhozy* and *sovkhozy* * intact, viewing them as the most suitable economic structures for extracting food and raw materials from the rural population. Those who expected the Germans to abolish the *kolkhozy* and restore private ownership of the land had a rude awakening. Nor did the Hitler regime restore church property that had been confiscated under Soviet rule.

Because of the growth of the partisan movement and the Germans' fear that the partisans might cut the Crimea off from the main forces of the German army, Nazi punitive operations became increasingly savage. The inevitable result was that the partisan movement spread more widely.

The Tatars who lived in villages with mixed populations, especially in the mountain district of the Crimea, took a negative attitude toward service in "self-defense" units and evaded it. The SD tracked down evaders and killed them. In response, there was even greater support for the partisans, as a rule. So it was, for example, in the villages around Bakhchiserai. The influence of the partisan movement grew. In the partisan camps Tatar sub-units were formed, and in nearly every Tatar village and "self-defense" group representatives of the partisan movement were present. The SD, together with regular German army units, began to destroy both Tatar and non-Tatar villages in the vicinity of the partisan zone. In response, the people of the villages went into the hills and joined the partisans. In one of the secret reports of the SD, the point was made that an entire company of Tatar "self-defense" troops had joined the partisans. Even such a Hitler accomplice as Kirimal admits that there were many Crimean Tatar victims of the "SD operations." [19] Toward the end of the occupa-

---

* *Kolkhoz (kollektivnoe khoziaistvo)*: a collective farm, the most common method of uniting the Soviet peasantry for the purpose of agricultural production. *Sovkhoz (sovetskoe khoziaistvo)*: a large state farm.

tion, in December 1943 and January 1944, the Germans burned down and destroyed 128 mountain villages in the southern and northern Crimea.[20] In January 1944 the inhabitants of Argin, Baksan, and Kazal—Crimean Tatar villages burned to the ground by the Germans—together with the inhabitants of Efendikoi, Kutur, and Neiman—Russian villages similarly burned—fled into the hills to join the partisans. A secret communiqué of the German High Command to the Ostministerium, dated February 28, 1944, pointed out that the Tatars had "recently" been showing "open dissatisfaction."[21]

Field Marshal von Manstein, commander of the southern group, wrote with a certain bitterness of the failure of the plan to use the non-Russian peoples in the occupied territories against Soviet power:

> If only we could realize the possibility of turning these auxiliaries into forces truly useful to our troops. Because thus far they have mainly taken to their heels at the threatened approach of the Russians. Of course it would be a big help to us if we could mobilize both Russians and non-Russians and used them against the Bolsheviks on a large scale. The most difficult question will always be what task to assign them, since their interests are opposed to ours and in the last analysis are bound to diverge. It is undoubtedly correct that we should have tried to cause divisions among them and, first of all, have laid the basis for that by appropriate conduct in the occupied areas.[22]

In his belated expressions of regret Manstein overlooks the fact, first, that any and all conquerors would be hated by the peoples of the USSR, no matter what blandishments they offered; and second, that the racist theory which exalted the German people as the master race and, most important, the accompanying racist practices in the occupied Soviet territories—mass murder, the annihilation of hundreds of thousands of people as "racially impure," the systematic extermination of prisoners of war in Hitler's camps, and the removal of populations to Germany for exploitation—provoked not only terror but indignation and hatred. The bestial and inhuman nature of the ideology, policies, and practices of the Third Reich absolutely ruled out any prolonged collaboration between it and even small groups of the Soviet population, let alone entire nations. Only those who became willing or unwilling accomplices in carrying out the fascist atrocities stayed with the Hitler gang to the bitter end, and were rightly brought to account for their crimes at last. Manstein himself, as commander of the Eleventh Army, was responsible for the criminal orders leading to the annihilation of the Jews in the Crimea.[23]

Even during the occupation of the Crimea, rumors began to circulate about the alleged total collaboration of the Crimean Tatars with the Nazis.

There were several bases for this fabrication. First, the special policies pursued by the occupation regime toward the Crimean Tatar population, the formation of the Muslim committees, and the participation of some Tatars in the "self-defense" units and other military formations; second, the false information provided by the partisan leadership of the Crimea to the leadership of the Crimean regional committee of the party and to the government of the Crimean ASSR on the situation within the partisan movement and the attitude of the Tatars toward it; three, the inaccurate information provided on this basis by the Crimean party leadership to the higher party bodies; and four, the reawakening of the traditionally suspicious attitude toward non-Russians within the Russian element of the population, an attitude that apparently had deep roots in the past.

The German occupation authorities, who began, as we have indicated, with the total physical extermination of the Jews and went on to form Tatar "committees" and "self-defense" units, at the same time organized guard battalions from the ranks of other nationalities and, somewhat later, waged a campaign to recruit Russians to the ROA.*

* Russkaia Osvoboditel'naia Armiia (Russian Liberation Army), the German-sponsored Russian collaborator units headed by General Vlasov [*translator's note*].

It's an old story—dividing the population along national lines and turning them against one another—and that was the Hitler regime's maneuver. One trick the occupation used was to carry off the stores of food from any partisan bases they uncovered and distribute these to the Tatar population. On the other hand, when partisans raided Tatar villages, the Germans used that as a pretext for compelling villagers to join "self-defense" units.

In July 1942 the leaders of the Crimean partisan movement, A. N. Mokrousov and A. V. Martynov, sent a memorandum to Marshal S. M. Budenny, commander of the southwestern front, containing the charge that "the overwhelming majority of Crimean Tatars in the mountain district and adjacent areas are following the fascists."[24]

The subsequent spread of misinformation was helped along by the ignorance of some local party workers, to whom, as the saying went, "All non-Russians looked alike." For them the term "Tatar" included Azerbaijanis, Georgians, Armenians, Uzbeks, Kirgiz, etc., not to mention Volga Tatars. It is difficult to distinguish here between deliberate, malicious circulation of false information and just plain ignorance.*

An example is the report to P. K. Ponomarenko, the chief of the Central Staff of the partisan movement at the General Headquarters of the Commander-in Chief, which asserted that in April 1942 fifteen thousand "Tatar volunteers" had completed their training in Simferopol.[25] In point of fact, these "Tatars" included prisoners-of-war from Central Asia, the Caucasus, Transcaucasia, and the Volga region, many of whom were forced to put on the Wehrmacht uniform however much they detested it.

We find confirmation of this both in the wartime documents and in those brought to light more recently. For example, "Brief Report No. 1," on the activity of the Simferopol underground

---

* Kurtlit Muratov, who was in charge of the Special Department of a partisan brigade in the Eastern army group, writes in his as yet unpublished memoirs: "No matter who attacked partisan detachments, whether Germans, Hungarians, Rumanians, the ROA, or others, the same term was used—it was the 'Tatars.' "

group led by Usman Bosnayev from January to March 1942, relates the following:

> After the Germans had formed Tatar and Ukrainian prisoners of war into battalions, the group set itself the task of trying to win over those prisoner "volunteers" to the Soviet side through explanatory work, so that at the right moment the "volunteer" battalions would turn their guns against the Germans themselves. Through explanatory work the group succeeded in recruiting a number of commanders—among them, Abdulla Kerimov, Fatkhullin, Mustafa Saranayev, and Ivan Leonchenko—and these in turn won over to the Soviet side the majority of soldiers in one Tatar battalion and one Ukrainian battalion, through painstaking work among the forcibly recruited Tatar and Ukrainian "volunteers." These battalions were prepared to move against the Germans, arms in hand. Only treachery thwarted these plans, and the battalions were disarmed, the above-mentioned leaders being shot.[26]

On the forcible recruitment of "volunteers" we find an account in one of the collections published in 1943:

> Through heavy pressure the Germans managed to enroll a not very considerable number of so-called volunteers. Their recruitment was accomplished through coercion. In the village of M. in 1942 the following incident occurred. The Gestapo arrived and began to try to persuade the Tatars to sign up as volunteers. They were called forward one by one and asked to enroll. Kandar Abliakim refused, and there and then, in front of everyone, he was shot down by a Gestapo agent. The Germans do not trust these "volunteers" and "self-defense" troops; they keep them under surveillance and deal harshly with discontented elements. In March 1943, 270 persons were shot, including 60 "volunteers" and "self-defense" troops.[27]

Despite such repression suffered by the Tatars, the seeds of hatred, mistrust, and suspicion against them, sown in various places and for various reasons, began to sprout.

R. I. Muzafarov quotes from a letter by a participant in the partisan movement in the Crimea, the historian A. Ya. Olekha, from Makhachkala, to the editors of the journal *Zvezda* (Star). We reproduce an extract from that letter:

> Hundreds of Tatar patriots, who fled from the occupation forces and wished to fight against them, arms in hand, were driven from the forest by Mokrousov and left to the mercies of the Hitlerites. Mokrousov was guilty of the deaths, among many others, of Abdurefi Seyt-Yagi, former president of the Supreme Soviet of the Crimean ASSR; the distillery manager Asan Seferov; and Nuri Asmanov, an instructor in one of the party's district committees. This "error," which played so perfectly into the hands of the enemy, cannot be regarded as anything but treason. Next came repressive measures against Tatar villages, ordered by these same chauvinist-minded partisan commanders, punitive actions accompanied by violence. In the Russian village of Mamut-Sultan, for example, a group of Russian partisans took reprisals against those inhabitants who gave aid to some Tatar partisans who had blown up a German armored troop carrier on the Alushta highway the day before.[28]

The following extract from a 1957 letter to the Presidium of the CPSU Central Committee from M. Selimov, R. Mustafayev, Sh. Aliadin, and other former partisans and military men reads as an outright indictment against the leadership of the partisan movement in the Crimea:

> Mokrousov and Martynov, in order to conceal their personal incompetence in the struggle against the occupation and to shift the blame onto the local inhabitants, frequently appealed to the military command to send planes to bomb such

peaceable villages and settlements as Stil, Kuchuk-Ozen-bash, and others. At the same time, they gave partisan units orders to burn down Tatar villages and wipe them from the face of the earth, and to destroy their inhabitants, who were guilty of nothing.[29]

By order of I. Vergasov, commander of a partisan region, par-tisans attacked the Tatar village of Merkur, in order to "raise the level of partisan combat activity," according to the same letter. Elsewhere the letter states:

> Partisans charged into the peaceful village of Merkur, open-ing fire on the peasants through the doors and windows of their homes. Along the approaches from Foti-Sala and Ur-kusta a barricade was set up. For more than an hour the par-tisans fired their automatics and threw grenades in the win-dows of the peaceful villagers' homes. . . . In the village of Koush, a group of partisans of the Fourth Region, in a state of intoxication, launched a pogrom, making no distinction be-tween friend and foe. Any citizen who happened to stray into the forests was shot.[30]

This same I. Vergasov, who became a writer after the war, himself reports cases in which partisans burned down Tatar vil-lages.*

In August and November 1942 the Crimean regional committee of the party, after a careful investigation of the facts concerning anti-Crimean Tatar actions by the partisan leadership, passed a resolution entitled "On Errors Committed in Evaluating the Be-havior of the Crimean Tatars toward the Partisans, and Measures for Overcoming These Errors and Strengthening Political Work among the Tatar Population." We reproduce this resolution in ex-cerpted form.

* I. Vergasov, *Krymskie tetradi* [Crimean notebooks] (Moscow, 1971), pp. 260–64. This and other books by Vergasov, openly hostile to the Crimean Tatars, continue to be published in the Soviet Union in large editions.

Facts at the disposal of the regional committee of the AUCP(B) [All-Union Communist Party (Bolsheviks)] attest that the Tatar population in many villages not only sympathizes with the partisans but has actively aided them. A whole series of Tatar villages in the mountain district and adjacent parts of the Crimea have given assistance to the partisans for a long time (the villages of Koktash, Chermalyk, Beshui, Ailanma, Ai-Serez, Shakh-Murza, and others), and the landing forces which reached Sudak in January 1942 obtained all their food from the surrounding Tatar villages of that region. Seleznev's band was based for four months in the village of Beshui and was supplied with food. Another fact cannot be left unmentioned, in characterizing the attitude of the local population toward the partisans. In August, three hundred partisans of the First Region spent three days waiting on the coast for a ship to pick them up, in full view of the local population, but none of the inhabitants reported them; on the contrary, when the detachment would come through, leaving its traces behind it, a Tatar herder (*chaban*) would drive his flock of sheep over the partisans' tracks in order to obliterate all signs of their passing.

Farther on, the same document cites numerous facts attesting to the loyalty of the bulk of the Crimean Tatar population. The conclusion reached by the bureau of the party's Crimean regional committee leaves no doubt about this:

An analysis of the facts, the reports of commanders and commissars of partisan units, and an investigation carried out on the spot all testify that the allegation of a hostile attitude by the majority of the Tatar population of the Crimea toward the partisans and the assertion that a majority of Tatars placed themselves at the service of the enemy has no basis in fact and is politically harmful.

The former leadership of the central staff of the partisan movement (Comrades Mokrousov and Martynov), instead of making a correct political assessment of these facts and exposing the base policies of the German occupation toward the Tatar population, wrongly asserted that the majority of Tatars were hostile toward the partisans, thus giving an incorrect and even harmful orientation to individual leaders of partisan detachments on this question.

The allegation of a hostile attitude toward the partisans by the majority of Crimean Tatars must be condemned as incorrect and politically harmful, and it must be explained that the great bulk of the Crimean Tatars are just as hostilely disposed toward the German-Romanian occupation as are all the working people of the Crimea.[31]

On August 11, 1942, at a session of the Crimean regional committee of the party, Mokrousov submitted a written statement repudiating his previous assertions that the majority of the Tatar population of the mountain district and adjacent parts of the Crimea had betrayed their motherland.[32] However, after the deportation of the Crimean Tatars (in 1944) Martynov succeeded in having the position of the regional committee reversed.

There is no doubt that reports from the Crimea denouncing the conduct of the Tatar population played a fatal role in Moscow in deciding their fate.

On May 17-18, 1944, the entire Tatar population of the Crimea was deported. The men were separated from the women and children beforehand and sent to serve in work battalions. All Crimean Tatars in the Soviet armed forces were demobilized and assigned to construction units.

The Crimean Tatars were shipped off to "special settlements" in Central Asia and Kazakhstan. Some of them ended up in the Urals. For over thirty years they have lived far from the Crimea, and throughout this time an undisguised propaganda campaign against the Crimean Tatar people has continued unabated.

What kind of people betrayed their country by collaborating with the Germans during World War II? In considering this question one would think it most important, first of all, to characterize them socially and psychologically, and to look at their nationality only after that—if it is of any importance at all. But it seems that the nationality to which this or that person belongs is exceptionally important precisely to those who are accustomed to emphasizing their international outlook at every appropriate opportunity. This is so important to some writers—it is time to speak plainly—that they become outright chauvinists: the collaborators they mention in their books are always exclusively Crimean Tatars, Chechens, etc. If a traitor of Crimean Tatar background is mentioned, it is obligatory to stress precisely that this was a *Tatar,* and so forth.* But when Russian or Ukrainian collaborators are discussed they are simply mentioned by name, without specifying their nationality.

Imagine what it would be like if books referred to the nationality of all Hitler collaborators, without exception. Here is an example of how such a text would look (the facts are taken from books by Soviet authors; I have indicated the nationality):

The **Russian** Andzheyevsky was *Burgomeister* of Feodosia before the **Russian** Gruzinov. Gruzinov's most trusted henchmen were the former **Russian** noblemen Pezhemsky, Kolkayev, and Miklashevich, and the **Ukrainian** Skripka.

Among the *Polizei* in the Crimea were the **Tatar** Usein Izmailov, the **Tatar** Cherman Seit Memet (in Alushta district), and the **Russian** Fyodor Ivanovich Salmin, chief-of-police in Yevpatoria, a native of the Cossack village of Voznesenskaya in Labinskii district of Krasnodar territory. The *Polizmeister* of Sevastopol was the **Russian** defector Lorchi-

---

* A representative book of this kind is A. Perventsev's *Chest' smolodu* (Honor since youth) (Moscow, 1957). In the 1975 edition of this book the references to the Crimean Tatars were deleted. On the other hand, V. Kucher's novel *Chernomortsy* (Black Sea sailors), published in Ukrainian in Simferopol in 1975, is full of abuse against the Crimean Tatars (see pp. 244, 246, 304, and elsewhere).

minov-Nekrasov, who initiated and directly supervised the mass murder of Soviet citizens in Sevastopol.

The names of the *Burgomeisters* of the major Crimean cities during the fascist occupation were as follows: in Simferopol, Sevastyanov; in Sevastopol, Supriagin; in Kerch, Tokarev; in Feodosia, Gruzinov; in Yalta, Maltsev; and in Karasubazar, Erudzhepov.

I. Genov, who was prominent in the partisan movement, writes the following: ''Notable for their savagery were Vasily Zadavi-svechka, the senior police officer Brazdnits, and the police troopers Ivan Sharko, Semyon Zhatkevich, and several others.''[33]

Just imagine what cries of outrage (fully justified, of course) we would hear if the nationality of all traitors, collaborators, etc., was consistently underlined.

It is officially a crime under the law in our country to stir up suspicion, ill will, and ultimately hatred against any people. The hate-mongering in regard to the Crimean Tatars is no exception. However, in no case has anyone yet had to answer for this crime.

The Crimean Tatars took part in the war against Hitler's Germany just as much as any of the other peoples of the USSR. The percentage of the Tatar population of the Crimea who served in the ranks of the Red Army, beginning with men called up in the fall of 1939, was the same as the percentage in other parts of the USSR.

Crimean Tatars were active in the partisan movement as well. Thus, according to the list of personnel drawn up by M. Aliyev, commander of the Eighth Partisan Detachment—who now lives in Kirovobad in the Azerbaijan SSR—his unit had 138 men: forty-eight Russians, thirty-eight Crimean Tatars, twenty-eight Azerbaijanis, thirteen Ukrainians, five Armenians, and one each of several other nationalities.

In two of the three major partisan formations operating in the Crimea, the commissars were Crimean Tatars. Likewise, there were Crimean Tatar commissars in two of the seven partisan brigades and ten of the twenty-eighty partisan detachments. Several partisan detachments were commanded by Crimean Tatars. For example, Abliaz Aedinov commanded the Third Red Army Partisan Detachment, and the commander of the Balashevsky Partisan Detachment was Gafar Gaziyev, who fell in battle in January 1942. The Sudak Partisan Detachment was made up primarily of Crimean Tatars, with Emarkhan Yusupov as commander and Abliaz Osmanov as commissar.[34]

How the Nazis dealt with Crimean Tatar partisans who fell into their hands may be seen from the fate of Seideli Murseitov. His corpse was found by partisans not far from Kolan-Bair. "His body, covered with wounds and bruises, was hanging from a tree. A red star had been carved into his chest, from which hung a sign, 'This is how all partisans will be treated.' "[35]

Immediately after the deportation of the Tatars practical measures were taken to eradicate all traces of Tatar culture in the Crimea, but not only Tatar culture.

On October 20, 1944, the bureau of the Crimean regional committee of the party passed a resolution providing for "the renaming of settlements, rivers, and hills whose names reflect Tatar, Greek, or German origins."[36]

The indicated reason is highly instructive, for it reflects the mounting chauvinism of the majority nation as the war drew to an end. On August 21, 1945, a decree of the Presidium of the RSFSR Supreme Soviet (No. 619/3), not for publication, was issued. It concerned the renaming of the village Soviets in the Crimea. In Azov district, ten were renamed; in Alushta district, ten; in Kuibyshevo district, nineteen; and in Yalta district, ten.

At the same time, new names were given to the villages of the Krymchaks, who had lived in Mariupol district since the late eighteenth century.

The following are some examples of the way places were renamed:

Old Local Name	*New Russian Name*
Korbeklinskii village Soviet	Izobilenskii
village of Korbek	village of Izobil'noye
Kuru-Ozen'skii village Soviet	Solnechnogorskii
village of Kuru-Ozen'	village of Solnechnogorskoye
Kuchuk-Lambetskii village Soviet	Kiparisovskii
village of Kuchuk-Lambet	village of Kiparisnoye
Ulu-Ozen'skii village Soviet	General'skii (!)
village of Ulu-Ozen'	village of General'skoye
Biyuk-Ozenbashskii village Soviet	Shchastlivyi
village of Biyuk-Ozenbash	village of Shchastlivoye

"This business of changing the old, local place names," wrote the noted Russian author Konstantin Paustovksy, "testifies to the absence of the most elementary culture and to contempt for the people and the country."[37]

This process was carried so far that in Simferopol, capital of the Crimea, a street named after Nariman Narimanov, one of the first presidents of the Central Executive Committee of the USSR, was renamed "Partisan Petrichenko Street." The street named after Mustafa Subkhi, a famous figure in the international revolutionary movement, was changed to "Krylov Street," and the Mustafa Subkhi Theater became the "Rodina [Motherland] Theater."

After the war an attempt was made to lure new settlers to the depopulated Crimea from the Ukraine. But from the start, things went badly. Meanwhile, the vineyards, the orchards, the gardens—everything that had been the glory of the Crimea for centuries—fell into ruin. It took many years and considerable resources before the Crimean economy was restored.

II

The Situation in
the Northern Caucasus,
and German Occupation Policies

IN THE SUMMER of 1942 the German army resumed the offensive, one of its aims being the conquest of the Caucasus and Transcaucasia.

The offensive began in the southern sector on June 28. It was marked by extremely heavy and bitter fighting.

By the end of the day on July 15, a breakthrough had been made in the Soviet defenses between the Don and the Northern Donets.[1] The offensive of the Germany armies extended across a front five hundred to six hundred kilometers wide.[2]

The Soviet troops managed to extricate themselves from an encircling maneuver by the fascist armies. On July 24, Rostov-on-Don was abandoned[3] and the Soviet forces withdrew across the Don.

On July 29 the Germans broke through on another sector of the front, in the Tsymliansk region. On August 2, the Germans began their drive on Salsk, on the part of the front held by the Soviet Don army group. The next day the Don group was pulled back across the Kuban River. On August 5 German units entered Stavropol. On August 11 Soviet troops abandoned Krasnodar. The Germans reached the Maikop region and took Belorechensk but failed to break through to Tuapse. Advancing to the south of Rostov, the German armies reached the Mozdok area on August 8 and the Piatigorsk area on August 9. On August 25 they occupied Mozdok.

Along the line of advance toward Tuapse, German forces broke through to the Black Sea on August 31 and took Anapa. Soviet troops were forced to abandon Novorossiisk on September 10, 1942. On the front held by the Soviet northern army group, during the period from August 17 to September 9, the Germans captured several passes in the sector from Mount Elbrus to the Klukhori Pass.[4]

On August 21 the Germans placed their flag with its emblem, the swastika, on the peak of Mount Elbrus. (There it waved until February 17, 1943, when it was torn down by Soviet soldiers and replaced with the state flag of the USSR.) On October 25 the Germans entered Nalchik.

They did not succeed in breaking through to Grozny. Likewise they were unable to gain control of all the passes in the Greater Caucasus range. Early in November the Germans were forced to go on the defensive.

In Hitler's plan of conquest the Caucasus was regarded above all as a source of oil supplies for Germany.* The projected Reichskommissariat Kaukasien was to cover a substantial territory—from Rostov-on-Don in the north, to the Black Sea in the west, to the Caspian in the east, and to the borders with Turkey and Iran in the south. This Reichskommissariat was, in turn, divided into seven lesser commissariats: Georgia, Azerbaijan, the Mountain region (Dagestan, Northern Ossetia, Kabardino-Balkaria, Checheno-Ingushetia, and Cherkessia), Krasnodar, Stavropol, the Kalmyk region (including Astrakhan and part of Rostov region), and Armenia.

The Germans established contacts with the Caucasian émigrés

* A special organization with the abbreviated name Konti Oel, headed by a representative of the Reich, Hermann Neubacher, was formed to carry out the economic exploitation of the Caucasus. Neubacher already had considerable experience in such matters, having organized the exploitation of the natural riches of Yugoslavia.

who had been living in Europe since the end of the civil war in the USSR. The intention was to utilize them in the German scheme.

Among the émigrés from the Northern Caucasus there was a group that had a pro-German orientation. It published the journal *Caucasus* in Berlin. One of the editors of this journal, Ali-khan Kantemir, offered his services to the Nazis. He drew up a memorandum examining the "Caucasian question" and submitted it to the Ostministerium in August 1941. A rival group of émigrés was headed by Said Shamil, grandson of the celebrated imam. Earlier, the Shamil group had been oriented toward France and belonged to the émigré Prometheus group. After the German attack on the USSR, Shamil tried to enlist the support of the Hitler regime for his plan to create an "independent Caucasus." In Berlin the idea of backing Shamil was found highly tempting, considering his origins.* But his program proved to be overly independent, and consequently Shamil broke off negotiations in the fall of 1942 and departed for Turkey. The Kantemir group, on the other hand, entered into active collaboration with the Hitler government. In addition to Kantemir, the Nazis won over the former White Guard General Bicherakhov, from Dagestan, as a collaborator. With the blessings and support of the Ostministerium, Kantemir and his followers founded the so-called Northern Caucasus National Committee. The Committee engaged in recruitment efforts among Soviet prisoners of war from the Northern Caucasus, persuading them to enroll in military formations of the German Reich. However, in the Northern Caucasus itself the émigrés' influence proved to be insignificant, their ideas being alien and unattractive to the Mountain peoples of the Caucasus.

Hitler's Germany sought to conceal its real plans for the Caucasus behind a mask of demagogic propaganda.

---

* The German fascist leaders were quite impressed by the prospect of collaboration with the bearers of such "distinguished" Caucasian family names as Prince Heracles Bagration and Prince Vachnadze, in addition to Said Shamil (Patrik von zur Mühlen, *Zwischen Hakenkreuz and Sowjetstern: Der Nationalsozialismus der sowjetischen Orientvölker im zweiten Weltkrieg* (Dusseldorf, 1971), pp. 125–27).

Early in the spring of 1942, in preparation for the renewed German offensive on the Soviet front, the question of policy in the Caucasus was discussed at length in Berlin.

In April 1942 the basic themes of the German propaganda line were laid down, as follows:

1. The German empire regarded the Caucasian peoples as friends.

2. The German armed forces took it upon themselves to "protect the Caucasian peoples" and to liberate them from "the Bolshevik yoke."

3. Without German aid it would be impossible to take the offensive against Bolshevik, Russian, and British imperialism, which had oppressed the peoples of the Caucasus for so long.

4. The national, cultural, and economic forces of the Caucasus would be allowed to develop freely. Their independent national and cultural development was in need of German protection. The age-old customs and traditions would be respected. The Caucasian peoples would use their native languages and have their own schools. In the realm of religion, all the Caucasian peoples and all their religious denominations would enjoy full freedom of worship. Churches and mosques would be re-opened.

5. Self-government would be granted, guaranteed by Germany.

6. The *kolkhozy* would be abolished.

7. Trade and free enterprise would be permitted without restriction.[5]

The proposed slogans were:

8. "Come over to the side of Germany, and support the German troops, at whose side your brothers are already fighting, united as one in the ranks of the German armed forces."

9. "Long live the free Caucasians in alliance with and under the protection of the Great German Empire of Adolf Hitler!"

The draft of this document met with strong objections from Rosenberg, especially Point 9, which seemed to promise freedom for the Caucasians. Rosenberg apparently succeeded in convincing Hitler that this slogan was ill-considered.[6]

However, in September 1942, when the German armies reached the Caucasus, the decision was made in Berlin to undertake the formation of local puppet administrations and, for propaganda purposes, to allow the use of such terms as "freedom," "independence," and "cooperation."

In contrast to the occupied territories of Central Russia, forced labor was not introduced in the Caucasus. Since the Caucasus continued to be a combat zone, power remained in the hands of the military command. In one of the orders of the commander of the First Tank Corps, von Kleist, dated December 15, 1942, instructions were given to treat the population "as friends" and not to create obstacles for the Mountain peoples if they wished to abolish the *kolkhozy* (in almost all the remaining occupied territory the Nazis preferred to retain the collective farms as economic units that would facilitate the extraction of food and raw materials to meet German military and economic needs); to permit the reopening of all places of worship; to respect private property and pay for requisitioned goods; to win the "confidence of the people" through "model conduct"; to give reasons for all harsh measures that would affect the interests of the population; and especially to respect "the honor of the women of the Caucasus." [7]

In issuing this order, von Kleist was trying to secure the rear of the German army in the Caucasus, especially because its position was increasingly threatened after the preponderance of Soviet arms had been established at the battle of Stalingrad.

Let us now look at the situation in some of the regions of the Northern Caucasus occupied by the German army in the fall of 1942.

THE KARACHAI AUTONOMOUS REGION

While the Red Army was trying to extricate itself from the enemy and to pull back from Rostov to the Greater Caucasus Range, it often happened that between the retreat of the Red Army units and the arrival of the Germans, several days of de facto interregnum would elapse, during which anyone who wished could assume power.

Thus it was in Mikoyan-Shakhar, then the capital of the Karachai Autonomous Region, that a former teacher, M. Kochkarov, appointed himself mayor.

The Karachai Autonomous Region was part of Stavropol territory in the RSFSR. It was founded on January 12, 1922.

Karachai was united with Russia in 1828. The Karachai people rose up in armed rebellion against the colonialist policies of tsarist Russia a number of times. The unending oppression of the Karachai by the tsarist authorities led, in the early 1870s, to a powerful movement in favor of resettlement in Turkey.

After the October revolution life began to change rapidly in the Caucasus, including in Karachai. At the time the Karachai Autonomous Region was established, there were 57,801 Karachai, 85 percent of the population.[8] Their numbers grew steadily and by 1939 there were 70,900 Karachai. However, their position relative to the population of the region as a whole declined substantially, to 28.8 percent,[9] while the Russian population grew rapidly both in absolute numbers and as a percentage of the whole.

In 1926 there were 2,916 Russians in the region,[10] but in 1939 there were 119,800.[11] In proportion to the rest of the population in the region, Russians increased from 4.5 percent to 48.3 percent during this period.[12]

In the Karachi Autonomous Region, which the German fascist army occupied at the beginning of August 1942, the occupying authorities tried to apply a "special" policy. Having confirmed the self-appointed Kochkarov in power, they decided to create a "Karachai National Committee." This "committee" obtained a pledge from the occupation regime that it would, in the future, be allowed to dissolve the *kolkhozy;* Soviet state property and public property were placed under the trusteeship of the Committee, which also had some voice in economic and cultural affairs—with the Germans, of course, retaining ultimate control. The Committee, for its part, made no little effort to justify the confidence of the German authorities and sought volunteers to form a squadron of horsemen for joint military operations with the Germans.[13] The Karachai Committee was the special protegé of the former German military attaché in Moscow, General Köstring.

During the occupation, a partisan movement developed in Karachai and Cherkessia. According to the evidence cited by Ch. S. Kulayev, thirteen partisan detachments numbering twelve hundred persons were operating in this territory.[14]

During the five months of the occupation the Nazis killed more than nine thousand civilian inhabitants of Karachai and Cherkessia, including many children.[15]

In late January 1943, units of the Thirty-seventh Soviet Army liberated Karachai and Cherkessia. Feverish but happy months of liberation and reconstruction began.

But unexpectedly, in November 1943, the entire Karachai population was deported from its native lands and shipped in closely guarded freight cars to "special settlements" in Central Asia and Kazakhstan. The Karachai Autonomous Region was abolished.

To make this dissolution of Karachai autonomy irreversible, two districts—Karachaiskii and Uchku-Lanskii—together with the former capital of the autonomous region (which now bears the name Karachaevsk), were transferred to the Georgian SSR and became part of Klukhori district. In December 1943, 2,115 Georgians were resettled here. The Russian population, numbering 5,672, remained in these districts.[16] The other part of the Karachai Autonomous Region (the districts of Zelenchuk, Ust'-Dzheguta, Pregrodnenskii, and Malo-Karachai) remained in Stavropol territory.[17]

The deportation of the Karachai occurred while the overwhelming majority of the male population was serving in the Red Army.

THE CHECHEN-INGUSH ASSR

Checheno-Ingushetia passed through several stages before December 1936, when it was finally transformed from an autonomous region into an autonomous republic. In 1939 its territory was inhabited by the following nationalities:

Chechens	368,100, or 50 percent of the total population of the ASSR
Ingush	56,500 or 7.8 percent
Russians	258,200, or 34.8 percent
Ukrainians	10,100, or 1.4 percent
Armenians	8,600, or 1.2 percent.*

The great bulk of the native (Chechen-Ingush) population lived in the rural areas. The working-class layer remained quite thin until the early 1930s and even by the beginning of the war had not greatly increased. According to official information, in 1937 there was a total of 5,535 Chechen and Ingush employees in the factories of Grozny, the capital of Checheno-Ingushetia.[18]

Collectivization undermined but did not destroy the age-old way of life in Chechnia.

Under the particular conditions in Chechnia—which had a clan system of kinship (the *teipa*)† and a system of land tenure based on common clan ownership, and where, among a certain part of the rural population, the distribution of land continued to be based on the principle of descent from either free peasants (*uzdenei*) or slaves (*lai*)—the policy of wholesale forced collectivization provoked resistance from the population. In turn, the authorities applied greater and greater pressure, with the result that conflicts became so greatly intensified that it probably would have taken many years to iron things out.

According to recently published information, sixty-nine acts of terrorism were recorded in Chechnia in 1931–33,[19] the victims being responsible party and government workers, activists, NKVD agents, etc. But there is no indication of what provoked these acts of terrorism. And did they actually occur on such a scale? After all, we know from Soviet history the extent to which accusations of terrorism were fabricated. In the spring of 1932 an armed uprising erupted in Nozhai-Yurtov district. The

---

* The results of the 1939 all-union census in reference to the autonomous republics were not published. The present statistics are taken from Korkmasova, p. 497.
† The Chechen term *teipa* means "clan" (plural, *teipy*).

strength and scope of this outbreak can be judged from the following official assessment of it: "This was the last armed action of the class enemy, who succeeded for a certain length of time in attracting a certain section of the peasantry to his side."[20] Here again we must wonder whether peasant protests have been inflated to the status of "armed uprisings" in order to justify the use of mass violence against them.

There is what we might call the unofficial view of the situation in Checheno-Ingushetia during collectivization. It takes as its starting point the fact that the clan system was still very strong there. Chechnia did not have private ownership of land. Only in the mountain *khutory* did families own a certain amount of property individually. In the lowlands everything was held in common—the land, the water, and the forests. Therefore, the term "kulak,"* applied to the concrete conditions in Checheno-Ingushetia, loses all meaning.

As for the 1932 armed uprising, those who support the unofficial view contend that no actual uprising occurred, that the whole affair was blown up on purpose to explain away the failure of the unintelligent policies pursued in Chechnia.

Periodically, military expeditions were made into the hills. Individual murders or attacks of a personal nature, not political acts, usually served as the pretext for these expeditions. Often these campaigns were simply a sham, and had the purpose of showing how loyal and indispensable the OGPU was for the Soviet system, enhancing the OGPU's power and prestige, and satisfying the personal ambitions of certain leaders. Here is the kind of story I have been told, the authenticity of which cannot be doubted.

One such expedition was undertaken in the winter of 1929–30 in connection with a rumor that many "kulaks" had gathered in the hills. Included in the expedition were *kursanty* (cadets) from

*The Soviet terms for the most prosperous peasants in the USSR, who exploited farm laborers. In 1929 those designated as kulaks were denounced as "class enemies," their property was confiscated, and they were sent to labor camps. Many thousands of so-called kulaks and their families died from starvation and violence.

the Vladikavkaz Infantry School for Middle-Echelon Officers, a cavalry regiment of Caucasian nationals, units of the Twenty-eighth Mountain Rifle Division (Russian units only), as many as two OGPU* divisions, and a number of other units. The expedition was headed for the Osinovskoye gorge, where—as OGPU information had it—many hostile elements had congregated. According to an eyewitness, Kh. U. D. Mamsurov, commissar of the Caucasian cavalry regiment (and in the future, a colonel-general and Hero of the Soviet Union), there turned out to be a total of fourteen "enemies." That evening, at their place of bivouac, Mamsurov overheard an OGPU agent (there was fully empowered OGPU representation in the Caucasus at that time, headed by the not unknown E. G. Yevdokimov, a man "renowned" for his cruelty) dictating a report to Rostov along the following lines: "Overcoming bitter resistance on the part of numerous bands, the expedition has reached . . ."—and then the name of the locality was given. When Mamsurov returned he appealed to A. D. Kozitsky, who had headed the expedition and was director of the Vladikavkaz Infantry School. Kozitsky's reply to Mamsurov was that he was not at all surprised, because in such cases the OGPU agents always resorted to lies to serve their own purposes.

Not long after, Mamsurov related this incident in public, in a speech at the regular party conference of the Northern Caucasus Military District, to which he was a delegate. As he told his story the auditorium rocked with laughter. However, it was not long before Mamsurov was summoned to Moscow, where he was severely reprimanded for publicly ridiculing the OGPU.

Exaggerated and inflated reports were made about the supposedly bitter "class struggle" in the mountains. There was a disturbance in the village of Goity, the population of which was

---

* Ob'edinennoe Gosudarstvennoe Politicheskoe Upravlenie (Unified Political Administration), the state security apparatus created in 1922 to replace the Emergency Security Commission (VCHK or Cheka, 1917–22). The OGPU was replaced in 1934 by the People's Commissariat of the Interior (NKVD). In our time, Soviet state security is delegated to the KGB (Committee of State Security).

famous for its resistance to the White Guards, who were never able to take the village during the civil war. The methods of forced collectivization had aroused the indignation of the inhabitants, among whom there were approximately 150 former Red partisans. They were dealt with severely, some even being shot.

Early in 1938, 490 collective farms were established in the territory of Checheno-Ingushetia, embracing 69,400 households. They covered three-fourths of the arable land in the republic (308,800 hectares out of 401,200). A large part of this arable land was located in the lowland areas—some 246,900 hectares.[21] Also in the lowland areas, fifteen machine-tractor stations, equipped with 571 tractors and fifteen combines, were established. However, such powerful advances against the backward forms of land cultivation did not apparently arouse great enthusiasm among the collective farmers: the productivity of labor remained extremely low. According to official statistics, in 1938 the number of collective farmers in the lowland areas who did not work a single *trudoden* (workday unit) was 17.4 percent; the number who put in up to fifty *trudodni* was 46.3 percent; up to 100, 15.9 percent; up to 200, 11.1 percent; up to 300, 5 percent; and up to 400, only 2 percent.[22] On January 1, 1939, 53 percent of the collective farms did not have any livestock sections, 68.2 percent had no dairy farming, and 75.3 percent had no sheep ranching.[23]

The system by which individual households worked their share of the commonly-held clan lands persisted almost everywhere despite collectivization. Alongside the elected administrative boards of the *kolkhozy* there existed underground bodies which actually ran everything, the "elected ones" merely serving as camouflage.[24] The audit of all agriculturally valuable lands in 1938, an official history reports, disclosed that in a number of lowland *kolkhozy* "no accounts were kept in regard to a large portion of the cropland and hay fields. . . . This made it possible for certain elements who had penetrated the leading bodies of individual *kolkhozy* to violate the land laws, to sell and rent land, and to maintain certain areas under crops secretly."[25]

In several districts (Achkhoi-Martan, Achaluki, Prigorodnyi, etc.) there were cases in which the best lands remained in the hands of individuals. Such holdings ranged in size up to as much as nineteen hectares per household, whereas on the *kolkhozy* there were only 2.5 hectares per household.[26] There were very small *kolkhozy* consisting of only twenty to thirty households, which actually remained *teipy,* having only changed labels.

In the upland areas, all the lands were categorized as "terraced." (These were narrow, flat, and not very productive strips hugging the slopes.) Here, despite the existence of 158 *kolkhozy* embracing 33,205 households, or 99.8 percent of all households in the upland regions, individual farming in fact remained the basic way of life.

Of the land suitable for cultivation, only 32 percent of the hayfields had been socialized. Pastureland, which amounted to 152,413 hectares, was not socialized.[27] In January 1940 in Chalanchozhskii, Itum-Kamenskii, and Cheberloyevskii districts, 67 percent of the land was being worked individually by so-called collective farmers, while about 90 percent of the horses and cattle and about 80 percent of the sheep and goats were owned individually.[28] One-ninth of the *kolkhoznik* (collective-farmer) households in the upland areas owned as much as 30 percent of the total number of cows (there were 9.3 cows per household on the average, 2.7 times more than the number of cows in the truck and dairy farming subdivisions of all *kolkhozy* in the upland areas).[29]

V. I. Filkin, a penetrating and thoughtful researcher, cites several examples, in one of his works, of trade in land on the *kolkhozy.* In 1937, in the settlement of Pliyevo, in Nazran district, the chairman of the administrative board of the Budenny *kolkhoz,* a certain Pliyev, sold two hundred hectares of land to *kolkhozniki* and individual farmers. In the same district the chairman of the "Twelve Years of the Workers' and Peasants' Red Army" *kolkhoz,* a certain Yevloyev, sold two hundred hectares of plowland and two hundred hectares of meadowland to *kolkhozniki* and individual farmers.[30]

The official history, *Essays in the History of the Chechen-Ingush ASSR, 1917–1970,* openly admits that "private farming remained the basic economic form among the Mountaineer peoples."[31]

One of the standard explanations for this is that "kulak and mullah* elements" infiltrated the leadership of the *kolkhozy*. This infiltration, in turn, is explained by the serious errors of the local Soviet bodies. What "serious errors"? It is said that these consisted in an incorrect understanding of the structure of Chechen-Ingush society, the denial of the existence of a kulak layer within the Chechen-Ingush population, and—as a result of such views—the continuation or preservation of kulak farms in many instances. Not so long ago, in 1973, at the Tenth Plenum of the Chechen-Ingush regional committee of the CPSU, the "non-class approach to the assessment of historical phenomena and the idealization of the past" were sharply condemned.[32]

The most frequently cited example of the influence of the Chechen-Ingush kulaks is the following: During collectivization most of the kulaks migrated from the lowland areas to the *khutory* (individually-owned farms) in the mountains. In 1938 the official count of individual farms in the mountains was three thousand. The authors of the *Essays* write that these "were formally *kolkhozy,* but in fact their owners, taking advantage of the absence of any checking by government authorities, arbitrarily took control of plowland, hayfields, and pastureland in forests belonging both to the local governments and to the national government, and there raised crops secretly and maintained large numbers of livestock."[33] Filkin adds that bandit groups often hid in the mountain *khutory*.[34]

Another explanation is that the leading bodies of many *kolkhozy* and village soviets "were riddled with hostile class elements."[35] In fourteen of the twenty-three *kolkhozy* in the Achkhoi-Martan district the chairmen were kulaks and traders or their sons.[36]

In the late 1950s and early 1960s another reason was added to help explain the rather complex situation in Checheno-Ingushetia,

* A Muslim religious leader or teacher.

namely, the weakness of the party organization as a result of the repression of the late 1930s. The first explanation is maintained in abridged form to this day. But when it comes to the effects of the repression, official historiography now makes only passing reference.

The party organization in the upland areas was particularly weak. Out of 824 Communists, 50 were totally illiterate (i.e., did not know even the alphabet), 265 had no primary school education, 275 had only primary education, and 153 had not completed secondary school.[37] In a number of districts the party organizations consisted primarily of the personnel of the party and government apparatus of the district and did not exceed twenty-five in membership. Thus, on February 1, 1939, the party organization in Cheberloyevskii district consisted of twenty-five people (eleven members and fourteen candidates); in Chalanchozhskii district there were eighteen and in Shatoyevskii twenty-three.[38]

The party organizational staff was completely contaminated. Both the party and state apparatus contained a good many self-seekers and careerists, i.e., the least reliable types in a complex and dangerous situation. In a number of district divisions of the NKVD, there were what V. I. Filkin calls "accidental people." Other NKVD agents, even "many" of them, as a resolution of the Chechen-Ingush regional committee of the party testifies, "underestimated the strength of the anti-Soviet elements and the harm they did by their work in subverting the measures taken by the Soviet government." This resolution also indicated that an incorrect assessment of the class struggle in the village had led to the use of "passive methods," for the most part, in the struggle against "bandits, kulaks, and anti-Soviet elements."[39] In other words, the regional committee was calling for harsher methods.

But where did the self-seekers and careerists in the party organization come from? The answer to that question is not difficult. The main wave came after the repression of 1937–38, when most of the old cadres were expelled and destroyed. Nowadays in the Soviet Union it is customary to evade this question with the use of doubletalk, but there can be no doubt that the crude administrative methods and harsh repression were among the main reasons for the complicated situation that arose in Checheno-Ingushetia at the beginning of the war with Hitler's Germany.

In Checheno-Ingushetia in 1938 all the directors of district land departments, fourteen out of eighteen machine-tractor station directors, nineteen chairmen of district executive committees, and twenty-two secretaries of district party committees were removed. In 1939, twenty-one chairman of district executive committees and thirty-three directors of district land departments were ousted. Most of them were arrested. Repressive measures were taken against party and government workers on the regional as well as the district level. [40]

At the time of the formation of the Chechen-Ingush Autonomous Region, in January 1934, the party organization had 11,966 members and candidate members. After the exchange of party documents 3,500 were expelled and 1,500 moved to other regions. As of April 1, 1937, there were 6,914 members and candidates remaining in the regional party organization. In 1937 and early 1938, 822 members were expelled, 280 of them being labeled "enemies of the people" or "Trotskyists." [41]

Repression continued in 1939 and in 1940, right up to the beginning of the war. This time the purge was carried out on the rank-and-file level and in the middle echelons. From March 1939 to March 1940, 129 chairmen and 130 secretaries of village Soviets, and nineteen chairmen and twenty-three secretaries of district executive committees, were replaced. [42]

On April 26 a resolution of the AUCP(B) Central Committee was adopted on the basis of a report on the work of the Chechen-Ingush regional committee of the party. The work of the committee was harshly criticized. [43]

If the close ties of the *teipa* kinship system are kept in mind, it is easy to imagine the attitude of the bulk of the population toward the repression and toward the authorities who carried it out.

Here, where age-old concepts of honor and mutual aid to one's kin still prevailed, where the custom of blood vengeance persisted, protests against the repression took the familiar patriarchal form—blood for blood. The injured parties or their relatives avenged their kin and fled into the hills. The system of mutual protection which reigned in Chechen-Ingush society provided fairly reliable concealment for these fugitives. Bands of the most oddly assorted elements formed in the hills, and it was no easy matter to combat them.

On the other hand, measures were taken to normalize agrarian relations, which were closely bound up with the relations between the different nationalities. In connection with the decree of the May 1939 plenum of the AUCP(B) Central Committee "On Measures to Protect Socialized Lands from Being Sold Off" it was revealed that 31,745 *kolkhozniki* had excessive holdings, and 8,410 hectares were taken back from them. Socialization of livestock, agricultural equipment, and harness gear was also carried out, although the authorities had refrained from this earlier. At the same time resolutions were passed to eliminate "'leveling" (*uravnilovka*) in payment for labor. A system of additional pay for crops of higher yields and for increased livestock productivity was instituted. But this measure was passed by the Council of People's Commissars and the AUCP(B) Central Committee literally on the eve of the war and could not have had much effect on the situation in the Chechen-Ingush ASSR.

In 1939–41 the party organization in the Chechen-Ingush ASSR, bled white by repression, once again reached its 1934 level in membership, i.e., had grown substantially. At the beginning of the war the organization had eleven thousand members and candidate members.[44]

In examining the factors that shaped the situation in Checheno-Ingushetia and affected the morale of its population at the beginning of the war, official historiography puts great stress on the Muslim religion as a powerful negative influence. At the time of collectivization in Chechnia there were 2,675 mosques and houses of prayer and 140 religious schools, as well as 850 mullahs and thirty-eight sheikhs financially supported by their congregations.[45] An enormous number of religious sects exerted their varied influences upon tens of thousands of people. The Muslim clergy, if the official view is to be believed, fought desperately against collectivization and against the establishment of Soviet schools and veterinary and health centers, and whipped up an atmosphere of hostility against the teachers, doctors, and veterinarians, condemning them to ostracism. Many of these victims could not endure this moral terror and preferred to leave.

In 1937 the mullah Bersanov, in the settlement of Atagi, forced a substantial group of *kolkhozniki* to swear on the Koran that they would not work on the *kolkhozy*. In the settlement of Valerik, in Achkhoi-Martan district, the Kunta-Hajji sect, through the chairman of the *kolkhoz*, Khasbek Ozdemirov, forced the *kolkhozniki* to swear on the Koran "to sabotage *kolkhoz* production by every means possible."[46] Probably these incidents actually did occur. However, the motives that prompted the *kolkhozniki* to follow the mullahs remain undisclosed. It should not be forgotten that the majority of village mullahs were peasants like the others. Only on Friday did they go to the mosques to read to their fellow villagers from the Koran. Belonging to a religion is seen as something reprehensible in the USSR. But isn't it ironic that in many foreign Communist parties membership is compatible with belief in God? If the leaders of the Communist parties of Italy and France, let us say, were to announce tomorrow that after they came to power religious adherence would be regarded in a purely negative way, their parties would rapidly decline in membership and influence.

It is no new observation that repressive measures only strengthen the hold of religion and increase its power of attraction.

Even in the light of the few, sparse facts that we know, the situation in Checheno-Ingushetia at the beginning of the war appears unusually complex.

It is undoubtedly true that a section of the native population, especially in the upland areas, was hostile toward Soviet rule. This, however, is not the same as saying they took a friendly attitude toward the Nazi army. Rather, they simply wanted to lead their own lives. Some possibly dreamed of a return to the legendary times before the Russian conquest of the Caucasus. However, their conception of those times was not only romantic but one-dimensional and far from accurate.

Filkin points out that with the outbreak of war "the remnants of the socially hostile elements, which had been shattered but not wholly destroyed, . . . intensified their resistance and began to commit terrorist acts against the best representatives and most active supporters of the Soviet regime and *kolkhoz* system and to undermine the *kolkhozy*." [47] Filkin emphasizes that "unconscious elements" [48] were drawn into the armed groups: he is referring to participation by various layers of the local population.

In 1940 the Sheripov band began to make its raids. Then there appeared the band of a certain Izrailov, formerly a Communist. Subsequently the two bands united. There were other armed groups or detachments "headed by inveterate anti-Soviet elements," wrote the newspaper *Groznenskii rabochii,* "such traitors and deserters as Badayev, Magomedov, Baisagurov, Gachirov, Shetsipov, Musostov, Alkhastov, Dakiyev, and others." [49] This very listing of the names of the leaders of the bands seems to point to the fact that the armed struggle in the mountains was not just some episodic occurrence, or merely a matter of isolated individuals.* The bands did not limit their actions to raids on the *kolkhozy* and government offices, nor were they content with merely plundering these organizations; they also terrorized the population and attempted to frustrate the authorities' efforts to mobilize against them.

At the end of 1941 the Chechen-Ingush regional committee of

---

* Evidence of the complexity of the problem of evaluating the bandit movement in Chechnia may be seen in the story of the alleged leader of the Sheripov band, younger brother of Aslanbek Sheripov, a famous hero of the civil war. The younger Sheripov was employed in the courts. According to his sister, Aisha Sheripova-Oshayeva, wife of the well-known writer Kh. D. Oshayev, her brother was sent into the mountains by the state-security organs to disrupt the functioning of a band and then "accidentally" perished in a crossfire. For many years she unsuccessfully sought an investigation into this case and the rehabilitation of her brother.

the party "placed a single task before all party organizations, the task of curbing the kulak-mullah elements."[50] People holding high posts in the party organizations of the committee were sent into eighty of the major *kolkhozy*, and representatives of the largest *kolkhozy* were added to the *nomenklatura* (the list of the most highly placed party personnel) of the committee. This represented a strengthening of the central government and at the same time the granting of broad powers and privileges to the chairmen of the *kolkhozy*. One hundred and fifty persons were sent from the towns to the *kolkhozy* to carry out a mass agitational campaign for a period of three months. In November 1941, by way of implementating the AUCP(B) Central Committee decree on the establishment of political departments in the machine-tractor stations and *sovkhozy*, over one hundred Communists were sent out into the rural areas. However, despite these exceptional measures, a year later, the armed struggle in the mountains, if the official reports are to be believed, was still in full swing.

Thus on November 22, 1942, in the settlement of Guni, in Vedeno district, a band of thirty-four attacked the "Red Livestock Breeder" section of a *kolkhoz*. The fighting, in which the *kolkhozniki* participated, went on for two hours, and several people were killed. Twenty-three of those who took part in the fighting were awarded certificates of honor by the Supreme Soviet of the Chechen-Ingush ASSR.[51]

More decisive measures were taken against the bands and deserters—special security units were organized, and the active party membership was everywhere mobilized to uncover and liquidate "the bandit groups and other counterrevolutionary elements."[52]

According to a much later report in the newspaper *Groznenskii rabochii*, the Soviet command was forced to withdraw large Red Army formations (*soyedineniya*) from the front lines and throw them against the armed bandit groups in the mountains. It is generally known that a *soyedinenie* is a troop unit of rather large size, a brigade or larger. On the basis of this it is easy to reach certain conclusions about the dimensions of the battle unfolding in the mountains.

In August 1973, Kh. Kh. Bokov, secretary of the Chechen-Ingush regional committee of the CPSU and later chairman of the Supreme Soviet of the Chechen-Ingush ASSR, said the following at a symposium on the book *Essays in the History of the Chechen-Ingush ASSR:* "It is important for the patriotic education of the working people of our republic not only to hold up models worthy of imitation but also to condemn with righteous anger the traitors, deserters, and enemies of the people who sought to hamper the struggle of the Soviet people against the foreign invader."[53]

Responding to this appeal, V. I. Filkin published an article in which he attempted to define the situation in which Chechen-Ingush society found itself during the war of 1941–45. He categorically asserted that the social base of "political banditism" was the kulaks, as well as the mullahs, sheikhs and—bourgeois nationalists![54] (As though "bourgeois nationalists" form some separate social layer.)

In Filkin's opinion, the middle peasantry, which constituted a substantial percentage of the population, supported all the measures of the Soviet authorities and rendered assistance to the authorities in the battle against "anti-Soviet elements." Another section of the middle peasantry, which was somewhat better off, is said to have observed neutrality, but at times offered "direct support" to the anti-Soviet elements. However, this schema seems rather abstract and greatly resembles the well-known schematic representation of the roles of the "kulak" and "middle peasant" given in the *Short Course of the History of the AUCP(B)* (1938). One question, however, remains unanswered: If class differentiation was so clearly expressed in Chechnia, what role did the "poor peasants" play? No place has been found for them in Filkin's schema.

As early as the fall of 1941 the reverses of the Soviet army in the south began to have unfavorable repercussions in the Caucasus. Fear that Turkey might strike a sudden blow from the south speeded up the mobilization effort. The events in and around Moscow on October 15–16, when tens and hundreds of thousands fled the capital out of fear that the Nazis would soon take it, heightened tensions in the south still further.

On October 22 the Grozny Municipal Defense Committee, headed by V. I. Ivanov, first secretary of the Chechen-Ingush regional committee, was formed. Thousands of people poured out to help erect defensive barriers around the city. A special sapper brigade was formed out of those of draft age. These efforts were not in vain: Grozny kept the Germans at bay in the fall of 1942. The German offensive slowed, and it died out at the approaches to the city. In mid-November 1941, formation of the 255th Special Ingush Cavalry Regiment and Reserve Division began. It should be remembered that part of the draft-age pool had already been called into the Red Army before the war began and were fighting all along the vast Soviet-German front. The formation of the new units took place amid the tensions created by the fighting in the mountains. V. I. Filkin, who was then one of the secretaries of the regional committee, writes that "serious distortions" occurred at certain district enlistment offices. The entire male population was called up, including old men and invalids who were absolutely unfit for military service. The draftees were often kept sitting in the barracks without rations, and sometimes they would leave without permission in order to have a decent meal at home. Absence without leave grew to such dimensions that the authorities became seriously alarmed, and in March 1942 the drafting of Chechens and Ingush of military age was discontinued. This decision was later acknowledged to have been an error, and of course was attributed to the machinations of Beria.* [55]

In August 1942 the decision was made to mobilize Chechens and Ingush into the Red Army on a voluntary basis. A second

---

* After Stalin's death in 1953, many of his crimes were attributed to Lavrenty Beria, head of the NKVD from 1938 until his execution in 1953.

mobilization was carried out from January 25 to February 5, 1943, and a third in March of that year.

A decree of the regional committee of the party and the Council of People's Commissars of Checheno-Ingushetia noted with satisfaction "the courage, fearlessness, and firmness" demonstrated by the Chechens and Ingush mobilized in September 1942.[56] In May 1943, summing up the results of the second and third mobilizations, a special commission of the Transcaucasian Front commented in a completely favorable way on the conduct of the Chechens and Ingush at the front, and the regional committee stated with satisfaction that the "call-up of Chechen and Ingush volunteers into the Red Army was accompanied by the demonstration of genuine Soviet patriotism."[57]

In addition, 13,363 Chechens and Ingush underwent military training in the ranks of the people's militia (narodonoe opolchenie). This represented about 40 percent of all those receiving such instruction in the autonomous republic.[58]

V. I. Filkin cites data which he considers incomplete on the number of Chechens and Ingush drafted into the active army. He gives the figure of more than 18,500, not counting those drafted before the war began.[59]

Several hundred Chechens and Ingush were part of the garrison of the legendary Brest Fortress.* But the attempt to play down this fact continues to this day.

Not long after the Germans were driven from the Caucasus reconstruction work began in Checheno-Ingushetia as elsewhere, and at the same time a purge of the party ranks and state apparatus began. Speaking at a plenum of the Grozny municipal committee of the party on February 19, 1943, the secretary of the committee, Berdichevsky, demanded "that mass political work among women, young people, Komsomols, and especially among the Chechens and Ingush, be decisively strengthened, and that the best people, those totally devoted to the cause of the party, be ac-

---

* Behind German lines, it was under siege for three months.

tively sought out and won to the party's ranks."[60] The importance of this declaration is obvious, for it, in fact, contains a positive assessment of the role of the Chechens and Ingush in the defense of the Caucasus. The continued expression of this point of view can easily be followed in the pages of *Groznenskii rabochii* for 1943.

At the end of the year the newspaper published a round-up article by G. Borisov and M. Grin entitled "The Friendship of Peoples Is the Source of Our Party's Strength," which once again confirmed the self-sacrificing struggle of all the peoples of the Caucasus, without exception, against Hitler's armies.[61] The newspaper recalled heroes of the war and the fact that fourteen million rubles had been raised to build an armored train named after the hero of the civil war Aslanbek Sheripov.[62]

February 23, 1944, was Red Army Day. Everywhere men were invited to meetings at the village Soviet buildings. No one suspected that disaster was at hand. Studebaker trucks rolled up (lend-lease from the American allies to help the Red Army). Soldiers holding automatics appeared. The Chechens were held at gunpoint. In every village the decree of the Presidium of the Supreme Soviet was read, announcing the total deportation of the Chechens and Ingush for treason and collaboration with the enemy. Twenty kilograms of baggage per family was the maximum that could be taken.

Bidding farewell to their native lands, the older people whispered the words of a prayer: *Allah il illahu* (Allah is great). Women wept; some children were happy at the prospect of getting a ride in a truck, but others were not sure and stuck close to their elders.

During the deportation terrible tragedies occurred. A certain Chechen writer has told of one.

The chairman of one of the village Soviets, the eighty-year-old Tusha, assisted in the removal of his fellow villagers, his own family being shipped off as well. Only his daughter-in-law remained with him, with her child at her breast. Addressing a Georgian officer, Tusha said in his broken Russian, "Me born here, me here die. Me no go anywhere!"

Tusha spread his arms out and stood before the gates of his home. The daughter-in-law understood. She cried out and, pressing her child to her breast, took hold of her father-in-law. She pulled him and pulled him toward our group, crying out all the while, "Daddy, Daddy, come on! They'll kill you." It all happened in an instant. The officer gave an order to a Russian soldier standing with his automatic at the ready.

"Shoot! All three."

The soldier blanched and trembled. He said, "The man I will shoot, but not the woman and child."

A TT pistol flashed in the officer's hand. Before the soldier had finished his last word he lay on the ground, shot through the head. Within the same instant, the officer had killed Tusha, his daughter-in-law, and her child. They drove us in haste down the path to the roadway. There trucks were waiting for us. Those who lagged along the way were shot. That is the way it was.*

Did this nameless Russian soldier know that the moment he refused to kill that woman and child he saved the honor of the Russian people?

It is not likely that he thought so. He was simply behaving like a human being. And his entire person rebelled when they tried to turn him into an animal. He was left there in the mountains, lying by the old man, the woman, and the child, a symbol of human brotherhood and its inseverable bonds. Someday at that place a monument will be erected to Mankind.

The lend-lease Studebakers rolled down out of the mountains. And then came the decree of the Presidium of the RSFSR

*Narushiteli ego voli [Violators of his will], unpublished manuscript. About two thousand resisters remained in the mountains. They wandered from place to place. They were hunted and killed, but they did not surrender. And the mountains hid many of them in safety.

Supreme Soviet on the changing of the names of the following districts:

Achkhoi-Martan	to Novosel'skii
Kurchaloyevskii	to Shuragatskii
Nazranovskii	to Kosta-Khetagurovskii
Nozhai-Yurtovskii	to Andalalskii
Sayasanovskii	to Ritliabskii
Urus-Martan	to Krasnoarmeiskii
Shalinskii	to Mezhdurechenskii

The district centers were also renamed accordingly.

The Chechen-Ingush ASSR was abolished. In its place Grozny region was created. The native population of Chechens and Ingush, which had numbered 425,000 before the war and had constituted more than 58 percent of the total population of the autonomous republic, was forcibly removed. Chechens and Ingush from Northern Ossetia and Dagestan shared their fate. Similarly, Chechens and Ingush in other cities and regions of the Soviet Union were deported. Only in Moscow did two Chechens manage to remain during the period of deportation.

Part of the territory of the autonomous republic, the Prigorodnyi district populated primarily by Ingush, was transferred to the Northern Ossetian ASSR. At the same time, by order of the authorities, tens of thousands of Russians, Avars, Dargins, Ossetians, and Ukrainians as well were resettled in Grozny region. There was one main reason for this—to make the restoration of the Chechen-Ingush ASSR impossible in the future. But this measure also served an immediate purpose—a utilitarian one, so to speak—to prevent the economy of Grozny region, especially its agriculture, from collapsing as a result of the depopulation of the territory.[63]

THE KABARDINO-BALKAR ASSR

The Kabardino-Balkar Autonomous Region was founded on September 1, 1921. Fifteen years later, on December 5, 1936, the autonomous region was transformed into the Kabardino-Balkar Soviet Autonomous Socialist Republic.

In 1939 the republic had 349,700 inhabitants. Of these, 150,300, or 43 percent of the population, were Kabardinians; 127,100, or 36.3 percent, Russians; and 39,000, or 11.2 percent, Balkars.[64]

The war reached the territory of the Kabardino-Balkar ASSR in the fall of 1942. On October 29, German troops took the capital of Kabardino-Balkaria, the city of Nalchik. Taking advantage of the brief interregnum, a former civil servant, Selim Zedov, assumed the post of mayor. Subsequently, under the aegis of the occupation authorities, a local administration was formed in which three émigrés played an active role—Prince Z. Kelemetov, Prince Shekmanov (Shaposhnikov), and a certain A. Uzdenov, whom Soviet sources identify as a kulak.[65] Besides these, the "government" included Prince Devlatgeri Tavkeshev, Makhdev, Khoshchishev, and Prizenko.[66] Entering the territory of the republic together with the occupation forces was the so-called Mountain battalion, commanded by T. Oberlander, a German creation composed of Soviet prisoners of war from the Caucasus. This battalion was an odd mixture of types, varying from outright enemies of Soviet power to prisoners of war who joined under pressure, unable to bear the murderous conditions in the Nazi camps.[67]

The occupation of Kabardino-Balkaria was relatively brief, from two to six months depending on the region. At its greatest extent, it lasted from August 12, 1942, to January 11, 1943. Wishing to ensure a stable rear area for its troops, the German command permitted the local administration, which it controlled, to open up the mosques and churches, hoping to win the support of part of the population in this way. On December 6, 1942, the occupation authorities issued instructions for a new system of land tenure, under which the dissolution of *kolkhozy* and *sovkhozy* was permitted in the upland cattle-raising areas (inhabited mainly by Balkars) and the dividing up of *kolkhoz* property; socialist property was abolished.[68] In an effort to demonstrate the supposed reciprocity of friendly feelings between the occupation forces and the Balkar population, a celebration of the Muslim religious holiday of Kurman was organized in Nalchik on December 18, 1942. Instructions were given by the local "government" to the *Burgomeister* of the village settlement of Lechinskaya to send festive national costumes to Nalchik for Kurman, as well as a horse in full ceremonial regalia (this was the one forwarded to Hitler as a gift), poultry, wine, fruit, sweets, and a select group of the most attractive male and female dancers.[69] At a later time this celebration of Kurman served as one of the bases for the charge of treason against the Balkars.

However, beneath this amicable exterior lay the cold and calculating policies of conquerors who saw in the peoples of the Caucasus merely an instrument for realizing their plans and an object of exploitation. The export of food and raw materials and the economic exploitation of the region was introduced on a wide scale with characteristic German efficiency and fascist ruthlessness.[70]

During the brief period of occupation, the Germans and the punitive forces made up of Soviet citizens recruited to German service killed 2,053 prisoners of war and 2,188 civilians in the population as a whole.[71] In the Balkar settlements alone, 500 people were killed, 150 of them children.[72] In one of the Balkar settlements, 52 of the 125 homes were burned down and 63 of the 512 inhabitants shot or brutally tortured.[73]

At the very beginning of the war, five thousand Balkars joined the Red Army and many of them died fighting for their country. More than six hundred men from the Balkar village of Gundelen, in Baksanskii district, fell on the various fronts of the Great Patriotic War.[74] A number of sources mention the participation of Balkars in the partisan movement, particularly in the United Partisan Detachment of the Republic. They also fought in the 115th Cavalry Division, formed in the fall of 1941.[75]

At the same time, part of the population did collaborate with the Germans. There were plans to separate Balkaria from Kabarda and to unite with Karachai (on the basis of their common language and Islamic religion) under a Turkish protectorate—an echo of the

Pan-Turkist schemes.[76] Several Turkish emissaries visited Bal-karia during the war.

On January 4, 1943, Nalchik was liberated by a Red Army reg-iment under a Major Okhman. On January 11, the last Nazi units abandoned the territory of Kabardino-Balkaria.

For fourteen months the population of the republic worked tirelessly to rebuild the economy and heal the wounds inflicted by the enemy invasion.

On January 4, 1944, the first anniversary of liberation from German occupation was triumphantly celebrated.[77] No one sus-pected that disaster was imminent.

But on March 8 the Balkar settlements were surrounded by troops, the Balkars driven away in trucks, then loaded onto cattle-cars and shipped off to Kazakhstan and Kirgizia.

Of course not a word of this appeared in print. Two days after the deportation of the Balkars, the newspaper of the republic pub-lished a telegram from Stalin in which the Leader sent "the frater-nal greetings and thanks of the Red Army" for the 15,300,000 rubles collected in the republic to outfit the tank column called "Death to the German Invaders"![78]

A month after the deportation of the Balkars the CPSU Central Committee passed a resolution replacing the party leadership of Kabardino-Balkaria.[79] Z. D. Kumekhov, former secretary of the regional committee, was transferred to the position of chairman of the Council of Ministers of the ASSR.[80]

On April 16, 1944, the newspaper of the republic, previously entitled *Socialist Kabardino-Balkaria,* began to come out under a new name, *Kabardinian Truth.* From then on the newspaper was referred to as the organ of the Kabardinian regional committee of the AUCP(B).[81] Thus the inhabitants of the republic learned that they now lived under an autonomous state structure of a different name—the Kabardinian ASSR. After another three days the newspaper published what was supposed to be a "militant and timely" editorial with the headline "To Be Vigilant Is the Duty of Every Citizen." At that very time the freight trains carrying the

Balkar population were already on their way. The inhabitants of Kabarda were warned that the Germans had left their agents behind in the liberated zones and that the penetration of alien elements into leading positions in *kolkhozy* and factories were not merely isolated occurrences. The newspaper urged that the authors of false rumors be exposed and brought strictly to account, and it called for the intensification of explanatory propaganda work (on what subject, however, it did not say).[82]

After another month, on May 20, 1944 (when the Balkars had already been settled in Central Asia) the newspaper appeared with an editorial entitled "Education of National Cadres." Kabarda had need of national cadres! In the entire republic there were only three Kabardinian doctors. Among agronomists there was not one Kabardinian with higher education; at the largest plant in Nalchik, the meat-packing complex, only one Kabardinian worker was employed.

In 1944 a total of only sixty-two Kabardinians completed secondary school. There were only twenty-six at the pedagogical institute, and the overwhelming majority of school-age children of this nationality were enrolled only up to the fifth or sixth grade.[83]

But how could this be? Where had the national cadres disappeared to? Had there been any in the first place? Perhaps the national cadres had been thoroughly eliminated during the repression of the 1930s.

The call for the advancement of national cadres was accompanied by a savage purge of the party and government apparatus of the ASSR. In September 1944 the former leaders of the republic, Kumekhov and Akhokhov, were removed from their posts. The charge against them was that

at the moment when the republic needed the highest degree of responsibility—during the fighting against the German fascist forces on the territory of the Kabardinian ASSR and under the temporary occupation—they committed a number of serious political errors. After the Germans were driven out, instead of providing leadership in a Bolshevik way for the struggle to successfully liquidate the consequences of the German fascist occupation, and to purge our ranks of alien elements and individuals unworthy of confidence, Comrades Kumekhov and Akhokhov took the non-party path of covering up for these people, and often promoted them to leading positions, including their own relatives who had committed crimes against the motherland.

The former leaders of the republic were also accused of selling state property.[84]

There can be no doubt that this resolution—and the ensuing decree of the AUCP(B) Central Committee Orgburo, in November of that year, on the work of the Kabardinian regional committee of the party, which contained the demand for intensified work "in liquidating the consequences of lying fascist propaganda which had influenced the backward section of the population"[85]—had only one purpose: to justify, after the fact, the total deportation of the Balkars as a people, and to shift the moral responsibility onto the former leaders of Kabardino-Balkaria.

III

What Happened in the Kalmyk ASSR

MUCH OF THE territory of the present-day Kalmyk Autonomous Soviet Socialist Republic (the Kalmyk ASSR) was in earlier times part of the Kalmyk khanate. After the historic migrations at the end of the eighteenth century, Kalmykia became part of the Russian empire. Even on the eve of the 1917 revolution, a large part of the native population of the Kalmyk steppes still followed a nomadic way of life. Raising cattle was the main source of livelihood for this not very numerous people. After the October revolution the situation in Kalmykia developed in quite a complicated way. The Kalmyks found themselves in the central stronghold of the White movement, and part of the Kalmyk population, primarily the better-off layers, followed the Whites. A crucial turning point was the 1919 uprising headed by nationalist elements. After this uprising was suppressed, political stability returned to Kalmykia and a period of economic reconstruction began.

In 1920 the Kalmyk Autonomous Region was founded, and in 1936 it was transformed into an autonomous republic. During collectivization the disruption of ancient patriarchal relations, with traditional kinship ties along the clan lines, proved painful and difficult. At the end of 1929, 315 large stock farms were expropriated, and in the summer of 1931 this figure rose to about

1,200. By 1937, *kolkhozy* comprised 95 percent of all households in the ASSR.[1] During collectivization, legality was crudely violated and acts of violence committed. This tendency culminated in the mass repression of the late 1930s, whose victims included even former leaders of the Kalmyk ASSR, those who had actually carried out collectivization. The attempt to uproot centuries-old customs and traditions overnight was not only unsuccessful but dangerous. M. L. Kichikov, a well-known Kalmyk scholar, puts it this way: "The ideas, customs, and habits of the past proved considerably more tenacious than the conditions that had produced them. Moreover, not all the *zaisangi* and *geliungi** or kulak sympathizers had been deported from Kalmykia. Members of the liquidated exploiter elements remained in the Kalmyk steppes and, to a certain extent, continued to have some influence with the backward part of the population, which had not assimilated the new ideological viewpoint sufficiently and had not yet freed itself of religious and *ulusist* (local) superstitions."[2] Kichikov's observations here are important because they help us to understand the reasons that led a certain section of the Kalmyks to collaborate with the German fascist army.

On the eve of the war the population of Kalmykia and the adjacent regions, according to the official figures in the 1939 census, was 220,684. Kalmyks constituted 48.6 percent of this number,[3] i.e., about 107,250.

Literacy in Kalmykia had risen from 2 percent before the revolution to 91 percent on the eve of the war. The substantial number of schools, the network of health-care and veterinary facilities, the adult-education institutions, etc., were indications of the cultural growth of Kalmyk society.

In the eyes of the central authorities the Kalmyks were considered unreliable for a long time after the 1919 uprising.

Until 1927 Kalmyks were not drafted into the Red Army. In 1927 the first 90 Kalmyks were called up. Ten years later the number was nearly twenty times that, having increased to 1,746.

**Zaisangi:* the clan nobility; *geliungi:* the local Lamaist (Buddhist) priesthood.

(Counting all nationalities, a total of 2,845 were drafted in Kalmykia.) In 1938 things stayed at approximately the same level—1,728 Kalmyks out of a total of 2,963 draftees. In 1939–40 there was a call-up of four age groups—4,200 people. M. L. Kichikov, in quoting these figures, informs us that the total number of Kalmyks in the Red Army when the war began exceeded 5,000.[4]

The war came close to Kalmyk territory as early as the fall of 1941, as Rostov-on-Don passed back and forth between German and Soviet hands, finally being taken and held by the Red Army.

The enemy actually reached Kalmykia in early August 1942.

There was no substantial resistance by the Red Army to the occupation of part of the Kalmyk ASSR, and some uluses* were not defended at all. It is important to remember this in order to understand the people's state of mind as they suddenly found themselves under foreign occupation.

Official Soviet documents have preserved for us some echoes of that tragic situation:

From August 1 to August 5, 1942, enemy troops in no great number, with no serious resistance on the part of our military units, took Zapadnyi and Yashaltu districts. On August 10, 11, and 12, Priyutnoye and the northern parts of Maloderbetovskii and Sarpinskii districts were taken, as was the capital, Elista, also on August 12.

For two to three weeks in July and August enemy airplanes flew with impunity over Elista and the villages of the above-named districts, strafing and bombing and setting the grassland and grain crops on fire. Several of the enemy's reconnaissance tank groups fired upon the population of Zapadnyi, Maloderbetovskii, and Sarpinskii districts. In this

---

* The Kalmyk word *ulus* refers to an administrative unit of the Kalmyk ASSR corresponding to a *raion* (district) in other parts of the USSR. Originally, *ulus* referred to the patriarchal clan community and the territory belonging to it [*translator's note*].

way the enemy disrupted the harvesting and removal of grain, wool, and hides, and the driving of cattle to the Volga.

The enemy advanced along the Voroshilovsk-Divnoye railway upon Elista without any resistance, since there were no units of our army in this area.[5]

Even before Nazi troops entered Kalmyk territory, rumors hostile to Soviet power began to circulate in a number of districts, and these apparently had an effect upon the mood of the populace. Kichikov reports that the former *geliung* M. Bazirov, for example, spread the rumor that Hitler was going to win in 1942 and that if he did not, the whole people would perish. Other rumors centered on the themes that Hitler Germany was sure to win and that the Germans treated non-Communists decently, although they were ruthless toward Communists and Komsomols.[6]

In a memorandum from the secretary of the Priyutnoye district committee to the regional committee of the party, there was a report that, through the actions of hostile elements in August 1941, a fire had broken out in *sovkhoz* no. 4 and eight grassfires on the steppe. Charges were brought against a certain accountant named Babenko, son of a former large landowner. It was said that the fires had been set, "not without his influence," because he had "openly expressed his anti-Soviet attitudes"![7] Of course this kind of statement sounds, more than anything, like an old-fashioned accusation of witchcraft.

The party placed "socially dangerous" elements—former kulaks, *geliungi,* White Guards, and nationalists—under surveillance.[8] However, the number of these "socially dangerous" types is not given.

After the first retreats of the Red Army, deserters began to appear in the Kalmyk steppelands. They began to join together in small bands and to engage in robbery and acts of violence. Larger armed bands appeared somewhat later—for example, the band of Bassang Ogdonov, which had between seventy and ninety members.[9]

In 1942, with the rapid advance of the German army toward the south, the number of deserters increased. New bands appeared in the nonoccupied districts: Yustinskii, Privolzhskii, Chernozemelskii, and Ulankholskii. According to official information, these bands attacked party and government personnel. As Soviet units withdrew toward the Volga, the number of deserters continued to grow. The same document of August 15, 1942, from the leadership of the Kalmyk ASSR, states that "in the Kalmyk steppelands, in the reed marshes along the Manych and Kuma rivers, and in the Privolzhskii district [along the Volga] deserters of various nationalities have found a hiding place."[10] However the document does not indicate whether or not these deserters engaged in armed combat against Soviet authority. It is more likely that the deserters at that time hid themselves, waiting to see how events would develop and wishing not so much to risk their lives as to preserve them at all costs.

In late autumn of 1942 collaboration between these bands and the occupation forces was established. The bandits stopped people attempting to flee across the Volga and drive their livestock off with them, and turned them over to the Germans.[11]

There is no question that the bands were emboldened by the weakness of the Red Army units defending Kalmykia. The symptoms of this weakness were everywhere in evidence.

On August 1, 1942, five days before the Nazi troops arrived, a petroleum storage dump and stores of food and raw materials at the Cossack village of Divnoye were blown up by Soviet demolition units; large quantities of gasoline were poured onto the ground despite the objections of the leadership of the Kalmyk ASSR.

The government and the regional committee of Kalmykia tried to alert the military councils of the Northern Caucasus and Stalingrad military districts to the fact that the road to Elista and Astrakhan was open to the enemy. Secretaries of the party regional committee were sent to the military district commands. Requests were made orally and by telephone for arms to be given out and for the Communists, nonparty activists, and local "destruction squads" (*istrebitelnye otryady*) to be armed, but these requests consistently met with refusal. The military command had no arms reserves. [12]

The Kalmyk steppelands were doomed.

Under these circumstances the actions of the leaders of the republic were contradictory and inconsistent. On the one hand, on August 2 the decision was made to evacuate all livestock to the other side of the Volga. [13] The evacuation was applicable to the populations of all the threatened districts. However, P. V. Lavrentyev, first secretary of the regional committee—as M. L. Kichikov reports—demanded that the secretaries of the party district committees in Beshantu, Yashaltu, Troitskoye, and Priyutnoye halt the evacuations, so that the harvesting of grain could continue: he accused the district leaders of being cowards and alarmists. "Such contradictory instructions," Kichikov concludes, "produced confusion and disorganization; yet all the while the motorized columns of the enemy and the gangs of bandits were cutting off the cattle trails, dispersing the cattle drivers, and rounding up the stock." [14]

The Zapadnyi and Yashaltu districts were occupied by the Germans on August 15. By November 1, 1942, five of the thirteen districts were completely occupied and three partly occupied, while in five of them Soviet power was maintained. [15]

The German army seized 670,000 head of cattle, 711 of the 963 tractors in Kalmykia, 410 of the 445 combines, and many motor vehicles that had been abandoned because there was no fuel to drive them away. Some four million poods* of grain and the greater part of the stock of wool and hides also fell into German hands. [16]

Nazi rule in the occupied parts of Kalmykia left its special mark with the annihilation of the not very numerous Jewish population of the territory. The Jews were gathered together in Elista, taken outside the city, and shot—all of them, including women, children, and old people. [17]

---

* One pood equals sixteen kilograms.

In view of the insignificant number of German units in the vast expanse of Kalmykia, the occupation authorities tried to pursue policies that would ensure safe conditions for their troops and communications. They counted on sowing antagonisms between the Kalmyks and Russians, causing them to fight among themselves and encouraging each to see the other as an implacable foe.

Assigned to the headquarters staff of the German Sixteenth Motorized Infantry Division were several persons who could speak Kalmyk—Professor Baron von Richthofen, the general staff officer Oberleutnant Halterman, and—last but not least—the Abwehr (military intelligence) officer Otto Doll, who had a fluent command of Russian and who now is the object of an attempt by contemporary West German historians to create a "T. E. Lawrence of the Kalmyk steppes," a man supposedly worshipped by the local inhabitants as a "demigod." Otto Doll (his real name was Otmar [Rudolph] Werva or Vrba) was from the Sudetenland, a former cavalry officer who served with Petlyura during the civil war in Russia. Later, Doll was a representative of the Abwehr at the German consulate in Odessa. In mid-August 1942 he was sent at the head of a small unit to establish contacts with the local population in Kalmykia.[18]

Doll succeeded in disposing a certain section of the populace toward collaboration. In contrast to the Hitler occupation policies in Russian and Ukrainian territories, the Germans promised to establish a "free Kalmyk state."[19] With this end in mind Prince N. Tundutov was sent to Elista as the head of a projected puppet "government." But at the same time there was a proposal to locate the seat of the *Reichskommissar* of the "Kalmyk region" at Elista. This did not jibe very well with the promises of a "free Kalmyk state." B. Tsuglinov was appointed mayor of Elista. At one time he had been a White émigré, but he had returned to Kalmykia and worked there as an accountant in the motor vehicle transport administration. Appointed as his deputy was a certain Truba who until then had worked as an agronomist at one of the *kolkhozy*. A group of émigrés around the Kalmyk Banner organization, headed by Sh. Balinov, also actively aided the occupation regime. In 1942 they founded a so-called National Committee, which in fact was an appendage of the German government agencies in charge of the captured Soviet territories. Contrary to the assertions of Joachim Hoffman,[20] neither this National Committee nor others like it enjoyed any independence. Their activities were completely controlled by the German authorities.

In early 1943 the "Committee" began to publish the magazine *Khal'mag* (Kalmyk). Leaflets and similar materials for the population of the occupied districts were printed. Several schools were opened, but instruction was reduced to a bare minimum. Fearing the spread of infectious diseases, the Nazis took a number of sanitary measures, sending a group of medical workers to Elista.[21]

The Nazis pursued carefully thought-out policies in Kalmykia. They counted on reawakening the instincts and traditions of nomadism. Thus they proclaimed the right of Kalmyks to own and raise as many cattle as they could, and to use any pasturage they wished, raising the tempting and totally explicit slogan "A hundred sheep and twenty head of cattle for everyone."[22] At the same time the dissolution of the *kolkhozy* was announced. In fact the Kalmyks were encouraged to take over former *kolkhoz* property. The Nazis even attempted to buy the support of the population, giving financial gifts to the "poor."[23]

However, the regime established by the Germans on the occupied territory of Kalmykia hardly differed from the regime in other Soviet areas occupied by the German army. Movement from place to place was restricted by a system of special passes and enforced with fines and penalties, including corporal punishment.[24] A broad system of informers was in operation.[25] In every place of habitation there was not not only a "specially selected" *Burgomeister* but also a chief of police appointed by the occupation authorities with an armed squad of *Polizei* under him, numbering at least fifteen.[26]

The Nazis did succeed in winning the collaboration of a section of the population.[27] This is discussed, for example, in a memorandum by representatives of the Central Headquarters of the partisan movement who had made an on-the-spot investigation of the situation.[28] The facts relating to collaboration are also noted in a memorandum of April 2, 1943, from the Kalmyk regional committee to the Central Committee of the party. There are documents that speak of the growth of the bandit groups and their intensified activity. One states that "groups of bandits turned back livestock and people from the *kolkhozy* and *sovkhozy* who were heading for the Volga, and betrayed them to the Germans."[29] The documents also mention that some of those recruited by the Germans were forced to agree to join the bands through death threats or blackmail. They also note, however, that the Germans "made fools of" the backward elements of the native population,[30] i.e., they actually acknowledge the effectiveness of the enemy propaganda.

What part of the population of Kalmykia was drawn into collaboration with the occupation forces? This is not a simple question. The chairman of the Kalmyk ASSR Council of Ministers, Gariayev, has asserted that only 1 percent of the population, i.e., twenty-two hundred people, collaborated with the Germans, referring to the population as a whole. If the Kalmyks alone are referred to, this figure becomes hardly more than one thousand. This highly dubious figure is obviously an underestimation. Kichikov cautiously observes in regard to this 1 percent that it is "Gariayev's count" and not his.[31] Our historian, in his own works, cites conflicting data.

On the other hand, among West German historians in recent years there has emerged a clear tendency toward exaggerating the facts in regard to collaboration by the non-Russian peoples, in particular the Kalmyks. Some West German historians have tried to portray the occupation policies of the Germans in Kalmykia as almost a blessing from on high and the collaboration between them and the Kalmyks as something quite idyllic. It is a characteristic feature of these works, moreover, to raise doubts about the reality of the crimes committed by Hitler's armies on the occupied territories of the USSR. At most, the crimes against the Jewish population of the USSR are admitted. Typical in this respect is the book by Hoffman, which we discuss in the "Note on Sources."

Hoffman asserts that the majority of the Kalmyk population demonstrated a friendly attitude toward the Germans, citing as proof the German military documents of the time.[32] However, another German scholar, Mühlen, regards as implausible the claim that half of the Kalmyk population collaborated with the occupation.[33]

These efforts to portray the majority of Kalmyks as friendly toward the Germans (a story first put into circulation by Doll and Halterman) are contradicted by the facts. First of all, at the approach of the Germans approximately 25 percent of the population of the republic withdrew to the unoccupied districts or to the other side of the Volga.[34] Subsequently many of those whom the Germans tried to recruit to Kalmyk military formations under their control also fled to the unoccupied districts.

Among the reasons for the flight of the population to the Soviet-held districts were the numerous cases of looting by soldiers of the Wehrmacht and of the Romanian units. Hoffman seeks to portray the Germans as "well-mannered" conquerors and cites documents pointing toward the possibility that all the cases of looting could be attributed to the Germans' allies, the Romanians. But one may conclude from these very same documents that the German servicemen were no strangers to robbery and violence either. In particular, an order of August 20, 1942, by General of the Infantry Ott, commander of the German Fifty-second Army Corps, acknowledges cases of looting by his soldiers.[35] A number of German orders of the day refer to looting by soldiers of the Sixth and Seventh Romanian Army Corps. A special conference was held on this matter, since the violence being committed by the soldiers was causing indignation among the Kalmyk population.[36] The German command realized very well that unauthorized looting and violence would lead to demoralization within the army and hatred for the occupation regime in the local population.

As everywhere, the Germans dealt harshly with discontented elements. In Kalmykia the Nazis shot approximately two thousand civilian inhabitants and prisoners-of-war.[37]

Of course, a social profile of the Kalmyk collaborators might help us arrive at an accurate picture of the dimensions and variety of collaboration with the Germans. But such information is in fact lacking, both in works by Soviet authors, most of whom are Kalmyk historians, and in those of Western scholars. The works by the Kalmyk historians, following the established clichés, assert that those who collaborated with the Germans were former kulaks, White Guards, and a section of the Lamaist clergy. Hoffman, too, speaks of the fact that Doll received much assistance from certain Lamaist priests, who acted more or less as intermediaries between the occupation authorities and the population. There was even a plan to send a delegation to the Dalai Lama in Tibet to obtain his approval for collaboration with the Germans.

Information is extremely scanty in regard to the social profile even of Doll's closest collaborators in the Kalmyk Cavalry Corps, which was formed in the fall of 1942. Facts on the social origins of the middle-echelon officers, noncommissioned officers, and rank-and-file of this corps are completely lacking. Something is known, however, about the professions of those in Doll's immediate entourage. For the most part they were teachers—one of the most common fields of specialization among the intelligentsia of Soviet minority nationalities. Most of them had served in the Red Army at an earlier time, and then deserted. In the senior command staff only one person, Bassang Ogdonov, commander of a cavalry troop, was obviously of peasant origin.[38]

The Nazis began the formation of Kalmyk cavalry troops in September 1942. According to a report of the Kalmyk regional committee of the party dated November 18, 1942, 200 to 250 persons were recruited over a two-month period. The same document gives the standard social characterization of the recruits, the accuracy of which it is impossible to verify—former *geliungi, zaisangi,* kulaks and "sub-kulaks" (*podkulachniki* *), bourgeois nationalists, deserters, and criminals.[39]

The same documents state that the Nazis sought to base themselves on former kulaks, priests, White émigrés, and nobles.[40]

---

* Poor peasants who are dependent for their economic survival on the kulaks.

A later document of the Kalmyk regional committee [41] points out that "during the occupation the membership of the bandit groups increased and their activity intensified."

Kichikov, in his published works, cites no further statistics on the "bandit groups" and the Kalmyk Cavalry Corps (KCC). However, in the manuscript of his dissertation he refers to a December 1942 memorandum from the Kalmyk regional committee to the Central Committee of the party, which says the following: "The fascists brought most of the bandit groups together into one unit—the so-called Kalmyk Volunteer Legion (ten cavalry troops with as many as fifteen hundred persons in all)." [42] This document also refers to reconnaissance groups. Our historian cites further information derived from what he describes as a captured German document. According to this, in the summer of 1943 the KCC consisted of four cavalry divisions, each of which had five troops as well as other subordinate units (*podrazdeleniya*). [43] Kichikov does not indicate the overall size. This is done by Hoffman, who cites several documents in his book, one of which is apparently the document used by Kichikov. According to these documents, the KCC originally numbered 2,200 soldiers. After retreating from Kalmykia the corps had about 3,000 men. In addition, there were 92 German military personnel in the corps. [44] In July 1944 there were 2,917 rank-and-file soldiers, 374 NCO's, and 147 officers of Kalmyk nationality in the corps. Hoffman guesses that at the end of the war there were no less than 5,000 in the corps. [45] However, it should be remembered that after the retreat from Kalmykia various elements hostile to Soviet power joined the corps, and they were not necessarily Kalmyks.

In January 1943 the KCC covered the retreat of fascist army units from the Caucasus. Later it served as the guard unit at the crossing of the Dnieper and took part in punitive operations against partisans. In the Ukraine the KCC committed many atrocities, with Ogdonov especially "distinguishing himself." At a later time he was in charge of a German diversionary group in the rear of the Soviet forces and was killed during mop-up operations against this group. The KCC came to the end of its inglorious road at Lublin. There it plundered, killed, and raped on such a scale that the German military command decided to dissolve it and placed a German colonel in charge (Doll having died by then). After the smashing of the KCC by Soviet troops and Polish partisans in the Radom-Kelce area in mid-January 1945, its remnants were evacuated to Bavaria. [46]

Together with the KCC the families of its personnel moved west, along with a section of the population that had been forcibly expelled by the Germans. (From Elista and Sarpinskii district alone, four thousand persons were driven into exile in the West.) [47] Before retreating from Kalmykia the Nazis and their collaborators spread rumors about the harsh reprisals that would await all Kalmyks at the hands of the Red Army. A certain section of the population, in fear and confusion, abandoned their homes and went west. The overwhelming majority later returned to their Kalmyk homeland. An insignificant handful of émigrés, many of whom were accused by the Soviet authorities of various types of crimes, founded the so-called Kalmyk Committee for the Struggle against Bolshevism, in Munich. [48]

Immediately after the liberation of Kalmykia, the work of restoring the economy and healing the wounds left by the war began. All the evidence points to exceptionally harmonious and intensive efforts throughout 1943.

There also began a purge of the party and government apparatus, encompassing all layers of the population and all levels of the apparatus without exception; the traitors who had collaborated with the occupation regime were exposed. The old cadres were replaced, and trusted people were sent into the districts to explain the real situation to the "backward sections of the population" and to obtain their support in liquidating the bands still active on the territory of the autonomous republic. Relatives of the bandits were sent into the bands to help break them up.

The purge touched everyone. On February 26–27, 1943, a plenum of the regional committee of the party relieved the first secretary, P. V. Lavrentyev, of his duties. The resolution indicated that Lavrentyev had not provided party leadership during the evacuation of the populace, livestock, and property or during the occupation of part of the territory. He was also blamed for short-comings and miscalculations in organizing the underground work and the partisan movement.[49]

The plenum resolution said further:

Many leaders of the district committees, the Elista municipal committee, and the base organizations of the party, not having a sufficient theoretical preparation and demonstrating political shortsightedness and negligence, had let mass political work slip at the most decisive moment of the military and political struggle, especially among the native population and the women. The result of this was that hostile agents and enemies of Soviet power attempted to influence an insignificant section of the peasantry, to revive past national animosities, and to inspire wavering and uncertainty among the politically backward sections of the population.[50]

An individual check on the behavior of every member and candidate member of the party during the occupation was carried out in the Kalmyk party organization. At the July 1943 plenum of the party the results were reported. They were shattering.

In 1939 the Kalmyk party organization numbered 5,575 Communists and 1,981 candidate members. By social composition, there were 1,433 blue-collar workers, 2,085 white-collar workers, and 2,255 peasants. Of these, 60.5 percent,[51] or about 4,500 people, were Kalmyks.

As it turned out, 78 Communists had been shot by the Nazis, 125 Communists had left with the occupation forces (!), 478 had remained in the districts after the liberation, and the rest had changed their places of residence (the majority being on active duty in the Red Army).

Up to May 5, 1943, 430 individual cases were reviewed and 181 members were expelled from the party as "unworthy of confidence."[52] This was a rather vague formulation. It could be interpreted in any way one wished. However, our Kalmyk historian makes a rather significant comment on these figures: "Among those expelled from the party were some who had not freed themselves from petty-bourgeois views and who had been taken in by the demagogic propaganda of the National Socialists.''[53]

It seems that Nazi propaganda proved fairly effective in Kalmykia.

One confirmation of this is the fact that the bandits continued their marauding in a number of districts, being especially dangerous in Ketcherovskii, Chernozemelskii, Troitskoye, and Yustinskii districts. A plenum of the Kalmyk regional committee of the party on June 12–15, 1943, acknowledged that the party organization, preoccupied with restoring the economy, had stood aside from the struggle against the bands, wrongly supposing that this was solely the concern of the NKVD. For their part, the organs of the NKVD were sharply criticized at the plenum for their insufficiently effective operations. The plenum called for the struggle against banditry to be combined with intensified political and educational work among the populace, emphasizing that it should be conducted with a sense of discrimination, taking into account ''such special factors as social and ethnic background, age group, etc.''[54] As a result of a whole series of operational and ideological measures, the bandit groups were largely liquidated during the fall of 1943.[55]

Still, irresistibly, the tragic outcome drew closer. As early as the fall of 1942, soon after the German troops had occupied several of the districts, rumors began to circulate about mass banditry in the Kalmyk territory and about the supposedly active collaboration of the mass of the Kalmyk population with the occupation. The leadership of the Kalmyk republic responded quickly: ''It is necessary to report to the Central Committee of the AUCP (B) that the question of banditry in Kalmykia has been greatly exaggerated by enemy spies,'' they reported to Moscow. As an example they cited the rumor that two thousand military personnel of the 110th Special Kalmyk Cavalry Division had gone off to join the bands. In fact the division, at that time, was fighting at the front with its full complement of troops.[56] Of course the phrase ''enemy spies'' was completely in the spirit of the times but hardly corresponded to reality. These rumors—or should we call them "denunciations"?—reached Moscow through various channels—party, government, military, and state-security. At a later time the responsibility for them was laid entirely on Beria. What remains unclear, however, is the role of the command staffs of the military districts and fronts.

The disbandment of the 110th Division on January 27, 1943, could hardly have occurred without the direct participation of the military command. And a number of other national and regional military formations of the Caucasian peoples were liquidated at the same time. Although the reason officially advanced for this was the sharp reduction in the native element within the division, it is easy to imagine the anxiety this caused the Kalmyk leaders.

This anxiety was reflected in a rigorous purge of the party ranks and state apparatus immediately after the withdrawal of the occupation forces and in the very harsh criticism and self-criticism at the January, February, April, and June 1943 plenums of the regional committee. The completion of the operation to eliminate the bandit gangs in the Kalmyk territory was insufficient to ward off the fatal turn of events.

In the summer of 1943 a section of the leadership of the Kalmyk ASSR began to express lack of confidence in the Kalmyk people in general. Kichikov rhetorically characterizes this as "a one-sided and unhealthy attitude toward shortcomings and difficulties, and toward the political and cultural backwardness displayed by part of the Kalmyk population."[57]

In August 1943 P. F. Kasatkin, cadre secretary of the Kalmyk regional committee of the party, sent the Central Committee a memorandum in which—to judge from the account in Kichikov's dissertation—he indiscriminately lumped together the actions of part of the Kalmyk population on the White side in the civil war, on the one hand, and the collaboration of part of the population with the Nazis, on the other. In so doing, as Kichikov puts it, Kasatkin made no class differentiation between the White counterrevolution and the working people of Kalmykia who took up arms to oppose both domestic and foreign counterrevolution during the civil war. Kasatkin also made no distinction between collaboration with the Nazis "by anti-Soviet, kulak, nationalist, and criminal elements," on the one hand, and the attitude of the bulk of the Kalmyk population, which remained loyal to Soviet rule, on the other.[58]

According to Kichikov's summary, Kasatkin pointed to "survivals of the past" linked with the particular characteristics of the Kalmyk way of life and the historical development of Kalmyk society, and interpreted them as manifestations of "bourgeois nationalism."[59] Kasatkin's memorandum became the basis for the charges soon brought by the Soviet government and the Central Committee of the party against the entire Kalmyk people.

Our Kalmyk historian, Kichikov, accuses the former cadre secretary of the Kalmyk regional committee of making insinuations against the political reliability of the Kalmyk people in general and the political and practical competence of most of the leaders of Kalmyk nationality. Kichikov also accuses Kasatkin of distorting the facts. For example, Kasatkin's memorandum made no mention of the fact that the plans of a fascist diversionist organization were disrupted thanks to the assistance of the Kalmyk population.*

Rumors reached Elista that a decision had been made in Moscow—or was being considered—to institute nationwide repression against the Kalmyk people as a whole. On December 25 the Kalmyk regional committee addressed a letter to the Central Committee describing the measures taken to combat the bandits and the effective elimination of them.[60] However, it is unclear whether this document reached the Central Committee before the Kalmyks were deported, since it is dated only two days before that event.

On December 27, 1943, Kalmyk party and government person-

---

* Kichikov, p. 326. Kichikov's point is not quite clear. If Kasatkin's memorandum was written in August 1943, he can hardly be reproached for not mentioning events of—October 1943! There is another matter worth noting—the report of the existence of a diversionist organization left behind by the Nazis in Kalmyk territory.

nel were informed orally that the Kalmyk people, without any exceptions, were to be resettled. Moreover, the reasons given for the dissolution of the Kalmyk ASSR, according to Kichikov, corresponded essentially to the negative remarks in Kasatkin's memorandum.[61]

Over a period of four days, December 27 to December 30, troops of the MVD (Ministry of Internal Affairs) carried out the forced deportation of the entire Kalmyk people. The freight trains made their way toward Siberia and Central Asia.

The operation was not limited to the territory of Kalmykia alone. On all the fronts, Kalmyk soldiers and officers were summoned from their units, gathered at certain assembly points, and shipped off to work battalions. The only exceptions made were in the cases of Colonel-General O. I. Gorodovikov, general inspector of cavalry of the Red Army and a hero of the civil war, and his nephew, Major-General B. B. Gorodovikov, commander of the 184th Dukhovishchinskaya Rifle Division.[62]

In concluding this section of our book it is necessary to say something about the contribution of the Kalmyk people to the war against Hitler Germany.

That the majority of Kalmyks not only remained loyal to the Soviet system but fought to defend it, arms in hand, is shown by the following facts.

On June 30, 1941 as many as 2,000 applications from individuals wishing to volunteer for military duty had reached the enlistment offices of Kalmykia. A people's militia was organized and by July 30, 1941, it numbered 8,664 persons (of whom 3,458 were Communists and Komsomols).[63]

In September 1941 the 189th Kalmyk Cavalry Regiment (2,000 sabers strong) was formed as part of the Seventieth Cavalry Division.[64] During the first eight months of the war 20,032 men were sent into the army, and by the beginning of 1943 23,000 soldiers from the Kalmyk ASSR were serving in the Red Army.[65]

From July 1942 to January 1943 the 110th Special Kalmyk Cavalry Division took part in combat operations in the Don region and the Northern Caucasus. Many Kalmyk soldiers fought on other sectors of the Soviet-German front. Kalmyks also participated in underground groups and partisan detachments, both on the territory of their republic and outside its borders.

In the Red Army the Kalmyks were regarded as good soldiers, and when in early 1944 the order came down to remove all military personnel of Kalmyk nationality from the front lines, there were commanders who quickly changed the records on the nationality of their troops and officers and thus kept them in their units. (Kichikov interprets this as a demonstration of internationalism and friendship among the peoples, as a result of which "a significant number of Kalmyk officers and a certain percentage of Kalmyk noncommissioned officers" remained in the active army. There are of course simpler explanations—the desire not to lose good soldiers or commanders, and, in some cases, considerations of personal friendship.)

Our historian gives the approximate figure of four thousand for the number of Kalmyks who remained in the Red Army until the end of the war,[66] but he does not indicate his source.

There were cases in which Kalmyk soldiers sent to construction battalions escaped and returned to the front lines, where they reintegrated themselves into the Red Army ranks.[67]

Many thousands of Kalmyks were decorated for valor, and several were honored as Heroes of the Soviet Union.[68]

Even if we accept as reliable the figure of five thousand—cited in many works by Western scholars—for the number of Kalmyks who served in military formations of the Third Reich, it can be seen that the overwhelming majority of Kalmyks living on Soviet territory, of whom there were 134,000 in 1939,[69] remained loyal to the Soviet system.

Since the Second World War there have been repeated attempts to create an idealized picture of Nazi occupation policies in the Caucasus and Kalmykia. In fact, however, the essence of the German occupation policies was the same wherever Hitler's armies imposed their rule. These can be characterized briefly as mass atrocities, violence, oppression and enslavement of the population, and organized plundering of the national wealth.

Alexander Dallin, a historian of high professional standards, has written in his study of this subject: "In spite of the special policy pursued, it would be historically false to depict German rule in the Caucasus as an idyll unmarred by abuse and brutality. Looting, physical maltreatment, and discrimination were widespread. Economic exploitation was attempted on a wide scale. In cases of doubt, military demands had priority over indigenous interests. German reprisals for killings or pillage of army stocks were as swift and savage as elsewhere in occupied Europe." [70]

If the crimes committed by Hitler's forces in the Caucasus were fewer than in the Ukraine, let us say, or Central Russia, or the Crimea, that is simply because of the shortness of their stay in that area. It was not because the Nazis had succeeded in winning over the Caucasian people.

IV

The Special Settlements

HUNDREDS OF THOUSANDS of inhabitants of the Caucasus and the Crimea were sent into exile. For thousands of kilometers railroad cars jammed the main rail arteries heading east. At major junctions where engines were changed and water taken on, passengers in oncoming trains, railroad workers, and local residents who happened to be in the vicinity stared at the poor unfortunates in fear and surprise.

Dmitry Gulia, the great Abkhazian educator, and his wife, Yelena Andreyevna, were traveling toward Moscow at that time. At one of the railroad stations in the Northern Caucasus they saw

an unbelievable sight: an extremely long train, made up of heated freight cars, jammed full of people who looked like Caucasian Mountaineers. They were being taken off somewhere toward the east, women, children, old people, all. They looked terribly sad and woebegone. . . . These were the Chechens and Ingush, and they were not traveling of their own free will. They were being deported. They had committted "very serious crimes against the Motherland.". . .

"These children too?" [Gulia burst out].
"The children are going with their parents."
"And the old men and women?"
"They're going with their children."
"But that sounds like the idea of the 'criminal population'
. . . it's been sixty years since I heard that." *

This meant the deportation of almost a million people! But for what crime? Nothing was said or written about that anywhere![1]

If you are a historian and are curious about this, take a look at the local newspapers *Groznenskii rabochii* (Grozny worker), *Sotsialisticheskaia Kabardino-Balkaria* (Socialist Kabardino-Balkaria), *Kalmystskaia pravda* (Kalmyk truth), *Stavropol'skaia pravda* (Stavropol truth), and *Krasnyi Krym* (Red Crimea) for 1943 and 1944. From the 1943 newspapers you will learn about the people's joy on the occasion of their liberation from enemy occupation and the feats of arms of the sons of Checheno-Ingushetia, Kabardino-Balkaria, Karachai, Cherkessia, and Kalmykia. You will read about the exploits of the Crimean partisans and such Red Army soldiers as the famed pilot Sultan-Khan, a Crimean Tatar who twice became a Hero of the Soviet Union; the Chechen sniper Khanashpe Nuradilov; the Hero of the Soviet Union Ibraikhan Beibulatov; the Balkar Konkoshev, also a Hero of the Soviet Union; and many, many others. Let us remember these names. They will appear again, but only fourteen years later, in the newspapers of 1957–58.

But from the newspapers of 1944 you will not learn much. And you will not find a single word there about the deportations— neither in the central press nor in the local press.

Nevertheless you can find out something from the newspapers. Thus, the twenty-fifth anniversary of the Chechen-Ingush ASSR

---

* The reference is to the tsarist deportations of entire village populations after the Crimean War.

fell on February 25, 1944. But there were no greetings from Moscow.[2] That was undoubtedly a bad omen.

And sure enough, on March 3, 1944, *Groznenskii rabochii* appeared for the last time as the organ of the regional committee and Grozny municipal committee of the party and of the Supreme Soviet of the Chechen-Ingush ASSR.[3] On Saturday, March 4, 1944, the masthead of *Groznenskii rabochii* bore the sole designation "Organ of the Grozny Regional and Municipal Committees of the AUCP (B)."[4]

Where did the Supreme Soviet of the Chechen-Ingush ASSR disappear to? Its deputies, along with the voters, were on their way to some rather distant places.

During those very days a session of the Supreme Soviet of the RSFSR was convening in Moscow. The Russian Federation, of course, included the autonomous areas of Checheno-Ingushetia, Kabardino-Balkaria, Karachai, and Kalmykia. But none of the deputies to the RSFSR Supreme Soviet rose from their seats to ask what had happened to their colleagues, the deputies from the autonomous areas of the Northern Caucasus, or why such a massive relocation of voters had taken place, or for what reason, after all, the autonomous areas had been liquidated. The deputies in Moscow, the chosen representatives of the indestructible bloc of Communists and non-party people, remained silent.

In order to transport the people of the Northern Caucasus and the Crimea to their new places of settlement some 40,200 freight cars were needed. You don't have to be a military specialist to imagine the scale of Operation Deportation or to understand what the removal of a great quantity of transport equipment from military use implied under wartime conditions in the fall of 1943 and the first half of 1944, how it affected military operations. Any commandant in charge of a railway station who delayed a train with military cargo could be court-martialed and convicted of sabotage with the full severity of the law in time of war. What punishment then should be meted out to a commandant who delayed hundreds of trains for several months?

We do not know, and will never know for certain, what were

the consequences of the shortage of transport equipment for Soviet troops, what effect it had on the situation at the front, or how many military personnel perished because of military supplies that were not delivered in time, military equipment that was left stranded, and troops who were not redeployed in time.

S. M. Shtemenko, the former deputy chief of the General Staff of the Soviet army, in his memoirs, makes it fairly clear that there were difficulties, for example, in transferring troops from the Crimea to other fronts after its liberation, and that these difficulties arose in connection with the forced removal of the Crimean Tatars. Shtemenko was in the Crimea from May 14 to May 23, 1944, i.e., at the time the operation to remove the Crimean Tatars was being planned and carried out. This is what he writes: ''The transfer of troops was especially complicated. There was not enough fuel for the use of motor transport to concentrate the troops at railroad stations. The distribution of railroad cars and other troop conveyances in the Crimea was wholly in the hands of General Serov, who was then the deputy people's commissar of internal affairs. The only way you could get them from him was with a fight. The main loading stations were in the Kherson and Snigirevka areas, to which the troops had to make their way, for the most part, on foot.''[5]

The Russian word *spetsialny,* borrowed from the West, refers to something unique, different from anything else, some property inherent only in a given object or in a particular situation or set of circumstances.

During the civil war in Russia this word, like many others in the Russian language, began to be abbreviated. Right at the start there appeared the contraction *voyenspets,* from the Russian phrase *voyenny spetsialist* (military specialist); then a whole avalanche of names and terms came crashing down, with the word-element *spets* acquiring quite a unique and important meaning. Thus there appeared the word *spetsovka,* meaning work clothes, overalls; *spetsotdel,* referring to the Special Department, a secret body in charge of the cadres and system of functioning in a factory, etc.; and *spetspayok,* the special food allowance, sometimes for particular categories of workers, but most often for apparatus personnel. Such word formations containing the element *spets* are quite numerous. In fact, *spets* acquired an independent meaning all its own, designating a specialist—not just any specialist but one with an engineering or technical background trained in the old, prerevolutionary school.

Then the time came when it was necessary to give a name to places of internment and exile for Soviet citizens who had gone wrong.

Thus the world was given a new word, *spetsposeleniye,* i.e., "special settlement." It was used for the places of penal exile or deportation where life went on, not in accordance with ordinary laws and customs, but under a special system governed by harsh regulations and instructions confirmed by the USSR Council of Ministers and the Ministry of Internal Affairs (MVD).

The special settlement system began to take shape as early as the time of collectivization, when hundreds of thousands of "de-kulakized" peasants were stripped of their property and civil rights and sent to Siberia.

The people deported from the Caucasus and the Crimea were also consigned to a life under *spetsposeleniye* regulations.

And there is something else to keep in mind—the deportation of a million people could not have been carried out if the state agencies involved had not accumulated a vast amount of experience in governing masses of people in the concentration camps, if they had not tested out the smallest details of people's behavior hundreds of times in places of exile and internment, if they had not learned that the life of a deported person was worth nothing, and if they had not been sure that at every level of the repressive apparatus they would enjoy complete immunity.

What were the reasons for the forced resettlement of these populations? What was the motivation behind it?

These questions are not nearly so simple as they seem at first glance.

The official charge was that the overwhelming majority of the deported people had collaborated with the enemy, the Nazi army and the German occupation regime.

But obviously we should also mention certain "theoretical" justifications for this and similar actions against entire nations put forward by the head of the Soviet state and the Communist Party, the central and infallible authority of the world Communist movement on the national question and every other question. Need I mention his name?

The documentation on this question is extremely limited. There are the officially published decrees and laws of the Supreme Soviets of the USSR and RSFSR on the dissolution of the autonomous republics, and there are accounts of unpublished laws found in dissertations and history books on the respective republics or in histories of the party organizations in these republics. A significant amount of work in bringing such documents to light, systematizing them, and partially analyzing them has been done by Kh. I. Khutuyev and R. I. Muzafarov. In addition to the decrees, the instructions on the regime of the *spetsposeleniye* and the modification of that regime have even greater importance.

On June 25, 1946, retroactively, two years after the event, the Presidium of the Supreme Soviet of the RSFSR issued a decree entitled "On the Dissolution of the Chechen-Ingush ASSR and the Transformation of the Crimean ASSR into the Crimean Region." We cite the text of this decree in full.

During the Great Patriotic War, when the people of the USSR were heroically defending the honor and independence of the fatherland in the struggle against the German fascist invaders, many Chechens and Crimean Tatars, at the instigation of German agents, joined volunteer units organized by the Germans and, together with German troops, engaged in armed struggle against units of the Red Army; also at the bidding of the Germans they formed diversionary bands for the struggle against Soviet authority in the rear; meanwhile the main mass of the population of the Chechen-

Ingush and Crimean ASSRs took no counteraction against these betrayers of the fatherland.

In connection with this, the Chechens and the Crimean Tatars were resettled in other regions of the USSR, where they were given land, together with the necessary governmental assistance for their economic establishment. On the proposal of the Presidium of the Supreme Soviet of the USSR the Chechen-Ingush ASSR was abolished and the Crimean ASSR was changed into the Crimean region.

The Supreme Soviet of the Russian Soviet Federative Socialist Republic resolves:

1. To confirm the abolition of the Chechen-Ingush ASSR and the changing of the Crimean ASSR into the Crimean region.

2. To make the necessary alterations and additions to Article 14 of the Constitution of the RSFSR.

Chairman of the Presidium of the Supreme Soviet of the
RSFSR I. Vlasov
Secretary of the Presidium of the Supreme Soviet of the
RSFSR P. Bakhumurov
Moscow, The Kremlin, June 25, 1946[6]

The charges against the Balkars were presented in a decree of the Presidium of the Supreme Soviet of the USSR dated April 8, 1944. The accusation was that during the occupation of the Kabardino-Balkar ASSR by the German fascist invaders the main mass of the Balkars had betrayed the fatherland, joined armed detachments organized by the Germans, engaged in subversive activities against Red Army units, assisted the Nazi occupation forces by serving them as guides in locating the mountain passes in the Caucasus, and, after the Germans had been driven out, joined bands organized by the Germans to combat the Soviet authorities.[7]

Ch. S. Kulayev reports similar accusations against the Karachai in his dissertation: ''The charges against the Karachai people were that during the occupation of their territory the bulk of them had allegedly betrayed the fatherland, joined detachments organized by the Germans, assisted the fascist forces by serving as guides to the Caucasian mountain passes, and, after the liberation of the Caucasus, joined armed bands organized by the Germans to combat the Soviet authorities."[8]

The allegations contained in the decree on the dissolution of the autonomous areas cannot withstand criticism. In the case of the Crimean Tatars, how can they be accused of participating in diversionist bands after the retreat of the Germans when every last Tatar was deported from the Crimea a week after it was liberated?

Also totally absurd is the charge that "the main mass of the population of the Chechen-Ingush and Crimean ASSRs took no counteraction against these betrayers of the fatherland." If that was so, it would mean that it was the Russian population of the Crimea, above all, and of Checheno-Ingushetia, that took no counteraction. The "main mass" of the population in the Crimea (approximately half) was Russian, the Tatars constituting only one-quarter. In Checheno-Ingushetia, on the other hand, about 35 percent were Russians, living alongside the 50 percent who were Chechens. But here too, Russians fall into the category of the "main mass of the population." Consequently, according to the logic of the authors of the decree, it is not only Chechens and Ingush (incidentally, there is not one word in the decree about the Ingush, but they were deported nevertheless; that is the level on which the law operates in the Soviet Union!), and not only Crimean Tatars, who should have been deported, but Russians too. Fortunately that did not happen.

Is it true that the Tatars, Chechens, and Ingush did not defend the "honor and independence of the Fatherland" during the war? Is it right to counterpose them to the "people of the USSR"? Don't they also belong to that category? The truth is that they were represented in the Red Army in as great a percentage as any of the other peoples in our country.

Finally, as N. S. Khrushchev acknowledged at the Twentieth Congress of the CPSU, there were absolutely no military·considerations necessitating the deportation of peoples, because the enemy was being rolled back everywhere under the blows of the Red Army.

These charges were not only absurd but grossly immoral and unjust. It is impermissible to spread public accusations of treason against every last member of a nationality, including nursing infants and their mothers and helpless old people.

Where did such accusations come from? After all, this type of thing could only reflect negatively upon the first multinational socialist state in the world, where, according to the constantly reiterated official doctrine, the ideology of internationalism, friendship, and brotherhood prevailed.

Perhaps Stalin's speeches will shed some light on this problem and help us probe the theoretical foundations of these arbitrary and lawless acts against entire peoples.

During the great purges of the 1930s the justification was advanced that the class struggle intensifies as the country advances toward socialism. This provided the rationale for the condemnation and elimination of individuals and even entire groups. In 1944 Stalin introduced a new element, providing the "basis" for possible repression against entire nations. He divided the nations of the world into "aggressive" and "peace-loving."[9] (This served the purpose, simultaneously, of justifying the lack of Soviet preparedness for the war with Hitler's Germany in June 1941.)

In 1949, in connection with certain considerations of the moment, Stalin referred to the German and Soviet people as people who "possessed the greatest potential in Europe for carrying out major actions of worldwide importance."[10] So much the worse for the other peoples of Europe!

Is there any need now to say that this way of dividing nations into different categories is totally indefensible? For if nations can be divided up this way, why not separate them into other categories, for example, revolutionary and nonrevolutionary, patriotic and unpatriotic, loyal and treacherous, etc., etc.?

Incidentally, Karl Marx during the 1848 revolutions (when he did not yet suspect that all his writings would become "classics of Marxism"!) wrote angrily more than once about nonrevolutionary nations (a category he applied, in particular, to the Czechs). Therefore, in principle, the possibility of classifying nations by categories relevant to one or another conjunctural consideration was always present in the arsenal of Marxism. For the sake of fairness and accuracy we should note that Lenin rejected such classifications and that his works in fact corrected the Marx of the pre-Marxist period.

On the other hand, charges of treason and betrayal, and the possibilities and ways of using such charges, fascinated Stalin throughout his long political career. During the civil war, he was never ashamed to bring such accusations against loyal military specialists. In the interwar period he sent hundreds of thousands of people off to a better world on charges of betrayal, and among these, political opponents constituted only a numerically insignificant minority. During the Great Patriotic War, in an effort to clear himself of responsibility for the setbacks in the initial phases, he applied the charge of treason to all Soviet soldiers and officers unfortunate enough to become prisoners-of-war. He simply wrote them off, refusing to recognize their existence. In replying to a toast by Churchill at the Teheran Conference (this happened on November 30, 1943, at a formal dinner in honor of the British prime minister's sixty-ninth birthday) Stalin said that in Russia even people of little courage, even cowards, had become heroes. And whoever did not become a hero was killed.[11]

However, we should discard the primitive notion that decisions taken at the highest level occurred unexpectedly and were made only because Stalin or someone else wanted them. In a state like ours, where the historical experience of bureaucratic rule has deep roots going back to Byzantium, and where the Muscovite officials were well versed in the ways of dragging things out for years without ever making any decisions, an extremely important role is played by the official "case" or "dossier," or, to use the modern term, the system of informing and denunciation.

Such an important decision as the forced deportation of peoples had to be, and in fact was, a kind of official endorsement of, or throwing of official weight behind, the great flood of reports about the situation in the various areas concerned. The reports were forwarded through various parallel channels—those of the party and government, of the military, the central headquarters of the partisan movement.

It is enough to read the documents published in collections dealing with Kalmykia and the Crimea during the war to see this. But thanks to the digging done by historians, we also have at our disposal unpublished documents of the party leadership in the Crimea and Kalmykia which show that the initial accusations came from party bodies in these autonomous republics. As we have said, the charge of treason against the entire Crimean Tatar people originated with the leadership of the partisan movement in the Crimea. But it is obvious that this information, which was sent to the Crimean regional committee of the party, was initially accepted by that committee as accurate and passed along as such. Only later, when it became clear that a goodly amount of misinformation was concealed in these reports, did the regional committee leadership try to correct its earlier point of view; but, alas, the "case" had already been started, and it moved along inexorably, following its own special bureaucratic laws, and heading toward the bureaucratically logical and inevitable culmination. The same thing happened in Kalmykia and, we must assume, in the other autonomous regions as well.

Thus, there are reports that the Astrakhan and Stalingrad regional committees insisted on the deportation of the Kalmyks and that the summary memorandum by P. F. Kasatkin, cadre secretary of the Kalmyk regional committee, lay at the heart of the "case" against the Kalmyks. There is very little information on the positions taken by higher bodies of the party in the other areas where autonomy was abolished.

One of the fundamental features of the phenomenon that is (not very precisely) called Stalinism is the provision and use of information organized on the principle of verisimilitude, true in part but seasoned with a goodly share of misinformation—that is, legally sanctioned eyewash.

Toward the end, apparently, both the Crimean and Kalmyk regional committees tried to forestall the fatal outcome. But, alas, they proved powerless to prevent it. The leaders of the autonomous regions themselves were forced to take the long road—not all of them, of course; just the ones in the appropriate national category. However, owing to another peculiarity of the Soviet system, caste privilege, the leaders of Kalmykia traveled to the areas of special settlement not in cattle cars but in first-class passenger coaches; some leaders in the Crimea were even allowed to travel to the railroad stations in their own official automobiles.

We do not have any accurate information on the circumstances under which the final decisions were made at the highest level. There is only the testimony of Colonel Tokayev, an Ossetian defector to the West. His account was first published in 1951 in *Sotsialisticheskii vestnik,* a publication sharing the views of the Socialist International; since then it has been cited in a number of works by Western scholars, including the book by Robert Conquest.[12]

There are two points worth noting in Tokayev's assertions: first, the recommendation of the Soviet general staff, made as early as 1940, that the situation in the Northern Caucasus made it necessary to take "special measures" in good time; and second, that the final decision to deport the Chechens was not the result of Stalin's unilateral action but the outcome of a discussion on the question at a joint meeting of the Politburo and the Soviet High Command on February 11, 1943.

Tokayev reports that two main points of view were expressed at this meeting. One view, supported by Molotov, Zhdanov, Voznesensky, Andreyev, and others, favored the immediate and public dissolution of the Chechen-Ingush ASSR. The other view, supported by Voroshilov, Kaganovich, Khrushchev, Kalinin, and Beria, and endorsed by Stalin, was to postpone the deportation until the Germans had been driven back. Only Mikoyan, who agreed in principle that the Chechens should be punished, expressed the fear that such a deportation would hurt the Soviet Union's reputation abroad. According to other reports, when the idea of deporting the Chechens and Ingush came up in the Politburo, the question was raised whether this would hurt the oil industry in the area. A most reassuring answer was forthcoming—that the entire engineering and technical staff was Russian and that only an insignificant number of Chechens and Ingush were employed as oil workers, in low-skilled jobs. We are unable to verify these reports and therefore will refrain from commenting.

At the Twentieth Party Congress, three years after Stalin's death, it was officially stated that the deportations of the Caucasian peoples, the Kalmyks, the Crimean Tatars, and even the Volga Germans were arbitrary acts associated with the "Stalin personality cult." But it took eleven years (from 1956 to 1967) for this acknowledgment to find official, legal expression, and the wrongs that were committed have not been fully corrected even to this day.

We sometimes forget, however, that deportation became a standard method of official policy not in 1943 or 1944 but much earlier, during collectivization, when the kulaks, or, more precisely, the millions of peasants who were listed as "exploiters," were deported from the central regions of the country, and from the Ukraine and the Northern Caucasus, to Siberia and Central Asia. Who can say exactly what a "kulak" was? No one. The victims of collectivization included not only the wealthier peasants who employed wage labor but also vast masses of other peasants, indiscriminately "de-kulakized" for a variety of reasons. This downtrodden mass of people, stripped of their possessions and all their rights, became the foundation on which the special settlements were built. The first instructions on special settlements appeared at that time. Simultaneously the first deportations along national lines began.

As far back as the early 1930s, Chinese and Koreans were resettled from the Far East and were also removed from the central regions of Russia. Some of them were openly accused of being Japanese agents. Later, in 1939–41, trainloads of "hostile class elements" rolled eastward from the newly annexed Baltic countries, the Western Ukraine, Western Byelorussia, Northern Bukovina, and Bessarabia. In the summer of 1941 German citizens of the USSR, the overwhelming majority of whom were from the liquidated Volga German ASSR, appeared in Central Asia. By the time of the war with Hitler Germany the regime of the special settlements had taken final shape, although this system continued to be modified in different ways—always in the direction of greater harshness.

In 1948 and 1949 a new wave of deportees from the Baltic and Moldavia reached Central Asia and Siberia. A campaign of wholesale collectivization, with "liquidation of the kulaks as a class" to accompany it, was then underway in those areas. These harsh measures might have resulted in what the authorities would regard as "a more homogeneous class society" in Latvia, Lithuania, and Estonia, but they were not taking any chances; they also wanted to water down the indigenous national population.

We should note that this wave of deportees involved people inhabiting the border regions of the Soviet Union. To replace them, people from Central Russia and the Ukraine were resettled in these areas.

The colonizing of the localities depopulated by the 1943–44 deportations involved mainly Russians, although in part local nationalities considered loyal were also brought in.

If Koreans and Chinese had at one time been suspected or accused of being agents of Japan, why shouldn't the Kalmyk Buddhists be regarded as potential agents of China? Stalin himself, in one of his speeches at the Twelfth Party Congress in 1923, said, "All we have to do is make one small mistake in relation to the small territory of the Kalmyks, who have ties with Tibet and China, and that will affect our work in a far worse way than mistakes in regard to the Ukraine." [13]

Did this express an internationalist understanding of the connection between national relations and international relations—or was this a Great Russian chauvinist speaking? Lenin gave a clear and unambiguous answer to that question in one of his last articles. * The leader of the Russian revolution regarded Stalin unqualifiedly as a Great Russian chauvinist.

It was precisely to Stalin, Ordzhonikidze's ally, that Lenin was referring when he wrote of a certain Georgian who "himself is a real and true 'nationalist-socialist,' and even a vulgar Great Russian bully." [14] Lenin insisted on distinguishing between the nationalism of oppressor nations and the nationalism of oppressed nations, the nationalism of big nations and the nationalism of small nations. In regard to the nationalism of small nations, Lenin wrote, "we, nationals of a big nation, have nearly always been guilty of an infinite number of cases of violence and insult." [15] And further on Lenin wrote, "That is why internationalism on the part of oppressors or great nations, as they are called (though they are great only in their violence, great only as bullies), must consist not only in the observance of the formal equality of nations but even in an inequality which obtains in actual practice. . . . In one way or another, by one's attitude or by concessions, it is necessary to compensate to the non-Russians for the lack of trust, the suspicion, and the insults to which the government of the 'dominant' nation subjected them in the past." [16]

* V. I. Lenin, "K voprosu o natsional'nostiakh ili ob 'avtonomizatsii' " [On the question of nationalities or 'autonomization'], in *Polnoe sobranie sochinenii* [Collected works], 55 vols. (Moscow, 1958–65), vol. 45, pp. 356–62. This article, or rather series of notes, embodies Lenin's last commentaries on the national question. The notes were dictated on December 30 and 31, 1922. They were written in response to the conflict between the Transcaucasian Territorial Committee of the RCP(B), headed by G. K. Ordzhonikidze, and the leadership of the Communist Party of Georgia, headed by P. G. Mdivani, over the question of whether Georgia should join the USSR directly or by way of the Transcaucasian Federation. Ordzhonikidze, who held the second view, became so rude toward his opponents that he slapped one of them in the face. Lenin, indignant at Ordzhonikidze's action, and at the conduct of Stalin and Dzerzhinsky, who gave de facto support to Ordzhonikidze, wrote this article, which later came into the hands of the Politburo. Lenin's letter was made known to the delegates at the Twelfth Party Congress, and Stalin was forced to include some of Lenin's points in the resolution of the Congress on the national question. But this was only for appearance's sake.

What was involved here of course was not Lenin's idealism or altruism, although such considerations should not be totally disregarded in evaluating his actions. Lenin was concerned about preserving the multinational state and about the influence its example could have in the future on the nations of Asia. A political realist and to a certain extent a pragmatist, the head of the Soviet state understood clearly that "crudity or injustice [these are Lenin's own words] toward our own *inorodtsy* [non-Russian nationalities]" would reflect negatively on the authority of the Soviet state among the peoples of Asia.[17] Even Lenin, to the end of his days, used the term *inorodtsy* (literally, "outlanders"), which had a plainly chauvinist ring in political parlance. That was the term the tsarist government had always used for the non-Russian peoples of the Russian empire.

At the Twelfth Party Congress Stalin was forced to acknowledge Lenin's reproach, and he warned in one of his speeches against the danger of degeneration on the part of responsible officials in the party and government apparatus, the danger of falling into Great Russian chauvinism, which he called a "growing force," a "fundamental danger," and the "most dangerous enemy" which "must be overthrown."[18] However, Stalin succeeded in including a point in the congress resolution on the need for a struggle against "local nationalism" as well. This phrase was widely used against any attempt to practice national self-determination on the local level. The danger of being accused of "local nationalism" always hung over the heads of party and government personnel like a sword of Damocles.

The history of the years that followed shows that Stalin's Great Russian chauvinist inclinations became firmly entrenched. The internationalism which he proclaimed in public served only as a cover for his "great-power" chauvinist policies.

At the same time, several generations of Soviet citizens had been raised on the ideology of internationalism, and it was precisely those whose views were formed in the 1920s and 1930s who felt this disparity between word and deed most painfully. The question arises whether the intensification of Great Russia chauvinism was not one of the consequences of the victory of the idea of building socialism in one country.

In the second half of the 1930s an avalanche of Russian super-patriotism swamped the cultural life of our society. The search for "great forefathers"; the wave of films praising Russian military leaders of the past, such as Aleksandr Nevsky, Suvorov, Kutuzov, and the Russian tsars Peter the Great and Ivan the Terrible; the flood of literary works that glorified the deeds of Ivan III and Dmitry Donskoi, that praised everything "truly Russian" and ridiculed *inostranshchina* ("everything foreign"); and the turn toward themes from Russian history in music, the opera, and drama, to the exclusion of almost everything else—all this testified to the fact that the development of culture in our society from then on would be strictly limited to the needs of this policy of Great Russian conformism.

Our society suffered the consequences of this chauvinism for a long time—even after the war with Germany had ended in victory for the USSR and the defeat of fascism. There came the "great days" of the struggle against "cosmopolitanism," the bellicose campaigns against the cultures of other people under the pretext of combating local nationalism—for example, the campaigns against the Kirgiz and Kazakh epic poems *Dzhangar* and *Manas*—and the totally groundless denial of the progressive nature of the national liberation movements of non-Russian peoples against the tsarist autocracy, such as Shamil's movement and the Andizhan uprising.

The killing of Mikhoels and the so-called Doctors' Plot*

* Solomon M. Mikhoels, a famous Soviet actor and a chairman of the Soviet Jewish Anti-Fascist Committee, was assassinated in January 1948 in Minsk, Byelorussia, by Soviet state security agents on the order of Stalin himself. This assassination was part of an anti-Semitic campaign in the USSR. The culmination of this campaign was the so-called Doctors' Plot in 1952–53, masterminded by the chiefs of Soviet state security. A group of prominent Soviet doctors, predominantly of Jewish origin, were arrested and accused of plotting against the lives of top Soviet leaders. During the investigation some of the defendants were tortured and died. Soon after Stalin's death in March 1953 the accusations against the doctors were officially withdrawn.

showed that the process of moral decay in our society had reached its limit. The "most dangerous enemy," far from being overthrown, had triumphed, at least for the time being.

Thus we must view the deportation of the people of the Caucasus and the Crimea, the Kalmyks, and, in part, the Baltic peoples not only as an expression of the arbitrary lawlessness of the Stalin regime, which of course it was, but also, and more importantly, as an inseparable part of the history of the Soviet state and of Soviet society and its intellectual culture.

The resettlement of nationalities also had a pragmatic purpose—to colonize border regions with a "reliable" Russian population. This aim by no means represented something new or unusual. From time immemorial the Russian state had sought to establish reliable buffer zones along its borders made up of "loyal" people and settlers who would block any possible enemy invasion.

Although times had changed, in principle the motivation remained the same. The deportation of the Muslims of the Caucasus and of the Crimean Tatars was undoubtedly related to the tensions that existed between the USSR and Turkey during World War II and to the pan-Turkist schemes of the Turkish chauvinists, which enjoyed the approval of Nazi Germany for a certain period. The overwhelming majority of the Muslim population, of course, had no knowledge of, or interest in, pan-Turkism or the ambitions for a Greater Germany. However, several Turkish emissaries did visit the Crimea and the Caucasus during the German occupation, and several thousand members of the peoples later deported did betray the Soviet government during the war by serving in German military formations. This proved to be sufficient grounds for accusing these entire peoples of high treason and charging them with collaboration on a massive scale.

If the Koreans and Chinese could be considered potentially dangerous in relation to Japan, and the Kalmyks in regard to China, then collaboration between the Muslim people of the Caucasus and Muslim Turkey could also be regarded as a potential danger, and was so viewed. The irrefutable proof that the repression was aimed against the Muslim people is that approximately eighty thousand Georgian Muslims were deported from Georgia to Central Asia in 1947. Some particularly zealous Soviet propagandists of the 1940s referred to the Crimean Tatars as "Crimean Turks," thereby unwittingly agreeing with the viewpoint of the émigré Tatar nationalists. That is how far one could go to "prove" the necessity of clearing the border regions of all "hostile populations."

How can we explain the deportation of the Greeks from the Black Sea coastal region in 1944? They certainly had nothing to do with pan-Turkist schemes. Their historical homeland, of course, was Greece. But what was Greece? A capitalist state with a monarchical form of government which maintained an alliance with imperialist England. In view of that, how could the Greeks be left in the coastal districts of our state?

And the Kurds—that nomadic people who did nothing but wander, crossing the state borders of the USSR whenever they had a mind to. What a golden opportunity for spies! But what about those Kurds who had adopted a settled way of life? Well, what about them—Kurds are Kurds, aren't they? And so the Kurds were sent off to Central Asia. And the Khemshins went with them. These are a settled people, to be sure, but most of them live in Turkey. And in general they are rootless cosmopolitans. But excuse us; that was later, and it referred not to the Khemshins but to the Jews!

We conclude that the deportation of peoples was regarded by the state as a preventive measure serving military needs (Volga Germans, Kurds, Turks, Khemshins, and Greeks), as a punitive measure (Chechens, Ingush, Balkars, Karachai, Crimean Tatars), but also as a measure with strategic implications, to create a more "reliable" border population. There is every reason to regard the deportations of 1943 and 1944 as a component part of Soviet foreign policy at the time. No sooner had the war ended than the Soviet government demanded of Turkey that it return Kars, Ardagan, and other areas that had gone to Turkey after World War I.

This border zone had already been cleared of "disloyal" Muslim peoples—against the possibility of armed conflict.

The wartime deportations were not isolated actions carried out under emergency conditions. There were deportations both before and after the war.

In the late 1940s and the early 1950s preparations were begun to deport all Jews from the main industrial and political centers of the country and send them to Siberia. As a propaganda convenience the Jews were referred to as "cosmopolitans." And the "cosmopolitans" were depicted as agents of American and "Zionist" imperialism. The political, ideological, and material preliminaries for such deportations had already been made. (But Stalin's death in 1953 put an end to this danger.)

In the Baltic region there was another mass expulsion of the native population along class lines, connected with the wholesale collectivization in those areas. Also, Greeks from other parts of the country were resettled in Central Asia. Several tens of thousands of repatriated Armenians were also expelled from Armenia.* And preparations were made to deport the Abkhazians from their Black Sea coastal region.

Thus the tragic policy followed toward the small nations of the Caucasus and the Crimea was in fact a continuation of a process begun long before the war and not ended to this day.

The deportation of entire peoples was made an essential component of nationalities policy in the final years of Stalin's rule. And it was one of the most important symptoms of the profound political and moral crisis that Soviet society and the Soviet state were passing through.

At the same time, deportation was not a completely new phenomenon in Russian history, although it had never before attained such massive proportions.

Shortly after the Crimean War (1854–55) tsarist officials

---

* Many repatriated Armenians who arrived in Soviet Armenia were settled in a town with the name—Beria! History often plays such nasty tricks.

brought wholesale charges against the Crimean Tatars for allegedly having helped Turkey. These charges were meant to divert attention from the inept performance of the tsarist government itself, and of its bureaucrats, during the war. They chose the Crimean Tatars as their scapegoat. Consequently, 100,000 Tatars were expelled from the Crimea at that time.

All of progressive public opinion condemned that brutal act of great-power chauvinism. On December 22, 1861, Herzen's *Kolokol* published an article entitled "The Persecution of the Crimean Tatars." It said in part: "And so the government has driven the loyal Tatar population from the Crimea in order to settle Russians there—and only when the 100,000 Tatars were no longer there did the government realize that Russians would not go to the Crimea. . . . The bloodiest battles and universal famine or plague could hardly have depopulated and devastated the territory in so short a time as the departure of the Tatars, speeded along by the administration." [19]

A well-known Russian historian of the late nineteenth century, Ye. Markov, decisively refuted the lie leveled against the entire Crimean Tatar population that they had betrayed Russia and supported the Turkish side during the Crimean War. This is what he wrote:

How strange! Instead of driving out the thieving bureaucrats and shooting them on the spot, the most honorable of the Crimean tribes, the Tatars, were driven out and shot. No one was hurt more by the war than this quiet and industrious people. It was dishonored by treachery. It was forced to leave its ancient homeland, where only a Tatar would be able to live happily without want. Anyone who has spent even a month in the Crimea can understand that the Crimea has perished since the Tatars were expelled. They alone could endure this hot, dry steppeland, knowing the secrets of how to find and bring up water, successfully breeding their cattle and cultivating their orchards. . . .

But perhaps it is true that the Tatars committed treason and that their departure was necessary, no matter how pitiable it was? That is what I thought when I went to the Crimea. . . . But I have not met a single long-time resident there who does not have the utmost contempt for all the vile allegations against the Tatars—which resulted in such a disaster for the entire region. They agree unanimously that without the Tatars we would have lost the Crimean War—all the means of local transport and vital necessities were entirely in their hands.[20]

Soon after the Crimean War a movement in favor of resettlement in Turkey began among the Causasian Mountaineers, partly instigated by the local feudal lords and Muslim clergy who were linked with Turkey. The tsarist government not only did not try to prevent this movement but even encouraged it, hoping to use the Mountaineers' lands as endowments for the Cossack villages the government was establishing in the region. From 1858 to 1865 some 500,000 Mountaineers resettled in Turkey. Half of them died from various diseases along the way, and a third of them, women and children, were sold into slavery.[21] Realizing that they had been cruelly deceived, the survivors sought to return to Russia as quickly as possible. The Chechens were particularly determined to return; many of them were even willing to accept the Orthodox faith as long as they could live in their homeland. The tsarist government tried to discourage the return of the Mountaineers in every possible way, although it could never break their indomitable will to regain their homeland. The bulk of the Chechens did return from Turkey after the Russo-Turkish war of 1877–78. From then on, the tsarist administration promoted the image of the Chechens not only as "savages" (something constantly reiterated even earlier by General Yermolov, the "conqueror of the Caucasus") but also as traitors who had sold themselves to Turkey. For the Mountaineers, the years in Turkey were remembered as a time of sorrow. Nevertheless, this stubborn stereotype of the Caucasian Mountaineer, as someone who was only waiting for a chance to defect to the enemies of Russia, still influenced those who in 1942–43 provided information to the highest authorities and those who decided these peoples' fate.

Historical experience suggests that decision-making is influenced to a certain extent by stereotyped ideas about events, people, and nations. The personal inner world, the cultural background and mentality of the decision-maker are of considerable importance. There can be no doubt that when the fate of the Chechens and Crimean Tatars was decided, the historical experience of the relations between these people and the Russian state played no little role.

Thus, for the second time in a century, the Chechens, Ingush, and other Mountaineer people and the Crimean Tatars faced the danger of physical annihilation.

The overall direction of the deportation of all these people was in the hands of L. P. Beria, member of the Politburo and the State Defense Committee, and people's commissar of internal affairs of the USSR. His deputies, B. Kobulov and I. Serov, had the direct responsibility for the compulsory resettlement operations.*

The preparations for the deportation operations were made with great care. The fundamental principle was surprise. Perhaps Hitler's surprise attack on the Soviet Union served as a model. Troops were brought in, the means of transport collected, and the routes for the truck columns established—all well in advance. The

---

* Kobulov and Serov accumulated quite a bit of experience in deporting people not only in the Crimea and the Caucasus but also in Bessarabia, the western parts of the Ukraine and Byelorussia, and the Baltic. For his outstanding "services" in the deportation effort, and, one must suppose, for his great "skill as a military leader" demonstrated in Operation Deportation, Serov was awarded the highest award for generalship, the Order of Suvorov, First Class. This order was generally presented to military leaders for the successful direction of operations on a scale no smaller than an entire front.

Kobulov was shot along with Beria in 1953. Serov, however—thanks to the part he played in the arrest of Beria, and to Khrushchev's patronage—became, for a time, the head of the state security agency, the KGB, and later was appointed deputy chief of the general staff. He rose to the rank of general of the army and became a Hero of the Soviet Union. Later he was reduced in rank and retired; today he lives happily on his pension.

operations were carried out by NKVD troops, convoy guards, and border guards. During the war, despite the colossal losses and the extreme need for people at the front, quite a few "special-purpose" troops remained in the rear.

In addition to the NKVD troops, however, three armies, one of them a tank army, were deployed to Checheno-Ingushetia a few months before the deportations.

The intention was to carry out the operations in the shortest possible time. The troops were trained to forestall resistance or to suppress it immediately if it broke out. The fulfillment of these aims was made easier by the fact that the bulk of the male population was absent from the territory, serving in the ranks of the Red Army and in partisan units, or languishing in German captivity. These people, of course, never suspected what fate was being prepared for their families and for themselves, that is, if they survived the war and the German camps.

In resettling these peoples no exceptions were allowed. Shortly before the deportation operations, members of the party apparatus in responsible positions were sent to the localities to assist in the deportation of their fellow tribespeople. They were warned that if they gave away the secret of the coming operations they would be severely punished under the law.

In Chechnia the men were taken directly from celebrations of Red Army day, where demonstrations of skill in horseback riding were given. The women and children were taken directly from the villages. In the Crimea all the men were called to the military enlistment offices, where they were held until their families had been transported to loading stations. Then they themselves were sent to construction battalions. In Kabardino-Balkaria, Russian, Ukrainian, and Georgian women married to Balkar men were offered the choice of breaking their marital ties and remaining in their homes or sharing the fate of their husbands and children. Not all were able to withstand this test—in some cases children were left without their mothers and husbands without their wives.

What tests people are forced to face, and what sufferings they are forced to bear, by others just like them!

The following incident occurred in Yevpatoria during the Nazi reprisals against the population after the unsuccessful Soviet landing of January 1942. On the outskirts of the town thousands of people were being shot and thrown into ditches. The land was soaked in blood. Sometimes the graves, hastily covered by the Nazi butchers, would stir—some were still alive when they were thrown into the ditches. The earth itself seemed to groan from the unbearable suffering. One man who had been shot—badly wounded but still alive—managed to reach the porch of his home at dawn. His wife opened the door and saw her husband, the father of their children. Bloody but unbowed, he had crawled back to their doorstep. What did the woman do? She called a *Polizei* and he finished off the poor unfortunate before her eyes.

But let us return to those who were being deported or perhaps already had been.

Tenzila Ibraimova, a Crimean Tatar woman who now lives in the city of Chirchik in Tashkent region, gives the following account:

> We were deported from the village of Adzhiatman in Frei-dorfskii district on May 18, 1944. The deportation was carried out with great brutality. At 3:00 in the morning, when the children were fast asleep, the soldiers came in and demanded that we gather ourselves together and leave in five minutes. We were not allowed to take any food or other things with us. We were treated so rudely that we thought we were going to be taken out and shot. Having been driven out of the village we were held for twenty-four hours without food; we were starving but were not allowed to go fetch something to eat from home. The crying of the hungry children became continuous. My husband was fighting at the front, and I had the three children.
>
> Finally we were put in trucks and driven to Yevpatoria. There we were crowded like cattle into freight cars full to overflowing. The trains carried us for twenty-four days until we reached the station of Zerabulak in Samarkand

region, from which we were shipped to the Pravda *kolkhoz* in Khatyrchinskii district.[22]

The following is the account given by a well-known Crimean Tatar writer, Shamil Aliadin, a veteran of the Great Patriotic War, at a hearing before the Central Committee of the CPSU in 1957:

> And now allow us to present a true picture of the deportation of the Tatars from the Crimea, which, in our view, may not as yet be completely clear to the members of the Presidium.
>
> At 2:00 in the morning of May 17, 1944, Tatar homes were suddenly broken into by NKVD agents and NKVD troops armed with automatics. They dragged sleeping women, children, and old people from their beds and, shoving automatics in their ribs, ordered them to be out of their homes within ten minutes. Without giving them a chance to collect themselves, they forced these residents out into the street, where trucks picked them up and drove them to railroad stations. They were loaded into cattle cars and shipped off to remote regions of Siberia, the Urals, and Central Asia.
>
> People were not allowed to get dressed properly. They were forbidden to take clothes, money, or other things with them. The agents and armed troops swept through these homes, taking these people's valuables, money, and anything they liked, all the while calling the Tatars "swine," "scum," "damned traitors," and so on.
>
> These people left their homes naked and hungry and traveled that way for a month; in the locked, stifling freight cars, people began to die from hunger and illness. The NKVD troops would seize the corpses and throw them out of the freight car windows.
>
> There was no order or discipline in the journey. Trains destined for Uzbekistan were sent to Siberia or the Altai region. But the bulk of the population ended up in Uzbekistan.[23]

The deportation of the other peoples was carried out in a similar way.

How many of the deportees died along the way? In all likelihood, there are statistics on this in the Ministry of Internal Affairs, but none have been published.

In the "Appeal of the Crimean Tatar People" quoted above it is said that the Tatars who perished constituted 46 percent of the population. This figure is apparently exaggerated. What exact information do we have? On May 17–18, 1944, 194,111 Crimean Tatars were deported from the Crimea.[24] Later it became known—through the court case brought by the Procuracy of the Uzbek SSR in 1968 against participants in the Crimean Tatar movement, E. Mametov, Yu. Osmanov, and others—that the procurator disputed the assertion, contained in a number of the documents of the Crimean Tatar movement, that 46 percent of the Crimean Tatars had perished during the deportation. The prosecution presented two very important documents on this question to the court.* Both of these documents were first published in *samizdat,* and then in New York in 1974.[25] We reproduce them in full.

SECRET

| Uzbek SSR Ministry for the Preservation of Public Order Tashkent | Copy no. _____ Investigations Department of the KGB of the Council of Ministers of the Uzbek SSR |

No. 7/3-2026 February 15, 1968   Here
Reference No. 3/184 of February 14, 1968.

There is no analytical data on changes in the composition

---

* Case no. 103 of the Procuracy of the Uzbek SSR, vol. 17, pp. 101, 102. In connection with this case the former Soviet army general P. G. Grigorenko, one of the most remarkable people of our time—a much-decorated military man, commander of a division during the Second World War, and subsequently a chief of department at the Frunze Military Academy—was summoned to Tashkent and then held by the KGB and forcibly subjected to "treatment" in a "special" psychiatric hospital of the prison type. After nearly six years in this "special" hospital Grigorenko was freed, not least because of the pressure of world public opinion.

of the people deported from the Crimea in the period from May–June 1944 to January 1, 1945, in the archive materials of the Ninth Section of the KGB and the Fourth Special Section of the NKVD of the Uzbek SSR.

One of the reports on the economic and domestic arrangements for special settlers from the Crimea dated April 9, 1945, mentions that from the moment of deportation of the special settlers from the Crimea to the Uzbek SSR, i.e., from May 1944 up to January 1, 1945, 13,592 persons, or 9.1 percent, died.

Head of First Special Section of the Ministry for the Preservation of Public Order of the Uzbek SSR, Colonel Kravchenko

Head of Third Department, Stokova
Received February 20, 1968

SECRET

Uzbek SSR Ministry for the Preservation of Public Order
Tashkent
No. 7/3-373 February 8, 1968
Reference No. 3/99 of January 29, 1968

To the Chairman of the KGB of the Council of Ministers of the Uzbek SSR, Lt.-Gen. S. I. Kiselev

Here

This is to inform you that the arrival in the Uzbek SSR of specially deported Tatars from the Crimea began on May 29, 1944, and was completed in the main by July 8, 1944. In the archive documents of the Ninth Section of the KGB and the Fourth Special Section of the MVD of the Uzbek SSR, the first data on the number of Crimean Tatars arriving at special settlements are for July 1, 1944. By that date 35,750 families had arrived, a total of 151,424 persons.

On January 1, 1945, the number of specially deported Crimean Tatars in Uzbekistan was 137,742, consisting of 36,568 families—21,619 men, 47,537 women, and 65,586 children under sixteen.

The situation on January 1, 1946, was: 34,946 families,

constituting 120,129 persons, of which 21,332 were men, 42,071 women, and 56,726 children under 16.

In the period from January 1, 1945, to January 1, 1946, 13,183 persons died, of whom 2,562 were men, 4,525 women, and 6,096 children under sixteen. The change in the number of specially deported Crimean Tatars is also to be explained by departures from the republic, removals from the register, escapes from places of settlement, and arrests for crimes.

First Deputy Minister for the Preservation of Public Order, Uzbek SSR, General, Internal Service, rank III, M. Beglov

Received February 9, 1968

From these documents it seems that the number of Crimean Tatars who died in Uzbekistan from July 1944 to January 1, 1946, amounted to 17.7 percent of all who had arrived there. The fate of the remaining twenty thousand is referred to rather vaguely here. But according to the information of the Crimean Tatar movement, the number of those who fled or were jailed was one thousand women and two thousand seven hundred children. Apparently many also moved, with the permission of the authorities, in order to be reunited with their families. Kh. I. Khutuyev reports the following, for example: "In the first two years after the war, as a result of long and painstaking efforts," approximately forty thousand people won permission to move from Kazakhstan to Kirgizia to be reunited with their families, and more than thirty thousand from Kirgizia to Kazakhstan.[26] We have no information on the other areas of resettlement, but apparently there were many similar cases in Siberia, Uzbekistan, and the Urals.

The bulk of the Crimean Tatars were settled in Uzbekistan, but some also ended up in Kirgizia, Kazakhstan, and the Urals. There are more precise details about where the Kalmyks were settled— in the Krasnoyarsk and Altai territories and in the Novosibirsk, Omsk, Tiumen, Kemerovo, and Khakas regions, while a small number were sent to Sakhalin region, Central Asia, and Kazakhstan.

The known number of Kalmyks in particular areas in May–June

1944 were as follows: Novosibirsk region, 17,100; Tiumen region, 14,174 (4,700 families); Khanty-Mansiisk, Yamalo-Nenets, and Tobolsk districts 8,587 (2,878 families). During the whole of 1944, 5,891 Kalmyks were brought to Khanty-Mansiisk district alone. The number of Kalmyks sent to Omsk region was 18,718; to Krasnoyarsk district, at first 3,000 and then another 21,000 families (the number of individuals is not known); and to Taimyr, 900 families.[27]

Thus, the Kalmyk people were dispersed over a vast territory, and it is rather to be marveled at that despite great human losses (about which more below), this people returned to its native land after fourteen years, having preserved its distinct character and inner sense of itself.

How many were deported altogether in 1943–44? Kh. I. Khutuyev gives analytical data on the number of *spetsposelentsy* (special-settlement inhabitants) in Kazakhstan and Kirgizia, drawn from the archives of the Ministry for the Preservation of Public Order of each republic. In Kazakhstan there were 507,480 and in Kirgizia 137,298.[28] Of the Crimean Tatars, it is known that 151,424 arrived in Uzbekistan. There are no general figures for the number of *spetsposelentsy* in Uzbekistan and the RSFSR. However, since we know the statistics of the 1939 census, and if we allow for the fact that the number of special settlers increased over time with the arrival of demobilized military personnel sharing the fate of their relatives, we can assume with a fair degree of certainty that the overall figure of those deported in 1943–44 was somewhat more than one million.

Half of them, if not more, were children under sixteen.

Among the Crimean Tatars in the special settlements of Uzbekistan, 15 percent were men, 32 percent women, and 53 percent children. Among the Balkars living in Kirgizia, men constituted 18 percent, women 29 percent, and children 52 percent.[29] The information on the percentages among the Karachai are similar.[30] In Osh region in the Kirgiz SSR, Balkar women and children constituted more than 70 percent, and in Frunze region they were 80 percent of all special-settlement residents.[31]

And so the wrath of the state descended primarily on women

and children. Can it be that they were "traitors" and "betrayers"? Or was this system of punishment for entire peoples simply an expression of the vindictiveness of authority and the complacency of power toward the weak and defenseless?

These are not just rhetorical questions. The Twentieth Party Congress, which condemned the deportation of peoples as an arbitrary and lawless act, did not make a profound analysis of what had happened or of its causes and consequences for the entire system of relations between nations within our country. Nor was that done at the Twenty-second Party Congress. Until a strict analysis, without any favoritism, is carried through and practical conclusions drawn from such an analysis (sooner or later this is inevitable), we cannot say that justice has triumphed. After all, it is not accidental that the Crimean Tatars still live far from their homeland and that the problems of the German population in our country have not been resolved.

In the deportation no exceptions were allowed. As Kh. I. Khutuyev wrote, "Everyone was subjected to these repressive measures—active participants in the civil war and Great Patriotic War, including injured veterans, men who had become invalids as a result of injuries on the job, the wives and children of those fighting at the front, Communists and Komsomols, leaders of party and government organizations and deputies to the Supreme Soviets of the USSR, the RSFSR, and the Kabardino-Balkar ASSR."[32] This was equally true of the other people whose autonomy was abolished.

The first years of life in the new locations were the most difficult for the residents of the special settlements. Hunger and disease swept down upon them, carrying thousands and thousands to their graves.

Here is how Tenzila Ibraimova describes life in the Tatar special settlements:

> We were forced to repair our own individual tents. We worked and we starved. Many were so weak from hunger they could not stay on their feet. From our village they de-

ported thirty families, and of these only five families, themselves stricken with losses, survived. In the surviving families only one or two remained, the rest having perished from hunger and disease.

My cousin Manube Sheikislamova and her eight children were deported with us, but her husband had been in the Soviet Army from the very first days of the war and was lost. And the family of this fallen soldier perished in penal exile in Uzbekistan from starvation; only one daughter, named Pera, survived, crippled by the horrors and hunger she had experienced.

Our men were at the front and there was no one who could bury the dead. Sometimes the bodies lay among us for several days.

Adzhigulsum Adzhimambetova's husband had been seized by the fascists. She was left with three children, one girl and two boys. Her family starved just as ours did. No one gave them either material or moral support. As a result the daughter died of starvation to begin with, and then the two sons, both on the same day. The mother was so weak with hunger she could not move. Then the owner of the house threw the two little infant corpses out onto the street, on the edge of an irrigation canal. Some Crimean Tatar children dug little graves and buried the unfortunate little ones. How can I speak of this? I can hardly even bear to remember it. Tell me, why were such horrors permitted?[33]

Shamil Aliadin gives this testimony: "Upon arrival in the town of Begovate, for example, fifty to one hundred people were shoved into dugouts where, before the Tatars, German prisoners had lived. Under these frightful conditions the Tatars began to die off. . . ."[34]

Kh. I. Kutuyev gives this testimony: "In Kazakhstan and Kirgizia, as a result of the unsatisfactory living conditions, exhaustion and emaciation, the abrupt change of climate, the inability to adapt to local conditions and the spread of epidemics, mainly typhus, a large number of those who had been resettled died. . . ."[35]

A. Dudayev asserts the following: "The most fearful and irremediable blow to the Chechen-Ingush people was struck in the first two or three years, when starvation and the most dreadful diseases obliged them to bury tens and hundreds of thousands of their fellow tribespeople in the steppes of Central Asia."[36]

Should the mortality rate among the Crimean Tatars for the first year and a half of deportation, i.e., 17.7 percent, be applied to the other people inhabiting the special settlements? That is doubtful because some suffered from this special settlement regime more than others. We will try to determine the numerical losses that these people suffered later on in this chapter.

The people of the special settlements lost not only their possessions and the roofs over their heads but also their fundamental civil rights as guaranteed by the Soviet constitution. They were even denied the right to an education. They did not have the opportunity to read in their own language, nor to publish or obtain literary works or periodicals in their language. Their intellectual life came to a standstill.

The iron regime of the special settlements bound them hand and foot.

On November 26, 1948, four years after the deportations, the Supreme Soviet of the USSR issued a decree (it was not published) which explained that all of these people had been deported permanently, without the right to return to their previous places of residence. For violations of the rules established for the special settlements, or of travel procedures, they were threatened with imprisonment, or hard labor for up to twenty-five years. Sentences were handed down by the MVD Special Board (Osoboye Soveshchaniye). Aiding and abetting or harboring an offender was punishable by five years at hard labor.[37]

According to the rules governing the special settlements, everyone, from nursing infants on up, was subjected to so-called special accounting. Residents of the special settlements had to register their addresses once a month with the special registration office of the MVD. No residents of special settlements could leave their places of residence without the knowledge and permission of the MVD commandant. For example, Chechens and Ingush could not travel beyond a radius of three kilometers from their places of residence.[38] A curious fact is that *spetsposelentsy* were brought to party meetings (a few of them were allowed to remain in the party) in trucks accompanied by armed guards. After each meeting the guards would deliver them to their homes. The settlements in which the *spetsposelentsy* lived were divided into groups of ten houses each, with chiefs placed in charge of each group. Every ten days they reported to the commandant on the state of affairs in the group assigned to them.[39]

Between the settlements, districts, and regions in which *spetsposelentsy* lived, roadblocks were set up, and commandant's offices and sentry posts for internal-security troops were established. At the boundaries between republics and territories, on the other hand, "their own special Chinese walls were erected."[40]

A system of passes was introduced, especially for *spetsposelentsy* who did not work where they lived but had to travel to other locations. These passes had to be shown the instant they were asked for. Failure to have one's pass with one could entail serious difficulties for the offender, ranging from fines to arrest and imprisonment.

"If a commandant, after stopping a bus at a roadblock and asking, 'Any aliens here?' (meaning deportees) received a negative answer, then all passengers would be checked for their passes without exception."[41]

In 1948 the rules were made more severe. Even officers of the Soviet Army, who earlier had reported to military registration offices, were placed on the special register for deportees."[42]

The "local authorities," namely the MVD commandants, interpreted the rules governing the special settlements according to their individual inclinations and flights of fancy. The petty tyranny and arbitrariness of the old tsarist town governors (*gradona-chalniki*), immortalized by Saltykov-Shchedrin, were resurrected here with Asiatic refinement and purely Russian verve.

The commandant of the village of Karkunduz in Dzhambul region, Kazakh SSR, arrested citizen Kenetat Kharunovna She-vayeva in the middle of her wedding because she was marrying citizen Anuar Mesostovich Elbayev without his, the comman-dant's, knowledge.[43]

During a family picnic in the Karadagovskaya Woods in Ka-zakhstan on May 2, 1948, an MVD special squad led by a captain came up and checked the documents of all present. When the doc-uments proved to be in order, the captain announced that it was forbidden to play and dance the lezginka (!), calling it "bandit music."[44]

Not all *spetsposelentsy*, of course, submitted to such humiliat-ing conditions. Some tried to protest; others ran away, hoping to reach their native grounds and hide out in the mountains. They would be caught and thrown into prison camps, and again would escape.

In the spring of 1945 the Ingush in Borovoye revolted. Che-chens took an active part in the celebrated prison uprising of Octo-ber 1954 known as the "rebellion at site 521." And the Crimean Tatar demonstration in Chirchik is well known.*

But the most commonly chosen form of protest was the letter to Stalin, for everyone knew he was the "Best Friend of All the Peo-ples" as well as their "Father." The newspapers never tired of

---

* Here is what the late writer A. E. Kosterin, a prominent figure in the Soviet civil-rights movement, wrote about that demonstration: "In Chirchik, in Uzbekistan, the Crimean Tatars wished to observe Lenin's birthday in their own way. They had good reason to show this man a special regard. He had given them autonomy and restored and strengthened their national dignity, language, and culture. And what happened? Our agencies of law and order turned upon these peacefully gathered Tatars with police clubs and streams of putrid water from fire pumps. As many as three hundred people were arrested." ("Razdum'ia na bol'nichnoi koike" [Re-flections from a hospital bed], manuscript [Moscow, 1968], p. 13.)

printing statements by workers addressed to the Leader with reports on labor accomplished, pledges to undertake new labors, and patriotic effusions. Thus, a statement addressed to Stalin was also the most natural form for a complaint to take. However, it was one thing to send greetings and something else to ask for justice and to complain about injuries or offenses committed by persons in authority. This kind of thing could easily be interpreted as slander against the Soviet state and social system. (And everyone knows what you get for slander.)

When a letter of complaint was sent to Stalin, the result was, in the best of cases, some "explanatory work" by agents of the government that is, a little "brainwashing" for the author of the letter. Thus in response to a letter by the Balkar writer Kerim Otarov, a wounded veteran of the war who had asked that the injustice done to the Balkars be reversed, an agent of the MVD of Kirgizia reported the following resolution of the problem: "I discussed a similar statement in person with Otarov. The correspondence is attached to his dossier."[45]

But there could be even worse variants—prison or a labor camp. The much-decorated Balkar combat officer A. Sottayev addressed a complaint to Stalin asking only an end to the rude and insulting treatment of special settlers (nothing more!) For this they gave him twenty-five years in the camps. A second Balkar, Bashiyev by name, likewise landed in prison for writing a complaint; he ended his days in confinement. And a third, named Karayev, spent six months in prison for a similar "crime."[46] There were quite a few such cases.

How did the local authorities and the local inhabitants receive the special settlers? And how did the life of the new arrivals develop?

Of course the local authorities were not prepared for such a huge influx of people. There were already many evacuees in Central Asia, Siberia, and the Urals who had arrived together with their factories and offices, or simply in a private capacity. There was a shortage of housing. All available living space was occupied. It is no wonder, then, that the newcomers found themselves in dreadful conditions, conditions which—it must be said—were absolutely unfit for human life.

In Kirgizia as of September 1, 1944, only 5,000 out of 31,000 special-settler families had been provided with housing. In Frunze region only 1,675 rooms could be found for 8,950 families, that is, one room for every five families.[47] In Kameninskii district eighteen apartments had been prepared for nine hundred families, that is, fifty families to an apartment! In Talas region 116 families had to live simply under the open sky. In Leninopolskii district, and also in Talas region, only 163 rooms were found for 625 families.[48] In Kurshabskii district two and three families lived in rooms of six to twelve square meters in size, with up to ten persons per family, that is, from twenty to thirty persons to a room.[49]

One would have to have a truly exceptional imagination to picture the full horror of the everyday life of the special settlers, who in Kazakhstan and Kirgizia alone numbered some 645,000. They were assigned to 4,036 *kolkhozy*, 254 *sovkhozy,* and 167 towns and workers' settlements, where they found work at 2,500 industrial enterprises.[50] Only after fourteen years, in 1958, had 93.8 percent of all the families forcibly deported to Kazakhstan and Kirgizia been provided with permanent quarters.[51] But by then it was time for them to leave again.

The work which special settlers obtained was, more often than not, heavy labor. The Kalmyks, for example, were sent to commercial fishing districts in Omsk region; in Krasnoyarsk territory, where they also did logging work; in Khanty-Mansiisk district; and in the Taimyr. In those areas the climate was cold and severe, quite different from the baking hot climate of the Caspian region. And the Kalmyks died in droves.

The special settlers employed in various kinds of jobs died from malnutrition and other diseases, from cold, and simply from homesickness.

The war was on, and everywhere a shortage of workers was felt. The local authorities were instructed to make maximum use of the new arrivals in industrial plants and in agriculture. Officials in the Central Asian republics, the Kazakh SSR, and the north and northeast of the RSFSR were allocated funds to build housing and provide minimal food and clothing allowances for the special settlers.

The average earnings of resettled persons were 20 to 30 percent less than those of skilled workers at the same factories. The newcomers often did not have the necessary skills and were not accustomed to the work. The same was true in the *kolkhozy*. In 1945 the average number of workday units (*trudodni*) completed by each special settler in the *kolkhozy* of Kazakhstan was 133.3, whereas for the local inhabitants the average was between 220 and 240. The reasons were everywhere the same—abnormal living conditions, work that was unfamiliar to most of the special settlers, and a climate they were not accustomed to.[52]

Nevertheless, those who were given steady jobs were lucky. In Uzbekistan, for example, it was often the case that Crimean Tatars simply would not be hired if their nationality became known, and if they nevertheless succeeded in finding work, it was not long before they were ousted from their jobs.[53]

Among the able-bodied population it was hardest for intellectuals who did menial labor. The Tatar writer Dzhavtobeli became a bricklayer. Another well-known Crimean writer, A. Dzhermendzhi, became a warehouse worker at a *sovkhoz* in Guryev. Constantly persecuted because of his nationality, Dzhermendzhi finally could bear it no longer and hanged himself.*[54]

There was a war on.

The special settlers were ill-clad, ill-fed, and ill-housed. Were the material losses they suffered as a result of the deportation cov-

---

* This was also the fate of a Russian poet, our pride and joy, Marina Tsvetayeva. Unable to endure life's cruelties, the hunger and the humilities, she too laid hands upon herself during the war, in Yelabug. And she did not live under the special-settlement regime; she had simply been evacuated. There were well-known writers in her circle and their wives as well. Did any of them offer her a helping hand or try to ease her burden? Which of them on that accursed night sensed with their inborn writers' intuition that a human being of rare, even divine gifts was about to die?

ered by the allotments for their support and material assistance? Left behind in the homeland from which they were forcibly expelled were their homes, farmsteads, cattle, farm equipment, home furnishings, libraries, personal belongings, money, and clothing. In fact, in 1943 and 1944 a million people were subjected not so much to expropriation as to pauperization. During the first years in the special settlements they were reduced to the status of disenfranchised and persecuted beggars. The homes of the deportees were taken over by new settlers. Their property was plundered. Their personal belongings were appropriated by those who carried out the deportation—Beria's MVD agents and the soldiers assigned to the deportation operation. Of the socialized property that was dissolved by the deportation, the state was able to make use of only half, and the other half was irretrievably lost. At a time of severe food shortages in the country, the livestock in the depopulated areas was left without any care or tending and a great many of these animals died.[55]

In Kazakhstan and Kirgizia the material difficulties of the first months prevented the special settlers from taking any active part in production. In 1944, out of the 219,665 able-bodied persons in the resettled population registered in Kazakhstan, 85,000 did not work. In Kirgizia, 14,216 persons counted as able-bodied did not work.[56]

The central committees of the union republic Communist parties, along with the regional committees and even the regional executive committees, were supposed to report regularly to the Central Committee of the party on the working and living arrangements for the relocated populations.

During the long years of forced exile, local and party bodies were sent quite a few official resolutions on economic and labor arrangements for the special settlers.

For example, a decree of the Council of People's Commissars and the Central Committee of the Communist Party of Kirgizia of September 11, 1944, entitled "The Situation in Regard to Economic and Labor Arrangements for Special Settlers," condemned those leaders of local party and government bodies who had failed to disperse to the special settlers the food allowances earmarked for them out of funds on the republic level and local level. The resolution gave this as the reason for the increasing frequency of deaths from undernourishment and infectious diseases among the resettled population.[57]

In a resolution dated October 12, 1945, i.e., a year later, the leadership of Kirgizia was still calling for more intensive measures to combat the massive epidemics that were causing a high mortality rate.[58] A decree of the Council of People's Commissars and the Central Committee of Kirgizia dated November 21, 1946, commented on the way in which the Bystrovskii district committee of the party had carried out the resolution of September 11. While it was acknowledged that the deportees had been fully provided with work, it was also noted that the funds allotted to bring their living conditions up to normal—specifically, to provide food, clothing, and housing, and to combat the epidemics—had obviously been insufficient.

In December 1945 the Council of People's Commissars and the Central Committee of the Communist Party of Kazakhstan appealed personally to Molotov to provide aid to the republic in completing the economic and labor arrangements for the deportees in the territory of Kazakhstan. But Molotov did not even consider this request. And a similar request from the Kirgiz leadership was treated in exactly the same way by the Central Committee secretary, Malenkov.[59]

Even four years after the deportations there were 118,259 special settlers counted as being in extreme need in regard to food in the following regions of the Kazakh SSR: Akmolinsk, Aktiubinsk, Kokchetav, Kustanai, North Kazakhstan, and Semipalatinsk. Among these 2,590 were suffering from dystrophy as a result of malnutrition and emaciation.[60]

Children! They constituted half the total category of special settlers. Thousands of them died. Those who survived had to be educated. But the school situation was rather complicated.

In Kazakhstan in 1944 only 16,000 out of the 50,323 school-age children of special settlers attended school, and in Kirgizia in 1945 the figure was 6,643 out of 21,015.[61]

Schools with instruction in the native language of the settlers did not exist. Publication of textbooks and supplementary materials was suspended. Most of the children knew no other language. And there were other obstacles. One of the party documents of that time stated: "The situation in regard to the schooling of children of the special settlers has improved somewhat by comparison with the initial phase; however even now it remains unsatisfactory. There are several reasons for this. Most of the children do not know the languages in which instruction is given in the location where they are settled; there are isolated cases of parents opposed to their children attending school; and because of inadequate shoes and clothing, the majority of the children attending school are forced to discontinue their attendance during the winter."[62] In Novosibirsk region, for example, as many as 30 percent of the children of Kalmyk nationality did not attend school.[63] But even the children who were fortunate enough to complete their primary school education (at most a seven-year course) could not count on continuing their education, because travel by special settlers was restricted and secondary schools with a full number of grades did not exist everywhere. This was not the only obstacle. There were others: for example, school directors who feared they might bring the anger of higher authorities down upon themselves if they accepted children from the oppressed nationalities; housing problems; and the problem of earning a living while in school.

And those who overcame all obstacles and entered specialized secondary schools or higher educational institutions were often denied stipends, not provided with dormitory rooms, and otherwise persecuted because of their nationality. Thus, M. Babayev, a student at the Kirgiz Pedagogical Institute, was expelled from his dormitory because he was a Balkar. The teacher Sh. Chechenov (later the minister of education of the Kabardino-Balkar ASSR) was arrested during classes at school and held for five days because he had overstayed the time limit on his pass, having been delayed longer than he had anticipated at an examination session at the Pedagogical Institute in the city of Frunze.[64]

D. Nominkhanov has tried to show in his dissertation and in a number of his published works that the Kalmyks were given the opportunity of studying in higher educational institutions even under special-settlement conditions. However, his works contain devastating statistics indicating exactly the opposite. For those who graduated from the Abakan State Teachers and Pedagogical Institute in 1947 he gives four names and adds "etc." During the years from 1948 to 1953 another four graduated from higher educational institutions "etc."[65]

At the Scientific Research Institute of Language, Literature, and History of Khakassia there was one Kalmyk working in the capacity of senior research fellow. At the above-mentioned Abakan Institute, one Kalmyk, a holder of a candidate's degree, worked as a senior lecturer. One Kalmyk defended his candidate's dissertation at Omsk. And at the Kazan State University one Kalmyk, the writer, Aksen Suseyev, defended his candidate's dissertation in philology.[66]

Essays in the History of the Kalmyk ASSR gives a list of the Kalmyks who graduated from higher educational institutions in the years of exile—essentially no more than one from each institution.[67]

After such "encouraging" statistics, Nominkhanov draws a conclusion that is far from optimistic: "Unquestionably, resettlement brought the cultural develpment of the Kalmyk people to a standstill."[68] Such a conclusion is justified in relation to the other repressed peoples as well.

Whatever the regime, one still had to work, to provide for oneself and one's family, in order to live, or rather to survive.

The desire to survive, to preserve the existence not only of oneself and one's dear ones, but of one's nation, so that someday it might be possible to return to one's native parts—this was both an unconscious instinct and a fully conscious aim.

People are made in such a way that even under the dreadful conditions of overcrowding, poverty, hunger, and spiritual oppression, they do not lose their human traits. So it was with the special settlers. For them, as for the people whose lives were relatively free, life went on not only with sorrows but with joys as well. They not only buried their dead and mourned them; they also started new families and raised children. They manufactured machinery and dug coal in the mines. And such labor, heavy as it was, helped them to survive—whether mountain people or steppe-dwellers.

The overwhelming majority of settlers remained obedient to the authorities who had torn them away from the land of their forebears and subjected them to unending insults and humiliations. Despite that, if anything was uppermost in their thoughts it was the desire for justice, which they were sure would be forthcoming from those same authorities.

In a sense these special settlers remained patriots. They did not rebel, there were only rare outbursts; they worked hard, they became shockworkers and exemplary workers and victors in socialist competition.* Gradually the local people got used to them, began to regard them as their comrades, gave them awards for work well done, held them up as examples to others, and (Allah be praised!) even wrote about their patriotic achievements in the realm of labor not only in wall newspapers and factory newspapers but also in the district and regional press.

A new generation was growing up that had never seen the Caucasus mountains nor the Caspian steppes nor the sea. This generation bore within itself such strong love and devotion to the land of its mothers and fathers that even if a thousand or even two thousand years went by, this longing, like the force of gravity, would continue, no matter what, and all obstacles on the road home from the Diaspora would be overcome.

Meanwhile the authorities on the whole were content—the special settlers were gradually becoming part of the labor force, mak-

* All terms for workers who overfulfilled their quotas.

ing themselves at home in their new locations, and becoming reconciled and accustomed to the new situation.

From Alma-Ata, Frunze, Tashkent, and remote Siberian territorial, regional, and district centers, regular reports flowed in to Moscow on the material conditions and the political and moral state of mind of the special settler population.

One of the documents sent from Kazakhstan to Moscow wrote about the special settlers as follows: "Most of them, both those employed in industry and those in agriculture, take a conscientious attitude toward their duties, participate in socialist competition, and are increasingly numerous among the ranks of shock-workers and Stakhanovites."[69] The *History of the Kabardino-Balkar ASSR* states: "The Balkars were resettled in Kazakhstan and Kirgizia. But in spite of this injustice, the Balkars demonstrated a high sense of patriotism. They joined in actively in the labor process, and the overwhelming majority of them worked honestly and conscientiously."[70] Another official publication comments: "The Balkars labored patriotically in Kirgizia and Kazakhstan."[71]

After the death of Stalin and the removal of Beria, a year passed before the situation of the special settlers was affected. In July 1954 the USSR Council of Ministers passed a resolution "On the Lifting of Certain Restrictions on the Legal Status of Resettled Persons." Those employed in socially useful labor were allowed to live freely in the region, territory, or republic where they were located. They received the right to travel freely on business (but not for personal reasons!) within the entire territory of the country under ordinary regulations. Registering with the appropriate MVD bodies was now made an annual rather than a monthly requirement.

The authorities made a demonstration of humaneness unheard of until then—they permitted all children under ten years of age to be dropped from the register for special settlers. At last, children in their younger years were freed of administrative surveillance and restrictions!

Young men and women over sixteen (i.e., those who would be

given an internal passport under the law) were also taken off the register if they were enrolled in educational institutions. They were allowed to travel to places of study anywhere in the country.

Fines and arrest for violation of special-settlement regulations were abolished.

Simultaneously, instructions were issued to bring special settlers into the trade unions and the Komsomol, to offer them incentives on the same basis as other workers, and to employ them according to education and profession.[72] There is no question that this resolution substantially improved the situation. But at the same time it gives evidence of the legalized arbitariness applied to the special settlers in the years preceding. The very fact that a resolution of the Council of Ministers of the USSR had to make a special point about removing children under ten from the special register speaks for itself.

The authorities felt it was important at that time to ease the bitterness and agonies of those who had been forcibly uprooted from their normal lives. It was necessary to help heal these deep and still-bleeding wounds as quickly as possible. What was proposed to accomplish that? Intensify educational work among the special settlers!

Yes, that is exactly how the question was posed even two years after the death of Stalin: not the immediate return of the injured people to their homeland but "the intensification of mass agitational and cultural-educational work among resettled persons"—that was the title of the new decree of the USSR Council of Ministers on June 26, 1955.[73] The question of whether or not there was to be a return to the homeland was still being debated at the top. Preparations were being made for a party congress that presumably would decide whether the USSR would move forward still carrying the old and dreadful weight of Stalin's heritage or discard this burden and step forward into the future. This was a time when, at sessions of the Presidium of the CPSU Central Committee, fierce clashes again and again broke out between the loyal comrades-in-arms of the deceased and those who supported N. S. Khrushchev in his desire to have done with the crimes of the past. This struggle, as Khrushchev himself relates, reached its peak while the Twentiety Party Congress was in session.[74]

Around this time there were more and more frequent cases in which Mountaineers would leave Central Asia and appear in the Caucasus without permission, asserting their rights to their own homes. However, the necessary preparations had to precede a general return to the homeland. It was also not at all clear who should be allowed to return. At that time, the idea of including the Chechens, Ingush, and Crimean Tatars was not even being considered. However, the decree of the Council of Ministers did affect all the deported nations. After the decree there began to appear posters, newspapers, and finally even books in the national languages; works of literature by the national writers and translations of Russian and world classics in the local languages were returned from the warehouses to the bookshelves. Many members of the younger generation of the resettled people held books in their native language for the first time in their lives.

There was a recommendation to promote resettled persons to local government bodies, not to very high posts, but at least to promote them.[75]

During the period of intensive preparations for the Twentieth Party Congress a new decree of the USSR Council of Ministers was handed down, a product of the unceasing and ever-growing pressure from the special settlers. Many of them had in the past been party workers, partisans, and participants in the Great Patriotic War and even the civil war. They demanded full correction of the injustice, that is, the right to return to their homeland and the restoration of their autonomous state structures. The unauthorized return of Chechens, Ingush, and Karachai increased in frequency, and nothing could force the returnees to leave. In a number of cases incidents involving bloodshed and violence occurred. Within the party leadership Khrushchev's course began to demarcate itself more and more sharply. The overwhelming majority of the party ranks supported this policy line. Only an uncompromising repudiation of the Stalin heritage and a public condemnation of Stalinist methods and practices could strengthen the position of the Khrushchev group and provide a moral justification for its aspirations to power.

Yet another decree of the USSR Council of Ministers, dated November 20, 1955, reflected the struggle inside the party leadership and the fear of making a complete break with the past on the part of an influential section of that leadership; and for that reason the decree had the features of a compromise.

The following were removed from the special register: veterans of the Second World War who had been decorated with awards and medals; the families of those who had died at the front; teachers in educational institutions; resettled women who had legally married local inhabitants; women of nationalities that had not been deported but who had followed their husbands into exile on the basis of marital ties which had ceased to exist at the time this decree was published (i.e., widows and divorcees); and invalids and chronically ill persons living alone and unable to ensure their livelihood by themselves.[76]

One might have thought that people in these categories would automatically have been granted the right to return to their former places of residence. But, as they say, "it didn't work out quite that way."

With time, new forces and new factors came into play. On the one hand, the mass departure of the resettled people from Central Asia, Kazakhstan, and Siberia was bound to affect the economic life of those regions unfavorably. On the other hand, a massive return to their former localities bore within it the danger of a worsening of relations between nationalities as well as an aggravation of the economic situation. For the homes, farms, and jobs of the deportees had long since been taken over by new settlers from other republics. Therefore the Council of Ministers of the USSR was at first inclined to forbid repatriation.[77]

As is evident from this decree, removal of some categories of deportees from the special register did not apply to their families. There was seething discontent over this among the special settlers. It seemed absolutely impossible to postpone the decision on this problem any further under those particular conditions. It had to be solved, if only partially. And that is what was done.

In Khrushchev's secret speech at the Twentieth Party Congress, well known even though it was never published in the USSR, he referred to the deportation of the Karachai, Balkars, and Kalmyks as "rude violations of the basic Leninist principles of the nationality policies of the Soviet Union." He emphasized the mass character of the deportations involving entire nations. Characteristically, Khrushchev did not refer to the fact that the overwhelming majority of the deportees were women and children, but he did not forget to stress the fact that there were Communists and Komsomols among them. He rejected the argument that the deportations were prompted by military considerations, since at that time the fortunes of war had shifted decisively in favor of the USSR. Khrushchev also referred to Stalin's intention to deport the Ukrainians. It turned out, however, that "there were too many of them and there was no place to which to deport them. Otherwise he would have deported them also." In concluding, Khrushchev did refer to women and children, but in his own special way: "Not only a Marxist-Leninist but also no man of common sense can grasp how it is possible to make whole nations responsible for inimical activity, including women, children, old people, Communists, and Komsomols, to use mass repression against them; and to expose them to misery and suffering for the hostile acts of individual persons or groups of persons."[78]

It is easy to see that Khrushchev's indignation for some reason did not extend to the three most numerous of the oppressed nations—the Germans, the Chechen-Ingush, and the Crimean Tatars. He did not say a single word about the fate of the Turks, Kurds, Greeks, Khemshils, the many tens of thousands of Armenians, the deported Balts, and the inhabitants of the Western Ukraine, Western Byelorussia, Moldavia, and Bukovina. Thus, the greater part of the deported populations remained outside the field of vision of the party leadership.

Nevertheless the public condemnations of the mass repressions against the people of the Caucasus and Kalmykia at the Twentieth Party Congress was of tremendous importance in principle for the future of all the deported nationalities. It also testifies to the sincere desire of the new leadership, or at any rate to leading elements within it, to correct the distortions in nationalities policy and to defuse the mounting crisis in this area.

This marked a good beginning and was a harbinger of important changes in the life of the Soviet Union's mutinational society.

A month after the congress, on March 13, 1956, another decree of the USSR Council of Ministers was issued by which the families of the special settlers covered in the previous decree were also removed from special registration status, and invalids were allowed to return to their former places of residence. Ten days later a prestigious constitutional obligation was restored to the special settlers—to be available for military service. Special settlers of draft age were removed from special registration and placed on military registration.[79] And events did not stop there.

On April 28, 1956, the Presidium of the Supreme Soviet of the USSR issued a decree entitled "On the Lifting of Special-Settlement Restrictions from Crimean Tatars, Balkars, Turkish Citizens of the USSR, Khemshils, and Members of Their Families Deported During the Great Patriotic War."[80]

The ice had truly broken if such an experienced and cautious government figure as A. I. Mikoyan began to receive representatives of the Chechens and the Ingush in the summer of 1956. Likewise, L. I. Brezhnev, who at that time was first secretary of the Central Committee of the Communist Party of Kazakhstan, had a friendly meeting with a delegation of Balkars. Officials in responsible positions in the central apparatus in Moscow were sent out to the localities where the special settlers lived to address public assemblies of special settlers and closed party meetings. The question of repatriation was openly discussed at the public meetings.

Within the top leadership a bitter dispute broke out over the question of repatriating the Chechens and Ingush. At first an attempt was made to organize mass recruitment of Chechens and Ingush for work in other parts of the country. But the Chechens and Ingush solidly ignored this proposal. The leaders of the Grozny region were consulted as to their opinions—the first secretary of the regional party committee, A. I. Yakovlev, and the chairman of the regional government executive committee, Kovalenko. Their opinions differed. Yakovlev expressed his opposition to the repatriation, while Kovalenko strongly favored the return of the Chechens and Ingush and the restoration of the Chechen-Ingush ASSR.* Party activists were mobilized to try to persuade the Chechens and Ingush to agree to the establishment of an autonomous republic in Uzbekistan with its capital at the city of Chimkent. When this plan also fell through, a new one was proposed: to let the Chechens and Ingush return to the Caucasus, but to have the capital of their republic be not Grozny but Kizlyar.

Meanwhile, as early as 1954 the Chechens and Ingush deported to Central Asia began to "force their way" back into Chechnia. They would be removed and arrested, but others would come and everything would start over again. In 1955 the number of those unauthorized returnees increased, and after the Twentieth Congress tens of thousands of Chechens and Ingush headed for home. Alarmed by Khrushchev's failure to refer to them in his speech at the Twentieth Congress, the Chechens and Ingush sent a delegation to Moscow. Thousands of Chechen families gathered at railroad stations, but an order was issued categorically forbidding the sale of train tickets to them. Despite all appeals and warnings, twenty-five to thirty thousand Chechens and Ingush returned in 1956. When they were not allowed into the homes that had belonged to them before deportation, they made dugouts alongside them and settled in. But, above all, those who returned restored the cemeteries where their ancestors had been buried, putting up fences, cleaning up the monuments, and burying the dead they had brought back from Central Asia with them. When

---

* Dzhebrail Kartoyev, a chemical engineer and a veteran of the Great Patriotic War, was officially authorized to assist in organizing the return of Chechens and Ingush from Kazakhstan to their homeland. He was a participant in the following incident: Yakovlev, in order to make a visual demonstration that the return of the Chechens and Ingush was impossible, filled a pitcher of water to the brim and said, "Can you pour any more water into this pitcher?" Kartoyev took the pitcher, poured out half of it, and then refilled the pitcher cup by cup. "There, you see," he said. "It can be done."

the Russian population saw that the cemeteries were being restored they realized that the Chechens had returned for good.

The determination shown by the Chechens and Ingush achieved results. They could not be ignored. Moreover, they numbered some five hundred thousand altogether. Thus the Chechens and Ingush won inclusion in the decree of the CPSU Central Committee of November 24, 1956, "On the Restoration of the National Autonomy of the Kalmyk, Karachai, Balkar, Chechen, and Ingush Peoples." The decree noted that the measures taken earlier to restore the rights of the deported peoples had been insufficient. The deportation itself was condemned as an arbitrary and lawless act. It was also noted that the measures already taken did not solve the problem of full rehabilitation and restoration of the deported peoples to equality with the other nations of the Soviet Union. Dispersed over a large territory and lacking their own autonomous structure, they did not have the necessary conditions for full development of their economy and culture. The Central Committee found it necessary to restore their national autonomy and to permit their return to their former homelands, but only on a voluntary basis; those who so wished could remain in their new places of habitation. It was proposed that repatriation be carried out in an organized fashion in order not to create difficulties in arranging for jobs and housing. A time period of two years, 1957–58, was set for the Kalmyks, Karachai, and Balkars (i.e., for the smaller nationalities) and a four-year period, 1957–60, for the Chechens and Ingush.[81]

On January 9, 1957, the Presidium of the Supreme Soviet of the USSR issued four decrees: "On the Reorganization of the Kabardinian ASSR to Form the Karbardino-Balkar ASSR," "On the Restoration of the Chechen-Ingush ASSR as Part of the RSFSR," "On the Formation of the Kalmyk Autonomous Region as Part of the RSFSR," and "On the Reorganization of the Cherkess Autonomous Region to Form the Karachai-Cherkess Autonomous Region." On February 11, 1957, these decrees acquired the force of law.[82]

But about the Crimean Tatars and the Volga Germans there was not one word. They might just as well not have existed.

V

The Return of the Punished Peoples to the Northern Caucasus and Kalmykia

SOME MEMBERS of the Caucasian peoples deported in 1943–44 began to return to their homelands as early as 1954, as we have said. They ran great risks in doing so, for such unauthorized movement was punishable by confinement in a prison or labor camp.

But there is a time for everything. And the time for repatriation had come. Neither threats nor intimidation could block or hinder this movement, these peoples' irresistible drive to return to their historic homes. Their unauthorized return hastened the adoption of official resolutions restoring the autonomy that had been abrogated.

If the Crimean Tatars had done as the Caucasians then did, had flooded back to the Crimea by the thousands, it is likely that they too would have won the restoration of their autonomous republic within the framework of the Ukrainian SSR. In this sense it seems that the Crimean Tatars missed a historic opportunity.

Not everyone managed to return to their extinguished home fires. Far from it.

At the time of repatriation it appeared that the deported peoples had been substantially depleted in number. The official statistics on this question, if they exist, are kept hidden and sealed with seven seals. However, scattered demographic data have appeared, enabling us to make a rough estimate of the losses. We will try to present these in the form of tables. Preliminary data are provided by the censuses of 1926, 1939, and 1970; by information on the percentages of the total Soviet population constituted by the various punished peoples; and by information on the population losses suffered by the country in general as a result of the war.

Table 1

Changes in size of population of the deported peoples of the Northern Caucasus and Kalmykia (based on all-union censuses [in thousands]).

	1926	*1939*	*1959*	*1970*
Chechens	319	408	419	613
Kalmyks	129	134	106	137
Ingush	74	92	106	158
Karachai	55	76	81	113
Balkars	33	43	42	60

Even this table gives a general idea of the disaster that struck these peoples between 1939 and 1959. We can picture the full dimensions of this tragedy in the form of another table:

Table 2

Net losses suffered by the deported peoples between 1939 and 1959 (after allowance for wartime losses [in thousands]). 1939 = 100 percent.

	Population growth normally expected as of *1959*		*Net losses*	
	In absolute terms	*In percentage terms*	*In absolute terms*	*In percentage terms*
Chechens	590	38	131	22
Kalmyks	142	7	22	14.8
Ingush	128	38	12	9
Karachai	124	63	37	30
Balkars	64	49	17	26.5

These figures are closer to minimal than maximal estimates.

THE RESTORATION OF THE KARACHAI AUTONOMOUS OBLAST

A month after the restoration of the Karachai-Cherkess Autonomous Region, a newly-elected Soviet of Workers' Deputies of Stavropol territory convened. Of the 162 deputies, 4 were Karachai, 3 Kalmyks, and the remaining 139 Russians.[1]

The composition of the population of the region had not changed significantly between the 1939 census and that of 1959.

The number of Karachai in the region had declined from 70,900 to 67,800, i.e., from 28.8 percent of the total population of the region to 24.4 percent. Russians remained the majority of the population as before—comprising 141,800 persons, or 51 percent, of the population, as compared with 119,800, or 48.7 percent, in 1939. The Cherkess population had also grown, by approximately one-third.[2]

In March 1957 the bureau of the Karachai-Cherkess regional committee of the party and the executive committee of the regional Soviet passed a resolution on accommodating the Karachai population on the territory of the region.[3] The same year, 6,500 individual homes and 2,644 temporary living quarters were purchased and built, and 2,805 Karachai families were housed in communal apartments and temporary quarters.[4] The arrival of about seventy-five hundred Karachai families was projected for 1958. An operational group headed by a deputy chairman of the regional executive committee traveled to Kazakhstan and Central Asia in order to carry out the population transfer in an organized way. The repatriation of the Karachai was essentially completed in 1959. Over forty-seven million rubles were allocated for housing construction and about seven million rubles for other forms of assistance. The construction of various types of cultural facilities expanded. On April 10, 1957, publication of a region-wide Karachai-language newspaper, *Kyzyl Karachai* (Red Karachai) resumed; and Karachai literature and art experienced a renaissance.[5]

Restoration of the Kabardino-Balkar ASSR

After the USSR Supreme Soviet passed the law on the reorganization of the Kabardinian ASSR to form the Kabardino-Balkar ASSR, in February 1957, the planned resettlement of the Balkars from Kazakhstan and Kirgizia began.

On March 28, 1957, at a session of the Supreme Soviet of the Kabardino-Balkar ASSR, the first secretary of the regional committee, T. K. Melbakhov, reported on the full rehabilitation of the Balkars and the restoration of the united autonomous republic. He warned: "The transfer of the Balkars to the Kabardino-Balkar ASSR can be carried out only in an organized way, according to a set sequence." At the same time the deputies learned that the transfer of twenty thousand Balkars, projected for 1957, was already underway. Completion of the resettlement operation was slated for 1958.

The plan was to place the returnees in three districts—Sovetskii, Elbrusskii, and Chegemskii—and in certain settlements in the lowland areas. It was expected that the Balkars would introduce socialized stock farming on a large scale in newly established *kolkhozy*.[6]

The Balkars returned to what were actually ruined areas. In an article entitled "Restore the Economy and Culture of Balkaria More Rapidly," I. Kazmakhov, the chairman of the State Planning Commission of the Kabardino-Balkar ASSR, openly acknowledged that after the resettlement of the Balkars in Kazakhstan and Kirgizia, the areas in which they had previously lived were completely abandoned for fourteen years. "As we know," he wrote, "at present Upper and Middle Balkaria, Karasu and Bezengi, Upper Chegem and Aktoprak, Upper Baksan, Terskol, and Khabaz are almost uninhabited, and the tremendous natural resources of these areas, in particular the rich alpine meadows and hayfields, on which large-scale livestock raising was based in the past, have not been developed well at all. In this connection we face the task of developing these areas and restoring the economy and culture of all of Balkaria."[7]

The construction of homes, schools, and veterinary centers in the republic was expanded. The repatriated Balkar families were granted home-building credits of ten thousand rubles per family, repayable within three years after occupation of the new home. Credits were also allocated for the renovation of old dwellings—up to three thousand rubles, with three years to repay—and for the purchase of cows—up to fifteen hundred old rubles, the equivalent of 150 new rubles.[8]

In the years 1957–59, 9,522 Balkar families, a total of 35,982 persons, returned, of whom 14,075 were in the work force.[9]

The restoration of the rights of the Balkar people applied to the republic as a whole. On March 20, 1957, the last number of *Kabardinskaia pravda* (Kabardinian truth) appeared, to be replaced on March 22 by the first issue of *Kabardino-Balkarskaia pravda* (Kabardino-Balkar truth).

The previously existing local place names were restored: Zarechnoye (Russian for "Town across the River") once again became Lashkuta, and the Georgian name Ialbuzi was dropped and Elbrus restored.[10]

The deputy chairman of the Council of Ministers of the Kabardino-Balkar ASSR wrote the following florid lines without even a sign of shame: "Nowhere have new settlers ever, in any country, enjoyed such attention or received such truly gigantic assistance from the state. Only in our country, having the highly-developed industry and powerful economy that it does, are such material and fiscal outlays to meet the needs of a newly resettled population [*pereselencheskogo naseleniya*] possible."[11]

And so it seems that the Balkars were simply new settlers (*pereselentsy*)!

"During the war," Kh. I. Khutyev grimly observes, "thousands died. Among them were representatives of the Balkar intelligentsia. A substantial number died during the time the Balkars were in Central Asia. The creation of a Balkar intelligentsia was effectively cut short."[12]

By the same token the cultural development of the Balkar people was held back because they were deprived for fourteen years of the normal attributes of a nation, its own culture, schools, literature, and art.

At the time the repatriation of the Balkars began, in 1957, out of 5,243 persons in the Kabardino-Balkar ASSR with a higher education only 74 were Balkars, and out of 6,915 with a secondary-school education only 140 were Balkars.[13] Among these, there was not one woman. Five years later, in 1962, the number of Balkars who had received a higher education had increased 2.6 times (to 193) and those with a secondary education 3.3 times (to 466), including 247 women in both categories.[14] These statistics testify not only to the rapid cultural development after repatriation but also to the colossal harm done to Balkar education in the years of deportation.

The roads of Kabardino-Balkaria are quite picturesque. Many trucks speed over them, and among the drivers are many Balkars. Glance into the cab of one of these trucks and you will see a photograph of Him. With his tender, watchful, and fatherly smile Stalin looks down upon the driver.

Truly, the ways of the Lord are mysterious!

The Kalmyk ASSR

On February 11, 1957, the USSR Supreme Soviet confirmed the law forming the Kalmyk Autonomous Region as part of Stavropol territory in the RSFSR.[15] In July 1958 Kalmykia was restored to its former status as an autonomous republic.[16]

Thus, fourteen years after their forced deportation the Kalmyks returned to their homeland. Repatriation began at the end of 1956.

It was projected that 14,000 Kalmyk families would be resettled in Kalmykia during 1957–58. In fact, however, more than that returned, many on their own initiative, in "non-organized fashion," so to speak—15,400 families, or 32,000 persons, of whom 23,650 were of working age and ability.[17]

By the end of 1959 the resettlement was essentially completed. 18,158 families had returned, amounting to 72,665 persons, of whom 30,056 were capable of working.[18]

How were they received by the local population? On this question even the official views, or those close to the official views, differ. *The Essays in the History of the Kalmyk ASSR,* published by the Nauka [Science] Press of the Academy of Sciences in 1970, asserts, for example, that "the Russian population welcomed the Kalmyks warmly. . . ."[19]

Actually, the attitude toward the repatriated Kalmyks varied. Many families who had occupied the homes of exiled Kalmyks and who had taken part of their property were eager to leave Kalmykia as quickly as possible. Others, who had been pumped full of official propaganda in the intervening years and had listened to all the stories about the "Kalmyk traitors and bandits," did not wish to live alongside such people. Others regarded them simply as alien interlopers.

Anti-Kalmyk attitudes must have been fairly widespread if such an important figure as M. A. Ponomarev, head of a party organizational section of the Central Committee of the CPSU in the RSFSR and, later, first secretary of the Kalmyk regional committee, could say at a session of the Supreme Soviet of the Kalmyk ASSR on October 28, 1958: "We have encountered certain individual manifestations of unhealthy relations between the newly arriving populations and those who have been living here. . . . We cannot have a situation in which teachers, agronomists, doctors, and other specialists leave our area. It is highly irregular that, in the case of *sovkhoz* no. 108 alone, some two hundred families have departed during the last two years. . . . Those Russian comrades who seek to leave the republic rather than work in harmony with the Kalmyks to rebuild the autonomous republic are acting incorrectly. . . ."[20]

By the end of 1958 more than fifty-five million rubles had been lent to families returning to Kalmykia for home-building, acquiring livestock, and temporary assistance.[21] On the average, this meant about three thousand rubles per family. Since no one has ever made an evaluation of the property the Kalmyks lost in the forced deportation, it is difficult to judge how adequate this compensation is, especially since prices for building materials, livestock, farm equipment, and other goods have risen sharply compared to prewar prices. The same is true of prices for personal belongings such as clothing, not to mention decorative and ornamental items.

During the first few years after repatriation there was a shortage of housing, and the situation in regard to new construction was poor. In Kaspiiskii district, for example, the new arrivals were lodged in dugouts. There were sixty-four hundred families without cows, although dairy products were the Kalmyks' main food.[22]

But, as we know, living standards can be improved with time. It is a much more complicated problem to raise a people's cultural standards.

Essays in the History of the Kalmyk ASSR says: "The period spent in the Eastern parts of the country did not pass without leaving its mark. But it did not break the Kalmyks' spirit or dim their devotion to the cause of socialism and communism. . . . Naturally, the removal of the bulk of the labor force from most of the districts of Kalmykia eliminated the possibility of a rapid economic and cultural advance and to a certain extent retarded the growth of the productive forces in Kalmykia and the economic development of its natural resources. The economic and cultural development of Kalmykia suffered a certain lag in comparison with neighboring regions."[23]

This quotation is indicative of much else, above all, of the attitude toward people who had suffered brutality, injustice, and lawlessness. Here they are regarded as some sort of abstraction— the labor force—the absence of which caused the economic development of the area to suffer.

But what about the offenses to their human dignity, the misery they suffered, the harsh fate of the younger generation, even if we consider only those who were from one to five years old at the time of the deportation and between fifteen and twenty years old after the repatriation? What was life like for young people who, just as they were coming of age, had to sit down at a school desk to learn to read and write their native language? But let us proceed. The authors of the *Essays* write: "Unfortunately, in connection with the deportation of the Kalmyks to Siberia and Central Asia the *educational process* both for primary school pupils and for those in secondary and higher educational institutions was *somewhat disrupted.*" (Emphasis added.) And here are the reasons for that: "The long road of relocation, difficulties with housing, the poor knowledge of Russian of *some* [emphasis added] pupils, and other causes prevented many students from completing the school year 1943–44 successfully and only an insignificant number continued their education. . . ."[24]

It is hard to know what lies behind such a description of the tragedy of deportation. Is it indifference, cynicism, or something else? Everything is reduced to this: that the "educational process" was "somewhat disrupted." But weren't the lives of these schoolchildren twisted and blighted by the violence, cruelty, and indifference displayed by those who ordered them removed and shipped under guard to their places of exile?

In 1940 there were 302 schools of all types in Kalmykia, with 45,357 students. Those Kalmyks who had received a specialized secondary education or higher education numbered 1,628 within the ASSR and another 160 outside the ASSR.[25]

Between the time of the dissolution of the Kalmyk ASSR and its restoration the number of students was cut almost in half, the number of schools by a quarter, and the number of teachers by 16 percent.[26]

During the fourteen years of deportation about 450 teachers of Kalmyk nationality graduated from pedagogical institutes.[27] This figure apparently includes teachers who received only a secondary-school education. The *Essays* reproduces a long list of those who completed their higher education or graduated from specialized secondary schools during the years of exile and discrimination. But a count of this list reveals only fifty-two people.[28]

Since the return of the Kalmyks a great deal has been done to reestablish education, cultural institutions, and health care, and to provide for representation of the Kalmyk nationality in government and party bodies. Kalmyk literature and printing has revived, and the sciences are developing successfully.

All possible measures were taken to erase from the national memory the years of exile and arbitrary rule.

How sore a topic the special settlements are may be seen, for example, from the fact that at the anniversary session of the Supreme Soviet of the Kalmyk ASSR marking the fortieth year since the establishment of Soviet power in Kalmykia, on October 29, 1960, neither the official documents nor the welcoming speeches referred to the tragic events of the last days of December 1943. Only one of those who spoke, Kh. I. Khutuyev, secretary of the Kabardino-Balkar regional committee of the CPSU, allowed himself to make such a reference, in a form befitting the occasion: "Your holiday is our holiday. . . . The road traveled by the Kalmyk people has not always been easy. There was sorrow and sadness on its historical road. We know what storms have swept down upon the peaceful Kalmyk dwellings over the course of centuries, threatening to destroy them and to extinguish the fires of their native hearths forever."[29]

A few years after this address, Khutuyev wrote a candidate's dissertation in which he told about the brutal and inhuman regime of the special settlements. Will this work ever be published?

Restoration of the Chechen-Ingush ASSR

The greatest difficulties arose in connection with the repatriation of the Chechens and Ingush, not only because of their large numbers but also as a result of their irrepressible determination to reoccupy their ancestral homes. The situation was further complicated by the fact that after 1944 the territory they had formerly inhabited was rather heavily colonized by new settlers from other regions and republics.

The decision was made to extend the resettlement of the Chechens and Ingush over a four-year period and to carry it out by moving only small groups at a time.[30] An organizing committee was established to take charge of the repatriation. It was headed by M. G. Gairbekov, later the chairman of the Council of Ministers of the Chechen-Ingush ASSR. But far more families kept arriving than had been planned for. This caused complications, and there were incidents resulting from housing problems and from the rapidly worsening relations between the nationalities in Grozny region and Northern Ossetia.

The return of 450 families to the city of Grozny was planned for 1957, but 2,692 arrived.[31] In the region as a whole, forty-eight thousand families returned in 1957, but only thirty-three thousand single-apartment dwellings had been prepared. In 1957 approximately five hundred million (old) rubles were spent to meet the needs of the returnees.[32] A significant portion of these funds went to establish *sovkhozy* for stock-farming.[33]

Individual assistance to the returning families seems not to have been substantial by comparison with the losses suffered by the Chechens and Ingush at the time of forced resettlement. Long-term credits per family were on the order of 1,000 rubles for home building, up to 300 rubles for home renovation, and 150 rubles for the purchase of cows. In the year of their repatriation, families were relieved of taxes and obligations for the delivery of agricultural products. At the same time arrears in rent on their former residences were forgiven. Insignificant sums (up to fifty rubles) were given in the form of outright grants.

The first year of the repatriation was especially tense. In a number of districts little attention was paid to arranging work for the newcomers, and housing construction moved slowly. According to official reports, mass cultural work was in a state of neglect.[34] Local leaders were especially concerned by the "inadequate propaganda work on the subject of friendship among the peoples." In mid-July 1957 the regional committee and the organization committee adopted a special resolution in connection with the unsatisfactory provision of housing for the repatriates.[35]

It was difficult to normalize relations between Chechens and Ingush, on the one hand, and those who had occupied their land, on the other. The return of the Chechens and Ingush was, to put it mildly, not greeted with special enthusiasm by the local population.

For example, in Mezhdurechenskii (now Shalinskii) district, of the four hundred families (with 669 able-bodied members) which had arrived by February 1, 1957, only ten had been accepted in *kolkhozy* and only twenty-one were provided with jobs at factories and offices.[36]

But energetic measures were taken "to exert ideological influence" on the repatriates. In the second half of July 1957 a republic-wide newspaper, *Leninskii put'* (The Leninist path) began to appear in Chechen and a similar newspaper in Ingush, *Svet* (Light). In rural areas lectures were given and meetings held on the theme of friendship among the peoples; these involved more than ten thousand people.[37] Selection and advancement of new cadres from among the Chechens and Ingush also proceeded.

On August 12, 1957, the sixth plenum of the Chechen-Ingush regional committee of the CPSU was held, at which a report was given by A. I. Yakovlev, first secretary of the committee, on the implementation of the decree of the CPSU Central Committee of November 24, 1956, on the restoration of the national autonomy of the Chechen and Ingush peoples. P. N. Pospelov, a secretary of the Central Committee, arrived in Grozny to explain to local personnel the tasks flowing from the restoration of the autonomous areas dissolved in 1943–44. Pospelov visited a number of districts where he spoke at public meetings. His visit was obviously connected with the worsening relations between the nationalities in the Caucasus. At the plenum there was a sharp exchange which, of course, was not reported in the press at the time but which has become known thanks to the later work of Dzhuguryants.[38]

Dzhuguryants, with a stenographic text of the sixth plenum of the regional committee at his disposal, described the incident as follows: "D. Malsagov, a member of the organizing committee, on the basis of isolated and episodic instances of incorrect attitudes toward the Chechens and Ingush, tried to imply that the leading party body of the republic held attitudes of the same kind. In regard to this speech P. N. Pospelov said that a wrong note had been sounded which was not conducive to friendship among the peoples. Also profoundly in error was a statement by another member of the organizing committee, Tangiyev, who called for reversal of the decision to transfer Prigorodnyi district to the Northern Ossetian ASSR.''[39]

There is no question that the poor relations between nationalities in Chechnia was one manifestation of the general crisis in the realm of nationalities policy, which was an essential part of the overall crisis of the Stalinist system, a crisis which began at the end of World War II and intensified in the first several years after the war.

At the time of the return of the Chechens and Ingush to the territory of Grozny region, over 540,000 inhabitants lived there already. During the next four years it was projected that the repatriation would add another 500,000. As early as April 1957 a number of settlers of Caucasian nationality—Avars, Dargins, Ossetians—who realized quite well what it meant to arbitrarily settle on the lands of one's neighbors and to take over their homes—appealed to the authorities to transfer them to Dagestan and Northern Ossetia, from whence they had come in 1944. There were seventy-seven thousand of these.[40]

Chechens from Dagestan (Aukhovtsy) also returned there. But their former settlements had been occupied by Laks, and a new district, Novolakskii (New Lak), had been formed. The Aukhovtsy settled on the lands of the Kumyks, a small nationality. Neither group objected.

Things were much more complicated in the case of the Ingush who returned to Northern Ossetia. When the Chechen-Ingush ASSR was restored, the decision was made to leave Prigorodnyi district as part of Northern Ossetia, since it bordered on the capital of the Northern Ossetian ASSR, Ordzhonikidze (formerly Vladikavkaz), on three sides.

In order to understand this problem better, we should look at the past history of the city for a moment.

Vladikavkaz had been founded on the right bank of the Terek on the site of three Ingush villages, the largest of which was the village of Zaur. On the left bank lived Ossetians. In the late eighteenth century Russian military authorities brought Ossetians who had been living in the mountains down to enlarge the garrison of Vladikavkaz. Early in the nineteenth century a fort was reestablished at the entrance to the Daryal gorge, and the Ossetians returned to their former homes. Later they were moved again, and this time they settled not far from Vladikavkaz, at Olginskaya. Under Soviet rule Vladikavkaz became the capital of the Mountaineer Republic. At the end of 1928 Stalin proposed that Ingush territory be joined to Ossetia, but the Ingush succeeded in demonstrating the inappropriateness of this idea. In 1932 Vladikavkaz was transferred to Ossetia. Half the Ingush population lived in the suburban settlement of Angushit, eight kilometers from the city.

The Ingush who had returned from deportation expressed their willingness to buy back from the new owners the homes that had belonged to them before their expulsion,* but the Ossetian authorities advised the local inhabitants not to sell. The Ingush were discriminated against in jobs and schools. But nothing could crush their determination to settle in their former home territory.

Unable to oppose the Chechens and Ingush in their powerful drive to recoccupy the places where they had lived before 1944, the authorities were compelled, "in order to facilitate and speed up the accommodation" of the Chechens and Ingush, to relocate 2,574 families, mostly Russian, to areas on the other side of the Terek.[41] They did this unwillingly because they wanted to avoid the spread of false rumors to the effect that the Chechens were driving out Russians. Nevertheless, according to data from the archives cited by Dzhuguryants in his dissertation, thirty-six thousand members of the Russian population did leave Checheno-Ingushetia on their own initiative.[42]

In the same work Dzhuguryants tells of the hostile and chauvinist attitudes toward the returning Chechens and Ingush held by a

---

* After the deportation of the Chechens and Ingush, their homes, with the exception of the villages in the mountains, which were blown up or knocked down, became objects of speculation, changing owners fifteen to twenty times.

certain section of the Russian population. "Individual party members," he writes, "took anti-party positions on the national question, tried to argue that it was impossible for the Russian and Chechen-Ingush populations to live side by side on the territory of the republic, and adopted a negative attitude toward the restoration of autonomy.[43]

It so happened that in the forefront of those who abandoned Checheno-Ingushetia there were Communists. Among them were leading party and government personnel, agricultural specialists, doctors, and teachers. They did this against the instructions of higher party bodies. For example, in Shalinskii district more than three hundred party members were stricken from the books during 1957.[44]

The further course of events showed that the incorporation of Prigorodnyi district into Northern Ossetia was a mistake and a source of dissatisfaction for the Ingush that has not ceased to rankle to this very day. At the time of the mass repatriation of the Chechens and Ingush in 1958 the situation was so tense that any incident at all could provoke a severe outbreak of trouble between the nationalities.

One such conflict erupted in Grozny on August 24, 1958. The immediate cause had nothing to do with politics—a Russian sailor on leave asked a young woman to dance, and an Ingush who had designs on her intervened. A fight began in which the sailor was killed. On the next day the sailor's funeral turned into a bloody mob action by the Russian population. The disturbances lasted four days, one of the worst racial clashes in the Soviet Union since the end of the war.

The crowd following the coffin to the cemetery consisted entirely of Russians. They marched up to the building housing the regional committee and demanded that the local party leadership and the government of Checheno-Ingushetia hold a memorial meeting. An attempt was made to carry the coffin into the party building. However, police who had arrived formed a line and no one was allowed to enter the party building. A truck with a public-address system appeared from somewhere and some dark-haired fellow began the rally. Meanwhile the crowd swept the police out of the way and burst into the party building. Two secretaries of the regional committee and a deputy chairman of the Council of Ministers (all Russians) appeared on the truck and said a few words. The city's Lenin Plaza, where these events took place, was crowded to overflowing. According to eyewitnesses, there must have been ten thousand people.

Some speakers called on people to join the strike that had allegedly been announced by the workers at the largest petrochemical plant in Grozny. A representative from the plant was given the floor. But when he told the crowd they were being wrongly informed and that the workers at the plant were not on strike, he was struck and knocked from the truck. Workers in the crowd, however, protected him from further reprisals.

Then a woman appeared on the platform of the truck. Declaring that she had formerly served in the regional committee and the Council of Ministers, she proposed a resolution with the following demands: 1) expulsion of the Chechens and Ingush; 2) mass search of all Chechens and Ingush, any found with weapons in their possession to be shot on the spot; 3) establishment of Russian power. The woman urged the crowd to go to the railway station, stop trains passing through, and tell the passengers that in Grozny the Chechens were attacking all Russians with knives.

Handwritten leaflets in block lettering were thrown from the windows of the regional committee building. Here are the approximate contents of one:

Comrades, brothers, Russian people!
Follow the example of the peoples of Jordan and Iraq.
Rise up and fight for the Russian cause!
Demand the expulsion of the Chechens and Ingush!
Read this and pass it on.
If you don't agree, tear it up.
People's Defense Committee.*

* The text of this leaflet has been reconstructed by the author. D. Malsagov, the member of the organizing committee mentioned above, immediately took a train

An empty bus drove by. In it were only the driver and the conductor. The driver stopped the bus, climbed up on the roof, and began to shout, appealing to the aroused mob. "The Chechens fired a volley at my bus. They killed a man and a woman, a young woman—they cut off her hands." (Actually, several pogromists had broken into the telegraph building. The chief of the guard in the building, a lieutenant, fired a shot after giving a warning, and wounded someone. The bus had passed by then and the driver had seen someone lying on the ground. His overheated imagination created all the rest.)

The crowd roared. An elderly man with plainly Caucasian features, wearing an astrakhan hat, was standing nearby on the sidewalk. He was seized and savagely beaten right in front of the soldiers guarding the government building. The soldiers simply looked on, without moving. The man was killed before their eyes. It was later found that he was a peddler from the village of Urus-Martan.

The Russian public, including Communists as well, pinned on red ribbons so that the rampaging pogromists would not take them for Chechens or Ingush. (How similar all this was to the pogroms

---

for Moscow to inform the Central Committee of the events in Grozny. While the train was stopping in Kharkov he saw a woman reading this leaflet out loud. Malsagov jumped out just as the train was leaving, snatched the leaflet from her, and took it to Moscow. There, through a certain R., he tried to submit the leaflet to the Party Control Commission, but R. did not deliver the leaflet. On May 8, 1959, Malsagov was expelled from the party and arrested. He was accused of anti-Soviet activity, of inciting racial animosity and slandering the Russian, Chechen, and Ingush peoples and the leading party and government personnel of the republic. He was also accused of dictating the text of this leaflet to his cousin. R. appeared as a witness for the prosecution. There was another "witness" as well, who later wrote a statement repudiating the testimony given against Malsagov. The court found Malsagov guilty and sent him to a labor camp at Potma, where he served five years. A protest by the deputy general procurator of the USSR was attached to the sentence, but subsequently the protest was withdrawn without any explanation. Malsagov was not restored to membership in the party. At the present time he works as an agronomist with the Ministry of Agriculture of the Chechen-Ingush ASSR. People who know Malsagov well insist that the case against him was a total frame-up.

against the Jews in tsarist Russia, except that then red ribbons were not worn.)

The Chechen population displayed exceptional restraint and did not respond to the pogromists' provocations. On the third day of the disorders in Grozny, looting began. Troops began to arrive. Gradually order was restored.

The chairman of the Presidum of the RSFSR Supreme Soviet, Yasnov, arrived from Moscow, along with General Pliyev, and N. G. Ignatov, a secretary of the CPSU Central Committee. The writer Khalid Oshayev, who had found a stack of leaflets of a pogromist character, tried to get an appointment with Ignatov in order to give him the leaflets, but Ignatov traveled off into the out-lying districts and did not receive Oshayev.

None of the pogromists were brought before the law for the disorders of August 1958 in Grozny, not even those who stood on the truck platform and incited the crowd to violence.

A year later, A. I. Yakovlev, first secretary of the regional com-mittee, was transferred to the post of inspector in the Central Committee apparatus in Moscow.

The 1958 disturbances helped to trigger smaller clashes. The regional committee bureau tried to normalize national relations somehow; it promoted local cadres and punished chauvinistic Russian leaders. In particular, R. K. Donskoi, first secretary of the Shalinskii district committee of the party, was reprimanded for negligence in mass political work, and the chairman of the Shalinskii district executive committee was removed from his post.[45] A number of Russian party members who had openly spoken out against the restoration of Chechen-Ingush autonomy were expelled from the CPSU. On the other hand, "manifesta-tions of national hatred" on the part of Chechen-Ingush party per-sonnel were much more severely punished.

A reflection of the deterioration in relations between the nation-alities may be seen in an article by V. Sklokin, deputy head of the party organizational section of the Chechen-Ingush regional committee. He wrote: "The party organizations must be espe-cially insistent in combating the serious shortcomings that have appeared in the course of the restoration of the national autonomy of the Chechen and Ingush peoples. It is necessary to intensify the education of the population in the spirit of the Leninist nationalities policy and of fraternal friendship among the peoples of our country, and to take more rapid measures to make arrangements for the Chechens and Ingush arriving in the republic in regard to jobs and domestic needs.''[46]

But, as subsequent events showed, the deportation of 1944 had a profound psychological effect not only on the Chechens and Ingush but also on the Russian and Ukrainian population of the area. Its negative consequences continue even today. In 1958 the writer A. E. Kosterin sent a letter to the CPSU Central Committee in which he cited instances of incorrect attitudes towards the repatriated Chechens and Ingush on the part of leading local party and government personnel. In particular, his letter referred to the mistaken decision to attach Prigorodnyi district to Northern Ossetia. Kosterin's letter circulated widely and had a big impact in Checheno-Ingushetia. The bureau of the party regional committee gave special consideration to this question and in a resolution of April 28, 1958, condemned Kosterin for his letter. The bureau asserted that the letter sowed discord and tended to inflame national hatred.[47]

Not only did the enforced exile of the Chechens and Ingush bring to a halt the struggle for atheism, reverse the decline in religious fanaticism, and preserve the influence of the Islamic religion and sects, it considerably strengthened the influence of religion. And what, after all, could the deported peoples turn to, if not religion? Certainly the authorities had left them in the position of pariahs. Cultural and educational work came to a complete stop—there were no newspapers, no books, and no motion pictures in the native language. All this created exceptionally favorable conditions for the increased influence of religion, an influence which historically had been to a certain extent both anti-Russian and anti-Soviet.

To this the authorities now added an exceptionally provocative measure, one which had deep social and political implications. In

1957 there began the systematic liquidation of the last *khutor* settlements of the Chechens, a process which was expected to take several years, lasting until 1963.[48] This measure may be regarded with some justification from the historical point of view as the completion of the "conquest of the Caucasus" begun 150 years earlier, allowing, of course, for the changes in the overall situation in the intervening years, the political shifts, and the radical transformation of the social structure of Russia (the Soviet Union) and the Caucasus.

On the other hand, a more concerted effort was begun to draw Chechens and Ingush into industrial production. This had a significant effect on the growth of the urban population and drew a part of the native population away from the traditions of its centuries-old way of life. Great harm was done to these people's cultural development. Even from certain fragmentary and far from complete statistics, officially published at different times, one can make an informed judgment on this question.

Of the 8,997 specialists with higher education listed in Checheno-Ingushetia in 1959, only 177 were Chechens and 124 Ingush. In the same year the number of people with a secondary school education was 14,150, of whom 403 were Chechens and 248 Ingush.[49]

The secretary of the Chechen-Ingush regional committee, A. I. Yakovlev, observed in one of his speeches in 1958 that as of January 1, 1958, approximately eight thousand Chechen and Ingush children aged eight to fifteen were not attending school. This amounted to 18 percent of the total number of schoolchildren in that age group. "The problem of introducing universal education," he stated, "is the problem of raising the cultural level of the Chechen and Ingush peoples further, rapidly overcoming harmful domestic and tribal survivals of the past, and involving all young people in active social and political life."[50] Z. S. Dudnik, a deputy to the Supreme Soviet of the Chechen-Ingush ASSR from the Alkhan-Kalinskii election district in Grozny, commented that in a number of places children were being taught in unsuitable buildings and that there were some who did not attend school at all.[51] R. I. Umayeva, a teacher and deputy from the Staro-Atachinskii election district of Urus-Martan district, said: "It hurts me very much when I think of the fact that we still do not have enough native teachers. For example, in Urus-Martan district there are only three teachers, young women. We still have too few rural personnel who know their jobs well."[52]

"In the period from 1944 to 1953," writes Dzhuguryants, "the Chechen and Ingush youth had extremely limited opportunities for entry into higher educational institutions and specialized secondary schools. This had a negative effect on the training of specialists from the ranks of Chechens and Ingush."[53] Of 8,000 teachers working in the Chechen-Ingush ASSR after its restoration, only 1,440 were Chechens and Ingush, and of these a mere 190 had higher educational degrees.[54] Moreover, according to the 1959 census the percentage of Chechens and Ingush in the population of the republic as a whole, although it had shrunk considerably by comparison with 1939 (when it was 58.4), constituted 41.1 percent.[55]

Rapid and energetic measures were taken. By 1957 there were 133 Chechens and Ingush studying at the pedagogical institute, 30 at the petroleum technical school, and 145 at the pedagogical school (on the secondary level).[56]

Even in the first years after repatriation, part of the Muslim clergy tried to turn the national sensibilities of the Chechens and Ingush in an anti-Russian direction. In a number of settlements teachers and medical personnel began to be harassed, and the local leaders in some districts—Vasilkov in Urus-Martan, and Krutov in Achkhoi-Martan—were inclined to regard this merely as an expression of hooliganism.[57]

The past, and the popular psychology connected with it, at some points in history proves to be more important than considerations of economic expediency. The fact remains that in spite of the enlargement of the territory of the Chechen-Ingush ASSR after the restoration of autonomy—three districts of Stavropol territory (Kargalinskii, Naurskii, and Shelkovskii) having been added to the republic, together constituting 27 percent of the entire territory of the ASSR (5,200 square kilometers out of a total of 19,300)—in spite of this the Ingush stubbornly continued to insist on the return of Prigorodnyi district, a territory of only 977.5 square kilometers.[58]

Fifteen years after the restoration of autonomy, on February 23, 1973, the anniversary of the dissolution of the Chechen-Inguish ASSR in 1944, a group of Ingush came to Grozny in organized fashion to demand that the authorities have Prigorodnyi district returned. This new sharpening of tensions was undoubtedly related to the discrimination against the Ingush, especially in regard to jobs, in Northern Ossetia, to which Prigorodny district now belongs.

A seventy-five-page appeal, signed by several thousand Ingush, lists cases of mistreatment and discrimination against Ingush living in Northern Ossetia. Among these are refusal to hire Ingush who live not in Ordzhonikidze but in nearby settlements, while at the same time non-Ingush people from villages twenty kilometers from the city are driven to work. The petition refers to restrictions in choosing a place of residence, refusal of permission to build or buy homes, and other forms of discrimination. For example, in one of the schools attended by Ingush children, the director, an Ossetian, supposedly sent a group of eighty children to a Pioneer camp, but in fact placed them in a boarding school for retarded children. Only after a year did the parents succeed, through great efforts, in having their children returned.

The Ingush requested that they be allowed to live where they wished, to buy homes and to build them, and, lastly, that they be allowed to establish their own cemetery. They stated that they were not seeking a change in the administrative status of Prigorodny district but asking only to be assured the same rights as other citizens of Northern Ossetia.

Ingush who lived in the Chechen-Ingush ASSR demonstrated in support of these demands. Demonstrations were held in Grozny over a period of several days. The demonstrators carried portraits of Lenin and Brezhnev and slogans with statements by these leaders on internationalism and friendship among the peoples. A big rally was held without interruption. One speaker followed another. There were no speeches of an anti-Soviet nature. The demonstrators organized their own marshal squad to prevent disorders. According to one account, the leaders of the republic, who had sent to Moscow in dismay for advice on what to do, received the vague but wise reply, "Do what you wish, but in no case use force."

Several highly-placed personages arrived in Grozny, headed by the chairman of the RSFSR Council of Ministers, Solomentsev. The events ended with buses being brought up, each with a sign bearing the name of a particular village. The demonstrators were advised to board the buses and return to their various homes. They were given assurances that no repression would follow. But several hundred, mostly young people, remained. Groups of firemen with hoses and police with clubs were turned loose on them.

The demonstration of February 23, 1973, was the biggest action by the Ingush since their repatriation. It showed once again that as long as the wrong that had been done was not completely corrected, it would repeatedly generate conflicts. There are constant smaller clashes, disputes, and expressions of dissatisfaction, but these do not become widely known or gain public attention.

True to the custom in the Soviet Union, the newspapers did not report the events of February 23, 1973. Only a few scattered articles filtered through and appeared on the pages of *Groznenskii rabochii* somewhat later on. However, these not only make it possible to infer the nature and scope of the events but also help us to understand the substance of relations between nationalities in Checheno-Ingushetia at the present time.

In mid-March 1973, articles, groups of news items, and other material directly and indirectly related to the Ingush movement for the return of Prigorodnyi district began to be published systematically in the pages of *Groznenskii rabochii*.

From these materials it became clear that a group of intellectuals and party workers formerly holding responsible posts, all of Ingush nationality, were taking part in this movement (and possibly providing its leadership). Among them were the popular

Ingush writer Idris Bazorkin; A. Gazdiyev, former secretary of the Nazran district committee of the party (Nazran is the center of Ingushetia) and subsequently deputy minister of culture of the republic; S. Pliyev, former chairman of the Sunzhenskii district executive committee; and the distillery director D. Kartoyev.[59] One of the participants in this movement, incidentally, was a graduate student at the Institute of History of the USSR under the USSR Academy of Sciences by the name of Parov. He was withdrawn from graduate work in the wake of these events.

Judging by the speech of S. S. Apriatkin, first secretary of the Chechen-Ingush regional committee of the party, at the tenth plenum of the committee, on March 27, 1973, the movement not only involved Nazran and Sunzhenskii districts; participants also came into Grozny city from Malgobek and Shalinskii districts and the rural part of Grozny district.[60]

After the plenum there was an extensive campaign against nationalism and religious influences upon the population. A series of gatherings dealt with these problems: the eleventh plenum of the Grozny municipal committee of the party, in April 1973; a meeting of all active party members in the republic, in late May the same year; the twelfth plenum of the Chechen-Ingush regional committee, on July 31, 1973; and the thirteenth plenum of the same organization, in November of that year.

The leadership of the republic was especially disturbed by the broad participation of young people in the events of February 23 and after. S. S. Apriatkin complained, at the plenum of the regional committee on March 27, 1973, for example, that in the above-mentioned districts mass political work had been poorly handled and had not reached a substantial section of the population, "especially young people, women, and the elderly."[61] A resolution of this plenum also stated: "In the towns and districts of the republic there are quite a few young men and women who do not work anywhere and are not going to school. Right in front of the eyes of Communists and Komsomol personnel, these young people pursue an improper and, in some cases, openly antisocial way of life."[62] Here, too, attention was called to the fact that some students graduate from higher educational institutions without having been "tempered ideologically."[63] At the second republic-wide methodology conference of Komsomol propagandists, held in Grozny in early June 1973, it was stated: "Certain politically and morally unstable young people, who have come under the influence of bourgeois propaganda and of adherents of reactionary survivals of the past, express themselves in a politically harmful way and distort the state of affairs in the republic. . . . Some young people from Sunzhenskii district have given vent to expressions of nationalism. The tractor drivers Alkhoyev and Khomatkhanov, on the Akhlangurskii *sovkhoz,* were expelled from the Komsomol."[64] Another young man, by the name of Arsamakov, a former secretary in the Komsomol organization of the Malgobek truck-and-tractor column, was also expelled from the Komsomol for "lack of political principle."

What were the reasons for the worsening relations between the nationalities in Checheno-Ingushetia, in the view of the party leaders of the republic? (This question pertains not only to the views of the local leaders, it would seem, for a deputy chief of the propaganda department of the CPSU Central Committee, Yu. A. Sklarov, spoke at the tenth plenum of the Chechen-Ingush regional committee.)

Their reasons were, first, the persistence and active influence of clan ties on social life. This was to no little extent the result of an underestimation—to use the words of the first secretary of the regional committee, S. S. Apriatkin—of the national peculiarities and the specifics of the historical development of the native population. He had to admit that the survivals of the clan system (the *teipa*) persist to this day, survivals which have an enormous influence on cadre policies too. The chairman of the KGB of Checheno-Ingushetia, V. I. Zhigalov, and the secretary of the regional committee, M. A. Kerimov, spoke at the plenum about the practice of promoting incompetent cadres and cynically transferring unsuccessful officials from one location to another. This cadre problem is what we would call a universal phenomenon, not something found only in Checheno-Ingushetia. The measures suggested for "correcting" this problem were to put a decisive stop to all attempts to "select cadres by kinship (*teipa*) ties" and to purge individuals "given to national prejudice and behaving in a two-faced manner." [65]

The second reason noted was the profound influence of Islam on a substantial portion of the population. Numerous Muslim sects and smaller sectarian groups exist and function in the republic. (By the unofficial count of the Georgian historian L. there are about 150.) According to S. S. Apriatkin, the sects encourage nationalist attitudes. In his words, the Kunta-Hajji sect in Shalinskii district called for a struggle against the "Russification" of the Chechen-Ingush youth. [66] At a conference at the Council of Ministers of the ASSR in April 1973 reference was made to the custom of pilgrimages to numerous "holy" places as a factor that intensifies religious fanaticism. [67]

Murid religious groups have "modernized" their activity and use the latest technology to illegally broadcast material with a religious content (this is severely punished under the law). Phonograph records and recorded tapes with religious content are also produced and circulated. [68] The extent to which religion influences the everyday life of the native population of the ASSR was discussed in a letter to the editors of *Groznenskii rabochii* signed by a group of young party and Komsomol workers—Yu. Aidayev, D. Akhriyev, B. Buzurtanov, M. Vedziyazhev, A. Karatayev, S. Sanguriyev, and M. Tochiyev. It was published with the heading "To Serve the People with Honor." It said: "A substantial part of the population is under the influence of religion. Murid communities of various persuasions, which are active in the republic, try to control the morals and customs, domestic and family relations, marital ties, and other relationships, and to strengthen their pernicious influence upon the youth." [69]

To judge from the pages of *Groznenskii rabochii,* the Muslim clergy seem to have become a kind of "shadow state" within a state. With its blessings, participation, and leadership, secret *khel* courts function quite actively; the customs of *kalym* (bride-money) and abduction of the bride from her parents flourish; and a cult is made of the traditions of blood revenge, mutual protection, etc.[70] At the tenth plenum of the regional committee, S. S. Apriatkin told of an especially curious case in which a *khel* court was counterposed to a people's court. In Nazran district the people's court brought a group of people to trial on charges of stealing grain from a *sovkhoz*. Later a *khel* court convened secretly and ruled that those who had testified in this case before the people's court should be fined seven thousand four hundred rubles—to go to the defendants![71]

However, it is hard to avoid the suspicion that the leaders of the Chechen-Ingush ASSR may be exaggerating the extent of the Muslim clergy's influence in order to cover up for their own inability to handle national problems and the fruitlessness of their attempts at solving these problems in concrete cases. Are they trying to exculpate themselves in the eyes of Moscow in this way?

The third official thesis is that there is a breeding ground for nationalist agitation in the "non-class approach to the evaluation of historical phenomena, the idealization of the past, the exaggeration of the merits of certain individuals out of all proportion, and the attempts to portray the Chechens and Ingush as peoples who had no class differentiation and never knew the class struggle."[72]

These points were later refined and enlarged upon in speeches by party leaders and, after them, by historians. Their main concern was to emphasize the positive aspects of tsarist policies in the Caucasus. M. O. Buzurtanov, a secretary of the regional committee, has stated quite seriously that the progressive significance of the unification of Checheno-Ingushetia with Russia was that otherwise it would not now be a socialist nation! Praising the exploits of General Yermolov, the strangler of the Caucasian peoples, Buzurtanov criticized writers and historians of Checheno-Ingushetia for their "one-sided treatment" of Yermolov's "founding of the fort of Grozny" and for failing to mention the importance of the fort "as part of the overall system of fortifications guarding against the danger that the peoples of the Caucasus, including the Chechens and Ingush, might be enslaved by the Turkish and Persian conquerors and the Anglo-French colonialists.''[73] Such unscientific pronouncements had not been heard for twenty-five years, not since the great-power chauvinist campaign against ''cosmopolitanism.''

K. Yefanov, a historian of the CPSU, spoke in the same vein as Buzurtanov. Not only did he repeat, without any solid scientific arguments, the thesis that there was class differentiation in Chechen-Ingush society and an intense class struggle, anathematizing all historical works that either denied this thesis or raised doubts about it; he also asserted that the popular movements in the Caucasus in the 1860s and 1870s had been provoked by Turkish agents in the interests of Turkey and Iran![74]

These and other similar statements are undoubtedly symptomatic of intensified Great Russian chauvinism in Checheno-Ingushetia. But at the same time, these statements testify to the dead end in which the leaders of the autonomous republic find themselves because they have pursued policies in the area of national relations that have been completely stereotyped and lacking in any perspective.

The official point of view contends, further, that it is necessary to wage a determined struggle against attempts to cover up ''negative processes,'' and not to hide the historical truth from the people, especially the youth. This historical truth allegedly consists in the fact that during the struggle for Soviet power and during the Second World War, class enemies organized in outlaw bands helped the enemies of the Soviet state and that the Soviet military command was forced to use front-line units of the Red Army to combat these bands.[75]

In May 1974 *Groznenskii rabochii* published a major article by V. I. Filkin headlined ''Hopes Built on Sand: For an Objective Treatment of the History of Checheno-Ingushetia During the Great Patriotic War.'' This article attempted to explain the complexity of the political situation in the region during the war. But it had a number of weaknesses. It gave no statistics on the number of people drawn into ''political banditry'' (a term Filkin introduced in place of the previously used term, just plain ''banditry''). It failed to discuss the question of participation by Northern

Caucasians in Hitler's military formations. And its attempt to describe the various positions of the different social layers during the war was too general and therefore unconvincing.[76]

The events of February 1973 supposedly revealed the existence of a great disparity: although the native population had acquired the material benefits of civilization, its need for cultural refinement had not been met. In the old days, on religious holidays, the Mountaineers used to prance about on horses decorated with yellow pennants. Now they decorate their Moskvich and Zhiguli automobiles. At the same time there are frequent reports from a number of districts that doctors, teachers, and members of other professions are harassed if they are not of the native nationality. For example, D. Banashev, deputy minister of internal affairs for the Chechen-Ingush ASSR, has written about such cases in Malgobek, Shalinskii, Nazran, and Nozhai-Yurtov districts.[77] A case was reported in the press in which specialists at the knitting mill who were not natives were harassed in Nazran in early 1973.[78]

Once again, however, we must ask: Why hasn't the press referred, at least after February 1973, to negative facts of the opposite kind, expressions of Great Russian chauvinism toward the Chechens and Ingush? Are there really no such cases? Don't the reports about hostility toward individuals who are not of the native nationality serve as justification for great-power chauvinism? It should be remembered that at the present time, according to the 1970 census, the Russian population in the Chechen-Ingush ASSR constitutes 34.5 percent, and the Chechen and Ingush 58.5 percent.[79] With this kind of population balance, the proper handling of the delicate instrument of nationalities policy requires special art. There are enough intelligent people in Checheno-Ingushetia to provide this skill, however. It should be noted that, in addition to calls for a struggle against nationalism, appeals for restraint have also been heard. A lecturer at the Grozny Petroleum Institute by the name of Ovcharov rightly condemned the tendency for "certain individuals" to make wholesale condemnations of an entire people because of the actions of a few "renegades." Ovcharov urged that "such tendencies be firmly stopped and that philistine nonsense be refuted objectively by dealing consistently with the historical truth, without going to extremes in one direction or another."[80]

In November 1973, at the thirteenth plenum of the Chechen-Ingush regional committee, first secretary S. S. Apriatkin declared that "the party organizations in the republic have succeeded in exposing the bankruptcy and harmfulness of the nationalist demands concerning Prigorodnyi district . . . and in exposing the organizers of the antisocial nationalist demonstration, showing that their actions were not in the interests of the people, but, on the contrary, were detrimental to its vital interests and aspirations. . . ."[81]

After this the plenum concentrated its attention on the fact that after the tenth plenum many scientists and scholars, especially of Chechen and Ingush nationality, had failed to speak up either orally or in writing. It was also revealed that during the assemblies held in all inhabited areas of the republic and at party, working-class, and Komsomol meetings, there had been "undesirable contributions." The plenum concluded that "the pathetic handful of nationalist elements had altered their tactics," and it called for a "strictly political response to the attempts to smuggle in harmful notions under the pretext of freedom of discussion."[82] It is evident that discussion had gone beyond the permitted bounds and that certain orders had been handed down accordingly.

After the events of February 23 the main effort in ideological work among the native population was to combat the cult of "the land of our forefathers," i.e., the historical claims of the Ingush to Prigorodnyi district. The results of this campaign were disappointing. At a plenum of the regional committee in June 1974 it was stated that too little had been done to deglamorize the "cult of the land of our forebears."[83] But looked at more generally, within the context of the present time in history, the idea that the Ingush could be persuaded to abandon their claim to their historic homeland seems highly dubious.

VI

Decisions That Cannot Be Avoided

NOT LONG before the liberation of the Crimea, P. Chursin, the Crimean regional committee secretary for propaganda, wrote in the newspaper *Krasnyi Krym* (Red Crimea): "If the Germans say they brought freedom to the Tatars of the Crimea, do not believe it! Today everyone realizes that dozens of Tatar villages were wiped off the face of the earth and hundreds and thousands of Crimean Tatars executed. The Germans came to the Crimea as enslavers and plunderers of the Tatar people."[1]

Four years later, in 1948, this same man, addressing a conference of historians of the Crimea, spoke of the Crimean Tatars in quite a different vein: "The Tatar population in the Crimea was never industrious. Therefore, after deporting the Tatars the Soviet government entrusted the restoration of the economy of the Crimea to Russian and Ukrainian collective farmers. . . . It is not right to criticize the Crimean Tatars by remaining silent about them. We must tell the truth about them, that is, expose their past as raiders and brigands, their parasitic way of life. . . ."[2] We must tell the truth, that is, expose! Here in this formula is the quintessence of the attitude which treats history as an instrument of politics and nothing more. And often, in the years that followed, was heard this call to "politicize history," in other words, to renounce history as a science.

Chursin's call was not only heard, it was taken as a guide to action in the field of historical scholarship. The historian P. N. Nadinsky wrote in *Essays in the History of the Crimea:* "The Crimean Tatars were so used to living off the proceeds of their thieving raids that they hardly ever engaged in productive labor themselves, and when they did it was with reluctance."[3] Other speakers followed Nadinsky's lead. Propaganda against the Crimean Tatars assumed vast proportions in the subsequent years, becoming, as it were, a common, everyday affair.

In 1968, R. I. Muzafarov and G. B. Fedorov, a doctor of historical sciences, wrote an extremely cogent review of Nadinsky's writings and of the collectively authored series *Essays in the History of the Crimea,* published from 1951 to 1967. The reviewers ridiculed Nadinsky's claim that "reunification with Russia [not just unification!] immediately and radically changed the face of the Crimean peninsula. It was as though it had sprung back to life after vegetating in a swamp for three centuries, as though social and economic life in the territory liberated from Turkish rule burst into full bloom."[4] Muzafarov and Fedorov commented: "Such raptures lead one to suspect that P. N. Nadinsky has culled his ideas about history 'from forgotten gazettes of the time of Ochakov* and the conquest of the Crimea.' But such 'opinions' were considered old-fashioned and reactionary even in Griboyedov's day." †

---

* Ochakov was a Turkish fort at the mouth of the Dnieper River on the Black Sea. It became a symbol of Russian victory over the Turks and Crimean Tatars when it fell after a long siege during the Russo-Turkish war of 1787–92. That war resulted, among other things in Turkish recognition of Russia's annexation of the Crimea. The quotation is from the Russian writer and diplomat Aleksandr S. Griboyedov (1795–1829), famous for his verse comedy *Woe from Wit,* which ridiculed the sterile superpatriotism of the early nineteenth century.

† Muzafarov and Fedorov, "Suzhden'ia cherpaiut iz zabytiykh gazet. . ." ["Their Opinions They Cull from Forgotten Gazettes . . ."], from unpublished page proofs for the magazine *Novy Mir,* 1959. The review was accepted by *Novy Mir,* set in type, and submitted as part of a proposed issue several times by the late editor Aleksandr Tvardovsky, but either the censor or someone higher up always threw it out. Thus the review never appeared.

Until 1954, writers, historians, and propagandists never stopped trying to prove that the Crimea had historically belonged to Russia. After the transfer of the Crimea from the RSFSR to the Ukrainian SSR, in 1954—perhaps as a kind of present on the three-hundredth anniversary of the "reunification" of Russia and the Ukraine—Ukrainian historians began to argue fervently that the Crimea had belonged to the Ukraine from "time immemorial" and to violently denounce the Crimean Tatars for every variety of mortal sin. The charges of "raiding," "looting," "brigandage," "treason," "perfidiousness" etc., re-emerged with new force.

But there was nothing original in any of this. Even in tsarist times it was the usual thing to dump the blame for military reverses on the non-Russians, the "outlanders" (*inorodtsy*). During the Russo-Turkish wars, and especially the Crimean War, as we have noted above, the Tatars were invariably accused by tsarist officials and other rank chauvinists of collaborating with the Turks. Thus arose the stereotype of the Crimean Tatar as an enemy of Russia and an agent of Turkey. This ready-made stereotype has found its way into the arsenal of propaganda against the Crimean Tatars in our day as well.

This propaganda against the Crimean Tatars has been going on now for more than thirty years. The kind of falsification done to certain documents on the history of the Great Patriotic War of 1941–45 in the Crimea is representative. Let us turn to a collection of documents published in 1973.[5]

Here are several examples of falsification:

1. *Document no. 164: report of the Crimean regional committee on the state of affairs in the partisan movement in the Crimea, December 18, 1942 (pp. 252–53).* The following sentence is omitted (without ellipses): "Mustafayev, third secretary of the party regional committee, has been sent to the forests, and with him a group of Tatar party workers, six of whom have already settled in at locations in Tatar villages." (See the Crimean regional party archive, collection 151, shelf 1, folder 134, sheet 47).

2. *Document no. 259: information on the raising of funds for*

the "Crimean Partisan" tank column, May 4, 1944 (pp. 373–74). The following sentence is omitted: "The following men and women of the Ikendzhi Bashsene *kolkhoz* in Ak-Shenskii district—Asan Muzakar, Elmas Asanova, Katishe Kililiayeva, and Kalil Bektashev—contributed a total of 13,000 rubles from their personal savings." (See the newspaper *Krasnyi Krym*, No. 35 (5808), May 4, 1944.)

3. *Document no. 146: from the report of the command staff of the partisan movement in the Crimea to the party regional committee on the activities of the partisan detachments from November 1, 1941, to March 21, 1942. Dated March 21, 1942 (pp. 217–19).* The following sentence is omitted: "The Tatar population in the steppe region, the Russians, and the Greeks await the coming of the Red Army impatiently and give aid to the partisans." (See the Crimean regional party archive, collection 151, shelf 1, file 19, sheets 49–51.)

4. *Document no. 152: from information sent by the Crimean regional party committee to the central headquarters of the partisan movement on the state of affairs in the partisan movement of the Crimea. Dated July 7, 1942 (pp. 223–32).* The following sentence is omitted: "At the same time it should be noted that the Tatars of the steppe region of the Crimea do not demonstrate such hostility toward the partisans as the Tatars of the mountain districts. Not infrequently they demonstrate their sympathy for the partisans. They do not support the German Fascists and look forward to the coming of Soviet power, and the Germans see this." (See the Crimean regional party archive, collection 1, file 22, sheets 1–3.)

5. In Documents 40, 51, 81, and elsewhere (see pp. 68, 75, 80, and 120–21) the names of the chairman of the Council of People's Commissars of the Crimean ASSR, M. Ibraimov, and the administrative assistant (*upravdel*) of the Council of People's Commissars, I. Seifullayev, have been omitted. Instead of their names, the word "signature" appears.

The names of Crimean Tatar activists in the partisan movement are either not mentioned or russified. Here are some examples from the materials of Muzafarov:

REAL NAME	ALTERED NAME

Seidali Agayev — *S. Ageyev*
(Active in the Sevastopol underground; arrested on October 13,
1943; shot by the occupation
authorities.)

(Source: I. Kozlov, *V krymskom podpol'e* [In the Crimean underground],
pp. 418–20.)

Seidali Kurtoseyitov — *S. Kursakov*
(Partisan diversionist; killed in
early 1944.)
(Source: Kozlov, p. 104.)

REAL NAME

Dzhetskhai-Kashik Nedzhibe
Battalova — *Batayeva*
(Teacher and underground activist
from the village of Dzhermai-
Kashchik; hanged by the occupa-
tion authorities.)

(Source: P. Meshalkin and K. Raspevin, "V logove vraga" [In the
enemy's lair], an article in the newspaper *Trud* [Labor], March 10, 1959.)

Alime Abdaknanova — *the scout Anya*

(Army scout from the village of   (The authors write that they could
Dzhermai-Kashchik.)   not establish Anya's last name.)

(Source: Meshalkin and Raspevin.)

Abdulla Seidametovich Dagdzhi — *Uncle Volodya*
(Leader of the largest underground   (Nickname; no last name given.)
organization in Simferopol; died in
1943.)

(Source: Kozlov, p. 93; N. Lugovoi, *Pobratimy* [Sworn brothers]
[Simferopol, 1965], p. 65.)

Neile Veliyeva — *Neile Veliyeva, a Tatar from*
(Crimean Tatar underground   *Kazan*
activist.)

(Source: Kozlov, *op. cit.*, p. 435.)

171

To complete this picture of falsification, distortion, and suppression of information, we will cite one last example: the author's abstract of the candidate's dissertation by G. Babichev.[6] Here statistics are given on the national composition of the participants in the partisan movement in the Crimea as of January 15, 1944. Babichev gives them as follows: Out of a total of 3,773, there were 1,944 Russians, 348 Ukrainians, 22 Byelorussians, 69 Armenians, 134 Georgians, and 66 Azerbaijanis. This adds up to 2,583 persons. But to what nationalities did the remaining 1,190 belong? After all, this is no small number—1,190 represents one-third of the total. Isn't it true, when all is said and done, that these were Crimean Tatars, Greeks, Krymchaks, and Jews?

After the rehabilitation of the people of the Caucasus it took another seven years before the Volga Germans were rehabilitated. A decree of the Presidium of the Supreme Soviet of the USSR on August 29, 1964, only two months before N. S. Khrushchev was removed from power, still bore fresh traces of the stormy period of struggle against the Stalin personality cult and of the resolutions at the Twentieth and Twenty-second Party Congresses concerning official abuse of power. The decree stated:

> In the August 28, 1941, decree of the Presidium of the Supreme Soviet of the USSR "On the Resettlement of Germans Living in the Volga Region," the charge of actively aiding and abetting the German fascist invaders was made in regard to large numbers of Germans who were Soviet citizens.
>
> Life has shown that these indiscriminate charges were unfounded and were an expression of the arbitrary abuse of power that existed under the Stalin personality cult.
>
> In reality, during the Great Patriotic War the overwhelming majority of the German population, together with the entire Soviet people, contributed by its labor to the victory of the Soviet Union over fascist Germany. . . ."[7]

All civil rights were restored to Soviet Germans, but their autonomous republic was not re-established.

Deep disillusionment over this half-measure led to the rise of a movement among the German population in the Soviet Union to emigrate to their historic homeland, Germany. Under the specific historical conditions of our time, for most Germans wishing to leave the Soviet Union, this means moving to the German Federal Republic. Things followed the usual pattern as with any movement in our country: petitions, demands, official repression, expressions of solidarity by democratic public opinion in our country, indignation on the part of world public opinion, and the addition of one more source of tension in relations between the USSR and the German Federal Republic. Yet this conflict would have been so easy to avoid. And it is still not too late to resolve it.

The rehabilitation of the Crimean Tatars was postponed even longer. The decree of the Presidium of the Supreme Soviet of the USSR withdrawing "the wholesale charges against all citizens of Tatar nationality formerly resident in the Crimea" was not handed down until September 5, 1967,[8] i.e., twenty-three years after the forced deportation of the Tatars from the Crimea.

Although the charges of collaboration with the enemy during the war were formally withdrawn, this action was qualified in certain fundamental ways. Above all, the decree referred to "citizens of Tatar nationality formerly resident in the Crimea." This implied that the concept of "Crimean Tatars" as a nation or national group had been nullified and this ethnic category replaced by the civil-law concept "citizens of Tatar nationality formerly resident in the Crimea." In effect, this phrasing eliminated the question of restoring autonomy to the Crimean Tatars, since if there was no such nationality, how could it have autonomy?

What we have here is subtle calculation, and not, as some students of the matter suppose, mere ignorance. To disarm and disorient the older generation of Crimean Tatars, who had lived and worked in their own autonomous republic, the decree stressed that the charges had been withdrawn "especially because a new generation has entered working life and the political life of society.'' In other words, this was being done not so much for those who had been repressed as for their children. What was this, then, rehabilitation or a condescending mockery?

The decree contained another assertion meant to counter the protests that were sure to follow, since the decree had remained silent about the restoration of the Crimean ASSR. This assertion was that the Tatars from the Crimea had ''put down roots'' in Uzbekistan and other republics. Such a vague formulation could be interpreted narrowly or broadly—narrowly, as simply referring to the areas where they were then living; broadly, as implying the assimilation of the Crimean Tatars in Central Asia, their loss of their own culture, language, alphabet, etc. But the fact was, of course, that they had never ''put down roots,'' and the decree could only be stating that they had resided in certain locations for a certain time, i.e., had been provided with residence permits and jobs by the authorities in those areas.

In the ''Appeal of the Crimean Tatar People to the Twenty-fourth Party Congress, the Soviet Press, and All Communists'' (March 1971) there is a report on the results of a poll of eighteen hundred Crimean Tatar adults in the Tashkent region on the question of returning to the Crimea. Only nine people were opposed to a return to the Crimea, and eleven refrained from expressing an opinion. Thus the overwhelming majority expressed themselves in favor of returning.[9] That is the real situation in regard to the Crimean Tatars ''putting down roots'' in Uzbekistan.

The decree of September 5, 1967, formally restored to the Crimean Tatars all the rights enjoyed by all other citizens of the USSR. But in reality, there remain unresolved not only the fundamental problem—the restoration of the Crimean ASSR—but also a whole series of civil rights guaranteed by the Soviet Constitution, from the right to live where one wishes (as a rule, Crimean Tatars are not given permits to move to the Crimea) to the right to instruction in one's own language.

In the Crimea before the war there were several hundred schools, both primary and secondary, with instruction in the Crimean Tatar language. More than sixteen hundred Crimean Tatars were attending higher educational institutions and technical schools (out of a total of eleven thousand such students in the Crimea). Many were preparing for careers as doctors and educators.

Nine newspapers in the Crimean Tatar language had been published. In 1940 the printing industry in the Crimea produced 1,487 quires, of which 938 were in the language of the Crimean Tatars. In addition, three magazines were published in this language. There was a national theater and a scientific research institute where work was done on Crimean history, philology, and culture.

Among the deputies to local Soviets in the Crimean ASSR there were 2,207 Tatars; 837 persons of Tatar nationality held high positions in party and Komsomol work, and 275 in government work.[10]

Today there is not one school, no national theater and no institute. In Uzbekistan, thus far, only one newspaper in Crimean Tatar is published (three times a week). In recent years literature in the Crimean Tatar language has begun to be published in Central Asia—as part of the effort to keep the Crimean Tatars in that part of the USSR.

In a period of nine months in 1939, fifty-eight textbooks in Crimean Tatar were published. Over a period of thirty years, from 1944 to 1973, only two such textbooks came out. During the years of "putting down roots" in Uzbekistan not a single study in Crimean philology or history nor a single Crimean Tatar dictionary appeared. Naturally such an abnormal situation is in flagrant contradiction to the Soviet Constitution and the Universal Declaration of Human Rights. It has produced a mass protest movement of the Crimean Tatar people, and the best representatives of democratic public opinion in our country have demonstrated their solidarity with the Crimean Tatars. Of these, we should mention at least three: P. G. Grigorenko, A. E. Kosterin, and Ilya Gabai. The savage reprisals against participants in this movement have done considerable harm to the international reputation of the Soviet Union.

The attempt to prevent all possibility of the Tatars returning to the Crimea by the redoubled colonizing of the peninsula with Ukrainian settlers will not solve the problem but only complicates it, further entangling the knot of contradictions built up around this question.

Even in 1975 the Crimean region was not very thickly settled, especially in the steppes. It is much less thickly settled than many other areas and republics of the Soviet Union. There is plenty of room in the Crimea—for Ukrainians, for Tatars, and for any others who might wish to settle there.

Sooner or later the Crimean Tatars will surely return to their homeland. It would be a wise policy to hasten this return and thereby make it as painless as possible for all. But it is a decision that cannot be avoided.

The deportation of peoples from the Caucasus and the Crimea at the end of the war was undoubtedly one of the manifestations of a profound crisis in the Stalinist system which became especially obvious after the war. In a multinational state such as the Soviet Union, a crisis in the system makes itself felt first of all in the area of national relations. History has shown this to be true.

In the twentieth century only two multinational empires have existed in Europe: the Austro-Hungarian monarchy and the Russia of the tsars. Austria-Hungary fell apart with its defeat in World War I, but the main cause of its disintegration was that the national contradictions of the Hapsburg empire had not been resolved. The ruling nation, the Germans, were a minority of the population, while the majority was made up of small nationalities. The ruling nation proved unable to counteract the centrifugal forces tearing the empire apart.

In tsarist Russia, the ruling nation, the Russians, constituted a relative majority, and this had a bearing on the fact that a significant part of the assimilated borderland areas of the empire were retained after the revolution in February 1917. And this was not only a matter of sheer physical force, because Russia had been weakened substantially by the war and internal conflicts. The

strong economic interdependence between Russia and the conquered borderlands, as well as the significant ideological influence of Russian culture, were also factors.

Within the Soviet Union, which arose from the foundations of
the shattered Romanov empire, there remained a high proportion
of those possessions which had been acquired during the three
preceding centuries. As history would have it, besides Yugoslavia, the Soviet Union was the only large multinational state left in
Europe. (More than one hundred nationalities live within its borders.) The whole problem of national relations in a multinational
state depends on the ability to reconcile the pressures and demands of the central authority (including the requirements for
economic development and statewide planning) with the growth
and advancement of each particular national culture. Lenin's idea
of "cultural assistance" to the smaller nations by the former
oppressor nation, so that each small nation can construct its "own
state,'' [11] was absolutely correct. But it collided with the pragma-
tism of the central authorities, who were seeking to strengthen the
power of their state. The entire system of relations among the nationalities was under constant pressure from centralizing tendencies, which on the one hand were objective in nature but on the
other hand reflected stereotyped conceptions inherited from tsarist
Russia about the ways of "regulating national relations." Energetic social reorganization without any special allowance for the
particular national features and conditions of each people produced an intensification of all the contradictions in the life of the
state as a whole and without exception. Under such conditions the
rise of conflicts between small and large nations became inevitable, up to and including armed clashes (the uprising in Georgia,
for example, and its bloody suppression; the elimination of the
"national deviationists"; the mass deportations of native populations on a social basis; and later, deportations of entire peoples on
a national basis).

The situations of sharp conflict on national grounds; the systematic ideological campaigns, now justifying tsarist Russia's
wars of conquest, now branding the national-liberation move-

ments of the conquered borderland peoples unjust and reactionary; the loud onslaughts against the national epics of various peoples, in fact, against their cultural heritage; the outbursts of anti-Semitism—all this essentially reflects the extremely weak "feedback" between the state and the various peoples.

As the smaller peoples (greatly aided by the central government) emerged from economic backwardness and downtrodden existence—with the elimination of illiteracy; the development of alphabets for many of these peoples and, consequently, of the printed word; the growth of spiritual culture, and not only of material refinements—there also arose an increasingly powerful desire for greater independence, cultural autonomy, and a broadening of local rights. People felt a greater respect for their own national history and culture, no longer because of some age-old attachment to the faith and traditions of their forebears but as a result of conscious reflection on the values inherent in the past history and experience of their nation. At this stage of national consciousness the desire for less supervision by the majority nation, if not for total liberation, makes its appearance.

However, during the time when the small nation travels this path, from the bare acquisition of the material benefits of modern civilization to the realization of the value of its own culture, other essential changes take place—involving migration, the mixing of populations, and partial assimilation. From the standpoint of general human progress, the natural process of the intermingling of populations—that is, without any forcible interference one way or another—is the kind of favorable soil in which the small nation's awareness of its culture as a part of overall human culture can best grow. Such interpenetration, and consequent interaction, between the cultures of various peoples and their mutual enrichment is perhaps the only sure road to the solution of the national question in general.

There are many obstacles along this road, and the biggest one is a policy of pressure or force on the part of the majority nation. Force, or a policy based on the possibility of its application at any moment, cannot be a long-standing or permanent factor contributing to unity in a multinational state, because the great-power chauvinism of the majority nation will exert a constant pressure. And that in turn automatically gives rise to resistance by the smaller nation and encourages it to withdraw into a narrowly nationalistic shell. Small nations instinctively and not just consciously seek to save themselves by defending even those traditions which hang like a dead weight upon them and which would, if not for the constant pressure from the central government or majority nation, gradually die away by themselves under the impact not of force but of a higher level of spiritual culture.

The actual encouragement of chauvinism and nationalism is the result of all our restrictive and discriminatory measures based on nationality, including administrative measures "regulating national relations"—from the stamp in the internal passport indicating the nationality of the bearer (of all the civilized countries, it seems, ours is the only one where such a barbarity survives) to the restrictions on residence permits on grounds of nationality, to quotas for admission to higher educational institutions and every kind of oral or written propaganda directed against a particular people, no matter what ideological camouflage it may be disguised in.

Every measure, even the most insignificant, which encourages chauvinism and inevitably leads to national alienation produces cracks in the structure of the national state, even if they are barely noticeable or microscopic. When too many of them have accumulated, they can bring on sudden tragedy.

Precisely such a tragedy was the forced resettlement of entire peoples in the 1940s. The impact of this tragedy still has not died away; it is still fresh in many areas of our life, but especially in the moral sphere.

It will take many years and considerable efforts before this wound is healed. And it is not the only one we have.

Conversation on a Train
(*In Lieu of an Afterword*)

IN THE MIDDLE of April 1975 I was returning to Moscow from Belgorod region after visiting the grave of my older brother, who died in the battle of Kursk in 1943.

It was nighttime when I managed to board the express from Makhachkala to Moscow at Kharkov station. I quickly climbed into my berth so that the other passengers, disturbed by my arrival, could go back to sleep. In the morning I discovered that I was sharing a compartment with three people: two women and a man.

One of the women was rather well dressed, a Russian lady, of that age where you can easily make a mistake by guessing a few years too many, or too few. Probably she was between forty-five and fifty. She had a rather pleasant face and slightly tinted dark hair. Several of her lower teeth were gold, detracting somewhat from her appearance. The other woman, who was about thirty, with large gray eyes and a longish face, turned out to be an Ingush. From the desultory conversation of the women I gathered that the Ingush woman had recently divorced her husband and was now traveling to Moscow either to her sister's or to a friend's. The last occupant of our compartment was a short, well-groomed man of about sixty with a smooth, almost polished, bald head. "A retired colonel," the thought occurred to me.

The women's conversation was mostly about the wives of well-known Grozny men, mainly writers.

When I heard the name of the author Bazorkin, I perked up and, addressing the Russian woman, said:

"Excuse me for breaking into your conversation, but I heard you mention Idris Bazorkin and I was wondering—do they still publish him after the 1973 events?"

The woman shook her head.

"That's what I thought," I responded, and added reflectively, "The fact that Prigorodny district was not returned to the Ingush has meant a lot of complications, and will mean a lot more."

At these words the Ingush woman looked at me closely but did not join the conversation. The Russian woman gave the impression that she half agreed with me, but I sensed that she really thought otherwise.

"Of course this business cuts both ways," she said. "I wonder whether two wrongs make a right?"

She obviously meant that although the deportation of the Chechens and Ingush in 1944 had been wrong, returning them to the Caucasus had also been wrong. Naturally I disagreed, stating my view that the mistake was not in the correction of the injustice done to the Chechens and Ingush but in the fact that it was not corrected immediately and thoroughly—all the lands where they had lived should have been returned to them.

The Russian woman's thoughts now took a new direction.

"I was living there then. I was just a little girl. And I saw it all with my own eyes. It was terrible. They rounded them up at six o'clock in the morning on February 23 and began loading them into the Studebaker trucks. They let the old people say goodbye to their native land. They said prayers and wept. Suddenly I saw a little child, limping, wandering from one woman to another. It made my heart ache. . . ."

The Ingush woman's dark eyes grew darker still, but she continued to listen impassively, not taking part in the conversation. Only her arms, crossed over her chest, seem to tense slightly.

"They began coming back in 1955," the Russian woman continued.

"I think it was 1956," I tried to correct her. "The decree restoring the Chechen-Ingush ASSR was issued in early 1957, and they began returning a year before that."

"They began returning in 1955," the woman reiterated. "Many Russian families began to leave in a hurry, especially the new settlers from the Ukraine."

"No," the Ingush woman finally broke in. "Many of the new settlers still live among us."

An argument quickly developed between the two women, each sticking to her opinion.

"Then a terrible thing happened in August 1958," said the older woman when she finally resumed her reminiscences. "There was a funeral procession down the Avenue of the Revolution. The coffin wasn't carried in the usual way, but like this. . . ." She raised her arms to show that the coffin was held high above the crowd of mourners, as though floating through the air by itself.

"There was no shouting, no weeping, just total silence."

I lost patience:

"Come on now, who were they burying?"

"A sailor on leave had come to visit. He went to a dance one evening and asked a girl to dance whom one of the locals was courting. This fellow snuck up on the sailor and killed him. It was the sailor they were burying."

"A Russian?"

"Yes."

The Ingush woman raised her eyes. She seemed to be trying to remember something.

"Yes," she said. "I know about that. The one who killed the sailor was my aunt's cousin by my father's brother." Her gaze traveled over us, as though to ask whether we understood what relation he was to her. We tactfully remained silent.

"He went to prison and never got out. Probably he's dead."

Everyone sighed.

But shortly the Russian woman continued her story: "The crowd came up to the party building and stopped. They demanded that someone come out and give a speech for the deceased. But no

one came out. The regional committee people quickly locked all
the doors and refused to show themselves. The mood of the crowd
turned ugly. Someone went up to the door and began trying to
break it in.'' Our narrator suddenly stopped and smiled, recalling
something she found amusing.

"A little girl lived in our building, about twelve years old. She
and other children from our block were running along after the
crowd, which by then was already storming the party building. Finally, the doors gave way and the crowd rushed up the stairs. Suddenly from the window of the third storey the little girl stuck out
her head and cried, 'Hurray for our side. We've won! We've
won!'"

"That's probably how revolutions happen," I thought to myself.

"The terrified committee people tried to get away or hide, but
the angry crowd grabbed them and started beating them.

"There was a history teacher who lived in our building. His
wife is a friend of mine. He was at the party building on business
that day. They grabbed him and began beating him. He was beaten savagely, beyond recognition. He begged and pleaded, telling
them he was just a teacher and not a party worker. They dragged
him home, and only after his wife brought out his teacher's di-
ploma and showed it to his torturers did they let him go.

"Then," she went on, "a truck with a sound system showed up
from somewhere. A woman teacher began shouting into the mi-
crophone, 'Why isn't there any butter? Why isn't there any food?'
The crowd demanded that Khrushchev come to Grozny. Police
appeared, and then troops. They managed to cut communications
between the center of town and the surrounding areas, and that
way prevented a clash between Russians and Chechens. Later
someone came from Moscow, but it was Yasnov instead of
Khrushchev."

With that she ended her story.

"But in 1973, it seems, everything ended peacefully, without
bloodshed," I said.

"Yes, there were no fights. They only broke the windows at the

Gastronome Supermarket. The Ingush simply marched to the government and party buildings and raised the demand that the lands given to Northern Ossetia be returned to them.''

"You know''—the Russian woman grew agitated—''they really were mistreating the Ingush in Ossetia. They wouldn't hire them and they kicked them out of the jobs they did have. The Dagestanis didn't treat the Ingush that way. As soon as the Chechens and Ingush showed up, the Dagestanis gave Vedeno back to them.''

"And what about Bazorkin—was he one of the leaders of this movement?''

"Well, I don't know whether it was spontaneous or was started by agitators.''

"It seems to me,'' I said, "that the situation was so hot that the so-called spontaneous elements very quickly became organized.''

I went on: "I was recently reading over the issues of *Groznenskii rabochii* for 1973, and a number of people in responsible posts were named there as alleged leaders of the movement. Among them were the first secretary of the Nazran district party committee and the former chairman of the Sunzhenskii district executive committee.''

"But the newspapers didn't write about those events,'' our narrator said with surprise.

"No, not directly. But there were articles later on which named names. . . .''

At that point the Ingush woman left us for a while.

"How did the 1973 events end up?'' I asked.

"Well, some people were rounded up.'' She gave an expressive sweep of the hand. "Even now they're still picking up a few quietly.''

"You sympathize with them,'' the lady went on. "But you know, the deportation did them good.''

"How so?'' both I and the man, who had apparently decided to join the conversation, said in joint astonishment.

"The Chechens used to be loaded with money,'' she explained. "But they never bought anything. After they lived in Kazakhstan, though, they acquired some culture. You should see how fashionably they dress now.''

The other man and I exchanged glances.

''What does culture have to do with it?'' I argued. ''They simply began to live in conditions they weren't used to, different from those they had known, and they learned the value or necessity of certain things. Did that make them more civilized? It has nothing to do with real culture.''

''And among Russians there are also quite a few who save money all their lives and live half-starving,'' the man remarked suddenly and rather emphatically.

''This 'acquiring of culture' certainly cost them enough. How many do you suppose died?'' I asked.

At that point the man went out into the corridor for a smoke, or perhaps for some other reason, and I and the Russian woman were left alone.

''But you know what General Yermolov said about them.'' my interlocutor quickly asked.

I looked at her inquiringly.

''He said that these people could not be re-educated, they could only be destroyed.''

I imagined for a moment, not the extermination of the Chechens and Ingush, but General Yermolov using the word ''re-educate,'' and I smiled involuntarily. ''Surely,'' I thought, ''there was no such word in his vocabulary.''

The woman paused, somewhat unsure, but immediately began again.

''And every year they blow up his statue.''

''There you see what 'culture' they've acquired,'' I laughed.

At that moment the Ingush woman appeared in the doorway, and immediately after her the man. ''Perhaps he's not a colonel after all,'' I thought. ''Maybe a professor or a lecturer.''

The Ingush woman had heard my ironic remarks about the ''acquisition of culture'' and, turning to the Russian lady, she said triumphantly:

''There, you see, none of the men agree with you.''

They both laughed.

The conversation came around to the Chechens again.

"You say the Chechens have suffered," said the Russian woman. "That's true. I am not defending anyone. To me all nationalities are the same—Chechens, Jews [giving me a meaningful look at that point], Ingush. But during the war there were so many bandits among 'them'; they killed so many people. Here's an example. They got hold of an NKVD chief named Dadayev [Dudayev?] and simply tore him apart, literally tore him apart; they ripped off his arms and legs. And not long ago a bandit appeared in the hills again, and they just can't catch him. The chairman of the state security committee was supposed to meet him, to negotiate, and imagine this, the chairman's car broke down, so that he didn't go, but the bandit was sitting in ambush, waiting for the car. Then the deputy chairman, Kuzakov, came along in another car. And the bandit let him have it with a cannon. . . ."

"What's that? A cannon?" we exclaimed.

"Oho, well done, boys!" Our male companion, for some reason, began to bounce up and down happily. ("No, he must be a colonel, after all," I decided.)

"Yes, a cannon. Certainly, a cannon." The woman insisted. But, seeing the dubious looks on our faces, she hesitated:

"Well, maybe it wasn't a cannon but what do you call them . . . a machine gun?" Everyone laughed.

The Ingush woman nodded. "Yes, they have lots of weapons. Almost of all them have pistols." "And submachine guns," added the Russian woman.

The Ingush woman looked extremely pleased, for some reason.

"He is like Zelim Khan," * she said referring to the bandit.

"Even she says"—the Russian woman nodded toward the Ingush—"it would take ten years to re-educate them."

"Ten?" I asked. "Or maybe fifty?"

---

* A legendary Chechen brigand of the early twentieth century who, like some Robin Hood of the Caucasus, stole from the rich and gave to the poor.

"Russians also have to be educated," our male companion said darkly. "How many loafers and drunkards there are among them. And why can't people be left to live as they wish, to follow their own tradition?"

Here our conversation turned to a discussion of custom and tradition. There were more anecdotes and stories, this time about the Chechen and Ingush customs of burying the dead. I asked the Ingush woman if the *teipa* traditions, the secret Islamic courts, and so on, still existed. She affirmed that they did.

"A man I know," our chief narrator broke in, "has spent many long years gathering material on the sects in Checheno-Ingushetia and their members. I think for a dissertation. He even attended some of their rites. He figured out that there are 150 sects there now."

"And you say ten years to re-educate them?" I turned to the Ingush woman. She smiled enigmatically.

The conversation then paused on the question of the moral training of the younger generation and the question of bribe-taking and corruption. I admitted that in Moscow, our capital, there was bribe-taking. Both women were overjoyed by that admission. It meant that even in Moscow everything was not so great.

The train pulled slowly into the station. We were in Moscow.

We parted as friends.

On the way home, thinking of how differently people perceive the same events, I remembered Goethe's lines:

> The truth, we are telling, the truth,
> And nothing but the truth!
> Our own truth it is, of course—
> What other do we know?

Appendix: The Case of Mustafa Dzhemilev

CAN WE REMAIN SILENT?

Mustafa Dzhemilev's trial in Omsk has just concluded.

A Crimean Tatar, Dzhemilev has devoted many years of his life to the struggle to restore the civil rights of the Crimean Tatars and to assist their return to their historical homeland in the Crimea from which they were deported by force in May 1944. Although the illegal nature of that act was later acknowledged by the Soviet government and the rights of the Crimean Tatars have been formally restored, they have not been allowed to live on the land of their forefathers.

Dzhemilev has repeatedly been sentenced to imprisonment for his actions in the service of his people. Now, just when his sentence was almost up, he has again been tried on a charge of anti-Soviet propaganda.

It is clear that they are afraid to release Dzhemilev.

At Dzhemilev's trial in Omsk on April 12–15, 1976, the indictment collapsed. The chief witness for the prosecution, a fellow convict named Vladimir Dvoryansky, retracted the testimony he had given during the preliminary investigation, and stated that he had signed those depositions under pressure from the investigator—pressure that had been applied for a whole year.

Dvoryansky gave the court frightening details on the way the investigation was handled; and despite continuing pressure, that young man of twenty-six found the courage to tell the truth in court. That is something we shall remember.

Naturally, the atmosphere of the trial in Omsk was permeated with a spirit of tyranny and contempt for human values. Of the sixteen friends and relatives of Dzhemilev who traveled to Omsk, only four were allowed into the courtroom. Two of them—Dzhemilev's brother and sister—were removed from the courtroom during his final plea. Academician Andrei Sakharov and his wife, Elena Bonner, who had come from Moscow to attend the trial, were not only barred from the courtroom but subjected to humiliations and physical violence.

Ignoring the facts and trampling on elementary norms of the law, the court convicted Dzhemilev and sentenced him to two years and six months in strict-regimen labor camps.

That sentence may prove fatal for Dzhemilev. His physical condition is critical: He is afflicted with partial atrophy of the liver and a serious heart disease. He began a hunger strike in June 1975, and discontinued it only on April 15, 1976, at the insistence of his family. He now weighs seventy-seven pounds.

Dzhemilev can be saved only if he is released immediately and receives prompt medical care.

The world has already witnessed the death of Yury Galanskov and the suicide of Ilya Gabai. Vladimir Bukovsky is critically ill in Vladimir Prison. And the fate of those cooped up in "loony bins" is frightful.

I appeal to everyone who considers himself a decent human being:

Do not close your eyes to this arbitrary and unlawful act.

And I ask you: Can we remain silent?

I appeal above all to my colleagues, to historians in the USSR and abroad who have a professional duty to tend the flame of truth ignited by Prometheus:

Let us stand up in defense of Dzhemilev, Bukovsky, Superfin, Kovalev, and others languishing in prison for their convictions.

Let us fight for a general amnesty of political prisoners throughout the world, but first of all in our own country. Today we must save Dzhemilev.

This is our duty—both our human one and our professional one.

And let us end our shameful silence.

Aleksandr M. Nekrich
April 17, 1976

Note on Sources

There are adequate materials in the archives—enough to accommodate several dozen historians, let alone one. But access to these archive materials has long been strictly limited. I, for example, could not even dream of working in the archives, where information could be found allowing judgments to be made about the number of people who collaborated with the enemy, their social makeup, and the reasons that prompted them to collaborate and betray their country. I presume that there is more or less accurate information on the number of people deported to the eastern regions of the country, on the assessed value of the property they lost, on the mortality rates and birth rates in the areas of resettlement, and on the judicial and extrajudicial reprisals that accompanied forced relocation.

On April 14, 1975, Professor R. I. Muzafarov sent a letter to the first secretary of the Crimean regional committee of the party, N. K. Kirichenko, requesting permission to use the materials in the Crimean party archives, permission which had been denied him earlier. In the event that this was not possible, Muzafarov requested that he might be informed, on the basis of the archive materials, of certain data or statistics on the participation of Crimean Tatars in the partisan movement and in the German military formations.

Muzafarov received the following reply, which I reproduce in full:

April 25, 1975

To Comrade R. I. Muzafarov
Moscow Region
Klimovsk 1
6A Zavodskaia Street, Room 10

In reply to your letter of April 14, 1975, we must inform you that the party archives do not have analytical data on the number of citizens of Tatar nationality enrolled in partisan detachments, underground organizations and groups, and the 152d Tatar Volunteer Batallion. It is not possible for us to make a special study of the documents on this question.

Director of the Regional Committee Party Archive of the Communist
Party of the Ukraine, I. Kondranov

bn.3

And so the documents exist; they have not been destroyed, but they also have not been published. Therefore on this topic—the deportation of the peoples of the Northern Caucasus and Crimea at the end of the Second World War—it is necessary to gather material grain by grain.

If you are lucky and do gain access to some archive materials, you still remain in the dark as to whether all the materials have been shown to you. The archive's assistant knows better than you what documents you need for your research. She brings them to you herself, and please, there is no need to ask her for a listing of all documents. How simple and convenient!

You wish to know whose signature is on the document. But what do you want to know that for? Exactly what good would that do?

And please keep this in mind as well—there were of course certain individual failings, isolated negative facts, and even acts of lawlessness in our past. But after all, why make generalizations about that?

The unpublished dissertations of historians working in the Caucasus and Kalmykia seem to me to be of the highest interest. One may familiarize oneself with these dissertations in the Lenin Library in Moscow, in the reading room for dissertations. Many of these dissertations were written and defended in the 1960s, when, under the favorable influence of a creative spirit in scholarship awakened after the Twentieth and Twenty-second congresses of the CPSU and the All-Union Conference of Historians in 1962, there began a rapid revival of Soviet historical science, especially in the field of Soviet history and modern Western and Eastern history.

(At first I wrote here: "A brief Golden Age in Soviet historical science! Nevertheless it left such profound traces that its influence can still be felt today." But alas, this is not correct. There was no "Golden Age." All that happened was that the dawn of a renaissance barely began to glimmer, then quickly died out.)

Still, it is true that in the late 1950s and early 1960s historical science began to be freed from the shackles that had bound it for at least thirty years. At that time the doors of archives, especially local ones, were opened wide. Under the fresh impact of the rehabilitation of the peoples of the Caucasus and Kalmykia, which had just occurred, historians and party workers in these autonomous republics sought to restore the truth about the part the deported peoples had played in the struggle against German fascism during the Second World War and to record at least some of the sufferings their fellow countrymen had been forced to bear during the bitter time of deportation. These dissertations were written by people who in many cases were secretaries of regional committees of the Communist Party of the Soviet Union (CPSU) or held local government positions, i.e., people who were intimately linked with the Communist Party. They belonged to the privileged layer in our society. They enjoyed free access to the archives in their homelands as well as to the archives of the Central Asian republics and Kazakhstan, where the Caucasians and Kalmyks had lived in special settlements for nearly a decade and a half. To judge from these dissertations the documents stored in local party archives are not only of local significance but have broader relevance as well. Among them are instructions on the regime for inhabitants of the special settlements, materials on the work to which they would be assigned, where they would be located, what the conditions of their daily existence would be, and information on education, etc.

The first to refer to the regime in the special settlements was apparently A. Kh. Dudayev.[1] But the dissertation defended by Kh. I. Khutuyev a year later proved to be the most important of all.[2] All who have dealt with this problem have drawn upon the material in this dissertation, including R. I. Muzafarov and the author of the present work. A. K. Dudayev and Kh. I. Khutuyev may justly be called the trailblazers in this field. Khutuyev, a well-known historian and philologist from Kabardino-Balkaria, was secretary of the regional committee of the CPSU and deputy chairman of the Council of Ministers of the Kabardino-Balkar Autonomous Soviet Socialist Republic (ASSR).

Khutuyev made use of materials in party, government, and institutional archives in the Kabardino-Balkar ASSR, Kazakhstan, Kirgizia, and in the USSR Ministry of Defense. He also brought together a number of memoirs by participants in the events. Khutuyev's dissertation, despite its exceptional value, still has not been published. But its main points have been presented in the author's abstract of the dissertation.[3]

Detailed materials on the history of the Kalmyks and the Kalmyk ASSR are contained in the dissertation by D.-Ts. D. Nominkhanov.[4] Among the sources Nominkhanov used were documents in the central party archives at the Institute of Marxism-Leninism of the CPSU Central Committee. Materials from Nominkhanov's dissertation have been published, in part, in a number of his works.[5]

Also to be noted is the dissertation by S. N. Dzhuguryants.[6] He unearthed some documents of great interest in the archives of the Chechen-Ingush Regional Committee of the CPSU. An abridged version of his study came out a year before he defended his dissertation.[7]

The history of Karachai and Cherkessia during the Second World War is treated in the dissertation by Ch. S. Kulayev.[8] He has made rather thorough use of the materials on the special settlements contained in the work of Kh. I. Khutuyev. Kulayev also cites local Karachai archives, archives of the Central Asian republics and of Kazakhstan, and archives of the Institute of Marxism-Leninism in Moscow. Unfortunately, Kulayev avoids the problem of the collaboration of part of the Karachai population with the occupation forces.

The dissertation by M. M. Bekizhev widens the scope of our knowledge of Karachai, especially after the period when autonomy was restored.[9] Khutuyev and the other historians from the re-established autonomous republics and regions faced the practical task of refuting the fabrications about the collaboration of their entire peoples with the Nazi occupation regime and of bringing out the facts about their participation in the common struggle against Hitler's Germany.

Long after the punished peoples had returned to their homelands there still appeared in the press both fabrications and one-sided treatments concerning their conduct during the war. The author of one dissertation, the Kalmyk historian M. L. Kichikov, writes that what impelled him to undertake his study of the history of Kalmykia in the 1941–45 period was the appearance in 1963, in the newspaper *Sovetskaia Kalmykia,* of an article by a certain A. Serbin entitled "Twenty Years Ago: The Tracks Lead Westward."[10] This article, as Kichikov put it, contained "a one-sided presentation of negative facts"; the article "caused alarm among the Kalmyk population of the republic, which had suffered on account of renegades from its midst during the period of the personality cult." Protests against the article poured in from veterans of the war. As a result, the Scientific Research Institute under the Council of Ministers of the Kalmyk ASSR was assigned to prepare a collection of documents dealing with the events of the war in Kalmykia (more on that collection below).

Justice compels us to note that not all historians have evaded the problem of the occupation and the collaboration with the enemy it involved. Kichikov, for example, undertook to explain the circumstances that led to the occupation of part of the Kalmyk ASSR territory by the German fascist armies and published materials on the struggle against the occupation forces by the bulk of the population in the republic. Under Kichikov's direction an extremely important collection of documents was prepared and published,[11] and memoirs by participants in the armed struggle against the Nazis were collected and published.[12] Among the especially important materials in Kichikov's dissertation—which he defended at Leningrad University in 1972—are documents of the Kalmyk regional committee of the party from the 1941–43 period. These documents, despite the fact that they are obviously compiled selectively, give a sufficiently clear picture of the situation in Kalmykia and shed light on the events immediately preceding the deportation of the Kalmyks.

The greater part of the documents did not appear in the book by Kichikov that was published in Elista.[13]

K. D. Korkmasova in her extremely interesting doctoral dissertation consigned (or was forced to consign) to a footnote the whole problem of the forced deportation of the peoples of the Caucasus.[14] Some information on the history of the peoples of the Northern Caucasus and Kalmykia during the events of 1942–43 and in the subsequent period can be extracted from a number of more general works.[15] Comparison of data derived from official statistical compilations for the prewar period, the war, and the postwar period allow one to obtain a clear picture of the dynamics of population changes in the Caucasus and Kalmykia, as well as changes in education, economics, etc.[16]

No small interest has been aroused by V. I. Filkin's works on the history of the Northern Caucasus. Filkin, a historian from Grozny, was at one time a secretary of the Chechen-Ingush regional committee of the CPSU. Former head of the department of CPSU history at the Grozny Petroleum Institute, Filkin is now a lecturer in that department. His many works are largely based on probing research into the archive documents, above all in the party archive of the Chechen-Ingush regional committee. Among his numerous writings, the most interesting to us are those directly connected with the history of the Chechen-Ingush ASSR from 1939 to 1945.[17]

It is necessary to speak separately about the manuscript by Professor Refik I. Muzafarov and about Professor Muzafarov himself.[18]

Professor Muzafarov has collected an enormous amount of material on the Crimean Tatars during the Great Patriotic War, on their life and situation after their deportation from the Crimea, and on the anti-Crimean Tatar propaganda and policies of the present time. In the fall of 1974 Muzafarov sent his manuscript to the CPSU Central Committee in the hope that after familiarizing themselves with the information he had compiled they would permit the Crimean Tatars to return to their historic homeland in the Crimea. Alas, as of May 1975 the manuscript had not yet had a great influence on the situation of the Crimean Tatars. True, certain isolated phrases or sentences in some literary works had been modified, certain parts of museum displays in the Crimea which were openly hostile to the Crimean Tatars had been removed, and recent editions of guidebooks for the Crimea had dropped the obvious slander against the historic past of the Crimean Tatar population found in previous editions. But that apparently was all.

Professor Muzafarov's own fate is of interest. He was born in 1928 in Simferopol, his father a civil servant employed in economic work. He was fifteen and a half when he was shipped off together with his fellow countrymen to exile in the Urals. The Muzafarov family was settled on one of the state timber industry establishments in Sverdlovsk oblast. Refik became an unskilled laborer. In 1946 he succeeded in moving to Uzbekistan, where he acquired skills as a machine operator and went to work in a factory. In 1953 he completed secondary school as an evening student and began his studies as a correspondence-course student in the department of Russian language and literature at the Tashkent Pedagogical Institute. At the same time he studied at a technical school for cultural and educational work, also as a correspondence-course student. He graduated from both schools and then worked in Kaluga. As an evening-school student at Kazan State University he wrote a candidate's dissertation entitled "Tatar Folk Sayings" and defended his dissertation in 1960. Subsequently he taught in institutions of higher education. In 1967 he defended his doctoral dissertation, "Essays in the Folklore of the Turks," at Baku. Thus Muzafarov became a doctor of philological sciences. Through his subsequent educational work he won the title of professor.

In 1957 he became an active participant in the movement of the Crimean Tatars for complete rehabilitation and the right to return to the Crimea. In 1967 the movement achieved a big success—the decree of the USSR Supreme Soviet restoring the civil rights of the Crimean Tatars. In 1972 Professor Muzafarov was deprived of employment because of his public activity. The newspaper *Trud* published an article about him, seeking to discredit him from a professional standpoint. From then until the fall of 1975, Professor R. I. Muzafarov, doctor of philological sciences, was denied regular employment. Nevertheless, he continued his scholarly work. In addition to the monographs he had written, Muzafarov compiled a Russian–Crimean Tatar dictionary and a Crimean Tatar–Russian dictionary. However, his attempts to have these published have met with no success. Now, after many years of hardship, he has been given a job at the Tashkent Region Pedagogical Institute in Angren, a city in Uzbekistan.

The materials issued by the Crimean Tatar movement provide another source of information about the Crimean Tatars. In part, these have been published in *Khronika tekushchikh sobytii* (Chronicle of current events), issued in Russian in 1974 in New York. These materials contain many important facts; however, the statistical data published in these materials should be handled critically. Precise data, verified to the greatest extent possible, about the losses suffered by the deported peoples in the USSR is sufficiently eloquent without overstating the case.

Of great importance for this book, as well as for all works on the history of Soviet society, without exception, are the stenographic records of the Twentieth and Twenty-second CPSU congresses.[19] Familiarity with these is necessary not only for an understanding of the new course in national policy in the USSR, i.e., the restoration of "Leninist norms," but also for a sense of the atmosphere at those congresses, when it seemed that the time of our unshackling had come. Khrushchev's secret speech at the Twentieth Congress was read to party members only at closed meetings and was not published in the USSR. It may be found in the supplement to Khrushchev's memoirs.[20] It was possible to extract some information from the newspapers of the Caucasian autonomous regions and republics and of the Crimea. As for the result of work with periodicals of the Central Committee of the Communist Party and the Soviet government on this question, it hardly justified the time and effort expended. Nevertheless that part of the work was absolutely indispensable.

As for the attitude of the official party and government leadership toward the deportation of the peoples of the Caucasus and Kalmykia and the subsequent restoration of their autonomy, one may form an opinion on this, within certain limits, on the basis of the relevant decrees, laws, and other materials of the sessions of the Supreme Soviets of the USSR and RSFSR, as well as the stenographic records of sessions of the Supreme Soviets of the autonomous republics.[21]

The rehabilitation of the Northern Caucasians and Kalmyks brought in its train not only a series of works by individual authors on the history of these peoples during the Patriotic War but also collections of documents, memoirs, and similar materials. The main purpose of all these publications was to attest to the loyalty of these peoples to Soviet power, to demonstrate their patriotism, and to show what contributions they had made to the armed struggle against Nazi Germany. In virtually all these publications there is information on the constructive labor and achievements of the deported peoples in their places of resettlement, but very little light is shed on their everyday life, and, of course, not a word is said about the strict regime in the special settlements or the consequences of that regime. Another particular feature of these works is that they omit any specific information on collaboration by part of the population with the Nazi occupation.

In my opinion, this is a serious error because silence on this question only contributes to the persistence of false notions as to the alleged treason of these peoples as a whole. What is in the interest of these peoples themselves is not suppression of the historical truth or evasion of the facts, but a calm and balanced study of the problems that arose in connection with the occupation of these areas. We have been made such fools of by empty-headed demagogy that we forget that not one of the nationalities of the USSR can be, or should be, made to pay for the crimes of individual members of those nationalities, or even for crimes of a group nature. From the legal point of view it is impossible to accuse an entire people of treason, since the concept of popular sovereignty removes all basis for that.

But is it really a question of our having *forgotten* this? Isn't it more honest to say that concepts of law and justice in the USSR have been so distorted that we ourselves have no clear conception of the actual meaning of the term *law?* And is such a phenomenon as the deportation of entire peoples possible in general in a state where there are legal norms?

It seems that, with the exception of M. L. Kichikov, hardly any Soviet historian has seriously taken up the problem of the collaboration with the enemy which arose as a result of the German occupation of a number of territories of the USSR.

Yet an enormous body of Soviet literature exists on the history of the partisan movement in the areas occupied by the fascist armies. Studies and memoirs and collections of documents have been published. They are not all of equal value, in either documentary content or quality. The collection of documents dealing with the Crimea is plainly biased against the Crimean Tatars.[22] Muzafarov's manuscript discusses this in detail.

And so it has been that all the problems related to collaboration with the enemy have been treated by foreign historians. They have had free access to German documents of the most varied sorts, from battlefield documents to the archives of Rosenberg's and Himmler's agencies. In addition, Western historians have compiled a great deal of testimony from persons directly involved in the workings of the occupation regimes on Soviet territory. All archival collections, on questions of any kind, have been at their disposal.

The vast majority of Soviet historians have been denied such opportunities. Only a few of them, a numerically insignificant group, have been allowed to make official trips to work in foreign archives, and it has been out of the question to make extended scholarly trips at one's own expense.*

---

* In my case, for example, during thirty years of work (including as a graduate student), first at the Institute of History and then at the Institute of General History of the USSR Academy of Sciences, I was never once allowed to take a trip to work in foreign archives or to participate in international conferences or symposiums. Moreover, even on Soviet territory it is by no means always possible to obtain permission to participate in symposiums with foreign scholars. In August 1970 I was forbidden to appear at the Twelfth International Congress of Historical Sciences, held in Moscow. Only after I protested in writing was this prohibition lifted. However, I was allowed to attend the sessions of the congress only as a guest. In April 1975 a number of Soviet historians were denied permission to attend (not to speak at, but to attend) a joint Soviet and West German symposium in Leningrad on the history of Soviet-German relations during the time of the Weimar Republic. Among those who were denied such permission in the most categorical fashion was the author of this book.

Willy-nilly one is forced to tag along behind one's foreign colleagues, making use of their advantage in gaining access to source material in the West. Such an undignified and even degrading position for Soviet historians does not, it seems, trouble our scientific and scholarly leaders at all, although they constantly call upon us to struggle for the primacy of Soviet historical science and to "refute the bourgeois falsifiers of history." The whole complicated pass system of various categories for work in archives, every possible kind of limitation in using the documents one discovers, the severe censorship which so often kills original thinking, the limitations on the choice of subject matter even for professional historians, and finally, as a result of all this, the habit of self-censorship and self-limitation—all of this greatly narrows the professional possibilities available to Soviet historians and prevents them from carrying out their basic professional duty: to serve the historical truth.

Among the works published in the West, Alexander Dallin's extremely thorough study of German occupation policies on Soviet territory, which came out eighteen years ago, still has not lost its significance.[23]

The English scholar Robert Conquest has concerned himself for many years with the problem of the deportations in the USSR.[24] He has done an enormous amount of work in collecting, interpreting, and drawing generalizations from materials available in the West on the deportations in the USSR. Quite a few books and memoirs have dealt with various aspects of German occupation policies in particular Soviet areas. Let us make special mention of the monograph by Luther, originally written at the Russian Research Center of Harvard University under Professor Philip Moseley; the works of von zur Mühlen, Littlejohn, and Hoffman; the memoirs of Gehlen, and the books of the Tatar nationalist Edige Kirimal.[25]

These books vary quite widely in their points of view and biases. I am not favorably impressed with the Freiburg study by Joachim Hoffman. Its overriding aim is to "rehabilitate" Hitler's policies and the actions of the German military and repressive organs in the occupied Soviet territories.

Certain materials used in the present work have been drawn from Soviet publications,[26] from the materials of the Nuremberg trials of the major German war criminals[27] and of the trials of lower-ranking leaders of the Third Reich on war-crimes charges,[28] from documents of the German diplomatic service,[29] and from a number of other primary sources.

Interviews with persons well informed about the events described in this book contributed greatly to an understanding of the situation that developed in the Northern Caucasus.

Notes

INTRODUCTION

1. Alexander Dallin, *German Rule in Russia, 1941–1945: A Study of Occupation Policies* (London, 1957), p. 427.

2. David Littlejohn, *The Patriotic Traitors: The Story of Collaboration in German-Occupied Europe, 1940–1945* (New York, 1972), p. 301.

3. *Ibid.*, p. 298.

4. *Khronika tekushchikh sobytii* [Chronicle of current events] (New York, 1974), p. 123.

CHAPTER I

1. S. Sulkevich, *Naselenie SSSR* [The Population of the USSR] (Moscow, 1939), p. 30.

2. *Trial of the Major War Criminals before the International Military Tribunal*, vol. XXXVIII (Nuremberg, 1949), no. 221-L, p. 87. Hereafter cited as *IMT*.

3. E. Kirimal, *Der nationale Kampf der Krimtürken* (Emsdetten, 1952), p. 311.

4. *IMT*, vol. XXXVIII, no. 1517-PS, p. 272.

5. Dallin, p. 256.

6. *Trials of War Criminals before the Nuremberg Military Tribunals under Control Council Law No. 10*, vol. IV (Ohlendorf) (Washington, D.C., 1952), p. 254. Hereafter cited as *Trials*.

7. *Akten zur Deutschen auswartigen Politik, 1918–1945*. Series E: 1941–1945, vol. 2 (Gottingen, 1964–1972), no. 132, pp. 225–226

(Schmieden to Schulenburg, comments on the propaganda conference, "Westphalia," April 13, 1942). Hereafter cited as *ADAP*.

8. *Dokumenty ministerstva inostrannykh del Germanii. Vypusk II: Germanskaia politika v Turtsii (1941–1943 gg.)* [Documents of the Foreign Ministry of Germany. Issue II: German policy in Turkey (1941–1943)] (Moscow, 1946), no. 25, p. 87 (Dittmann to Tippelskirch, August 5, 1942). Hereafter cited as *Dokumenty*.

9. *Ibid.*, no. 15, p. 51 (Erkilet to Hentig, Istanbul, November 27, 1941).

10. *ADAP*, ser. E, vol. 2, no. 115, p. 197 (von Papen to the Foreign Ministry, Ankara, April 6, 1942).

11. *Dokumenty*, no. 17, pp. 65–66 ("Memorandum to Herr General Warlimont").

12. *Ibid.*, no. 27, p. 100 (von Papen to the Foreign Ministry, Ankara, August 27, 1942).

13. *Ibid.*, no. 30, pp. 116–120 (Ribbentrop and Hewel to "Werwolf," Fuschl, September 12, 1942).

14. M. Luther, *Die Krim unter deutscher Besatzung im zweiten Weltkrieg*, in *Forschungen zur Osteuropäischen Geschichte* (Berlin, 1956), vol. 3, p. 60; Dallin, p. 260.

15. Luther, p. 61.

16. R. I. Muzafarov, "Vdali ot krymskikh gor. Anatomiia deportatsii" [Far from the Crimean hills: anatomy of a deportation], manuscript (Moscow, 1974), pp. 94–97.

17. Kirimal, p. 314.

18. Luther, p. 62.

19. Kirimal, p. 315.

20. *Ibid.*, p. 316.

21. *Ibid.*

22. *Dokumenty*, no. 36, pp. 135–36 (Manstein to Dirksen, May 9, 1943).

23. *Trials*, p. 508.

24. From Protocol no. 6 of the August 11, 1942, session of the Bureau of the Crimean regional committee of the party, cited in Muzafarov, p. 64.

25. *Krym v period Velikoi Otechestvennoi voiny 1941–1945 gg.* [The Crimea during the Great Patriotic War, 1941–1945] (Simferopol, 1973). Document nos. 279, 287, 289.

26. Muzafarov, p. 89.

27. *Nepokorennyi Krym* [Crimea undaunted], a publication of the political administration of the Black Sea Fleet (1943), p. 9.

28. Muzafarov, p. 96.

29. *Ibid.*, p. 112.

30. *Ibid.*, p. 113.

31. Resolution of the Crimean regional committee of the AUCP(B), November 18, 1942, cited in Muzafarov, p. 66.

32. Muzafarov, p. 67.

33. I. Genov, *Dnevnik partizana* [Diary of a partisan] (Simferopol, 1963), p. 250.

34. From materials supplied to the author by R. I. Muzafarov.

35. E. Stepanov, *Partizanskimi tropami* [Partisan paths] (Ulan-Ude, 1967), p. 271.

36. Protocol no. 60 of the session of October 20, 1944, of the bureau of the Crimean regional committee of the AUCP(B). See Muzafarov, p. 198.

37. K. Paustovsky, *Sobranie sochinenii* [Collected works], vol. 5 (Moscow, 1968), p. 566.

CHAPTER II

1. K. Trippelskirch, *Istoriia vtoroi mirovoi voiny* [History of the Second World War] (Moscow, 1955), p. 233. Russian translation of a 1951 book by a German ex-general.

2. A. A. Grechko, *Bitva za Kavkaz* [The Battle for the Caucasus] (Moscow, 1971), p. 52.

3. Tippelskirch, p. 52. Tippelskirch writes that Rostov was taken by the Germans on July 29 (p. 236).

4. *Velikaia Otechestvennaia voina Sovetskogo Soiuza 1941–1945. Kratkaia istoriia* [The Great Patriotic War of the Soviet Union, 1941–1945: a short history] (Moscow, 1970), pp. 177–81; Grechko, pp. 74–89, 157–64.

5. *ADAP,* ser. E, vol. 1, document no. 127, pp. 216–17 (Consul-General Bräutigam of the Ostministerium to Ambassador Grosskopf, Berlin, April 10, 1942).

6. *ADAP,* ser. E, vol. 2, document no. 147, pp. 246–47 (notes of Weizsäcker for Ribbentrop, Berlin, April 17, 1942).

7. Dallin, p. 241.

8. Umar Aliev, *Karachai (Karachaevskaia avtonomnaia oblast)* [Karachai (the Karachai Autonomous Region)] (Rostov-on-Don, 1927), p. 33.

9. K. D. Korkmasova, "Natsional'naia gosudarstvennost' v SSSR (osnovnye gosudarstvenno pravovye problemy)" [National statehood in the USSR (fundamental problems of public law)] (dissertation, Rostov State University, Rostov-on-Don, 1971), p. 498.

10. Umar Aliev, p. 33.

11. Korkmasova, p. 498.

12. *Ibid.*

13. Dallin, p. 246.

14. Ch. S. Kulayev, "Partiinye organizatsii Karachaia i Cherkesii v period Velikoi Otechestvennoi voiny Sovetskogo Soiuza (1941–1945 gg.)" [The party organizations of Karachai and Cherkessia during the Great Patriotic War in the Soviet Union (1941–1945)] (dissertation, Voronezh State University, 1968), p. 125.

15. *Ibid.*, p. 156.

16. *Ibid.*, p. 179.

17. *Ibid.*

18. *Ocherki istorii Checheno-Ingushskoi ASSR, 1917–1970 gody* [Essays in the history of the Chechen-Ingush ASSR, 1917–1970], vol. 2 (Grozny, 1972), p. 175. Hereafter cited as *Essays in the History of the Chechen-Ingush ASSR*.

19. *Ibid.*, p. 155.

20. *Ibid.*

21. *Ibid.*, p. 208.

22. *Ibid.*, p. 209.

23. *Ibid.*

24. V. I. Filkin, *Checheno-Ingushskaia partiinaia organizatsiia v gody Velikoi Otechestvennoi Voiny Sovetskogo Soiuza* [The Chechen-Ingush party organization during the Great Patriotic War of the Soviet Union] (Grozny, 1960), p. 18. Hereafter cited as Filkin (1960).

25. *Essays in the History of the Chechen-Ingush ASSR*, p. 209.

26. *Ibid.*

27. *Ibid.*, p. 210.

28. Filkin (1960), p. 17.

29. *Ibid.*

30. V. I. Filkin, *Partiinaia organizatsiia Checheno-Ingushetii v gody bor'by za uprochenie i razvitie sotsialisticheskogo obshchestva (1937– iun' 1941 gg.)* [The party organization in Checheno-Ingushetia during the struggle for the consolidation and development of socialist society (1937–June 1941)] (Grozny, 1961), p. 72. Hereafter cited as Filkin (1961).

31. *Essays in the History of the Chechen-Ingush ASSR*, p. 210.

32. *Groznenskii rabochii* [Grozny worker], April 3, 1973.

33. *Essays in the History of the Chechen-Ingush ASSR*, pp. 210–11.

34. Filkin (1961), p. 70.

35. *Ibid.*, p. 71.

36. *Ibid.*, p. 76.

37. Filkin (1960), p. 19.

38. Filkin (1961), p. 71.

39. Filkin (1960), p. 19.

40. Filkin (1961), p. 79–80.

41. *Ibid.*, p. 114.
42. *Ibid.*, p. 117.
43. *Ibid.*, p. 118.
44. *Ibid.*, p. 114.
45. *Essays in the History of the Chechen-Ingush ASSR*, p. 145.
46. Filkin (1961), p. 77.
47. Filkin (1960), p. 15.
48. *Ibid.*
49. *Groznenskii rabochii,* June 27, 1973.
50. Filkin (1960), p. 20.
51. *Ibid.*, p. 23.
52. *Ibid.*
53. *Groznenskii rabochii,* August 4, 1973.
54. *Ibid.*, May 19, 1974.
55. Filkin (1960), p. 42.
56. *Ibid.*, pp. 42–43.
57. *Ibid.*
58. *Ibid.*, p. 46.
59. *Ibid.*, p. 43.
60. *Groznenskii rabochii,* February 21, 1943.
61. *Ibid.*, December 24, 1943.
62. *Ibid.*, February 4, 1944.
63. S. N. Dzhuguryants, "Deiatel'nost' Checheno-Ingushskoi partiinoi organizatsii po osushchestvleniiu leninskoi natsional'noi politiki na osnove reshenii XX i XXII s"ezdov KPSS (1956–1965)" [The activity of the Chechen-Ingush party organization in implementing Leninist national policy on the basis of the decisions of the 20th and 22nd CPSU congresses (1956–1965)] (dissertation, Dagestan State University, Makhachkala, 1966), p. 84. Hereafter cited as Dzhuguryants, dissertation.
64. *50 let Kabardino-Balkarskoi ASSR. Statisticheskii sbornik* [Fifty years of the Kabardino-Balkar ASSR: statistical handbook] (Nalchik, 1971), p. 12.
65. Kh. I. Khutuyev, "Balkarskii narod v gody Velikoi Otechestvennoi voiny i poslevoennyi period (Vosstanovlenie avtonomii balkarskogo naroda)" [The Balkar people during the Great Patriotic War and the postwar period (the restoration of the autonomy of the Balkar people)] (dissertation, Rostov State University, Rostov-on-Don, 1965), p. 76. Hereafter cited as Khutuyev, dissertation.
66. *Sotsialisticheskaia Kabardino-Balkariia* [Socialist Kabardino-Balkaria], January 3, 1943.
67. See I. V. Davydov, *Partiinaia organizatsiia Kabardino-Balkarii v period Velikoi Otechestvennoi voiny 1941–1945 gg.* [The party organiza-

tion of Kabardino-Balkaria during the Great Patriotic War, 1941–1945]
(Nalchik, 1961), p. 80.

68. *Sotsialisticheskaia Kabardino-Balkariia,* January 3, 1943.

69. *Ibid.*

70. Dallin, p. 248.

71. *Sotsialisticheskaia Kabardino-Balkariia,* January 5, 1944.

72. *Ocherki istorii balkarskogo naroda* [Essays in the history of the
Balkar people] (Nalchik, 1961), p. 199.

73. See Khutuyev, dissertation, p. 76.

74. *Ibid.*

75. See I. T. Khatukayev, *Boevoi put' 115 kavaleriiskoi divizii* [The
fighting road of the 115th Cavalry Division] (Nalchik, 1965).

76. Khutuyev, dissertation, p. 73.

77. *Sotsialisticheskaia Kabardino-Balkariia,* January 4, 1944.

78. *Ibid.,* March 10, 1944.

79. *Ocherki istorii Kabardino-Balkarskoi organizatsii KPSS* [Essays
in the history of the Kabardino-Balkar organization of the CPSU] (Nalchik, 1971), p. 242. Hereafter cited as *Essays in the History of the
Kabardino-Balkar Organization of the CPSU.*

80. *Sotsialisticheskaia Kabardino-Balkariia,* April 11, 1944.

81. *Kabardinskaia pravda,* April 16, 1944.

82. *Ibid.,* April 19, 1944.

83. *Ibid.,* May 20, 1944.

84. *Ibid.,* September 16, 1944.

85. *Essays in the History of the Kabardino-Balkar Organization of the
CPSU,* p. 242.

CHAPTER III

1. *Ocherki istorii Kalmytskoi ASSR. Epokha sotsializma* [Essays in the
history of the Kalmyk ASSR: the epoch of socialism] (Moscow, 1970),
p. 211. Hereafter cited as *Essays in the History of the Kalmyk ASSR.*

2. M. L. Kichikov, "Sovetskaia Kalmykia v Velikoi Otechestvennoi
voine 1941–1945 godov" [Soviet Kalmykia during the Great Patriotic
War] (dissertation, Leningrad State University imeni A. A. Zhdanov,
1972), p. 14. Hereafter cited as Kichikov, dissertation.

3. *Ibid.,* Appendix 3, p. 393 (data from 1939 census).

4. Kichikov, dissertation, pp. 57, 97.

5. *Kalmykiia v Velikoi Otechestvennoi voine 1941–1945. Dokumenty i
materialy* [Kalmykia during the Great Patriotic War, 1941–1945: documents and materials] (Elista, 1966), pp. 141–43. Hereafter cited as *Kalmykia during the War.* The quotation is from document no. 90, excerpted
from a memorandum of the Kalmyk ASSR Sovnarkom and the regional
committee of the party, to the party's Central Committee and the USSR

Sovnarkom, on the military and economic situation in Kalmykia as of August 15, 1942; dated "Astrakhan, August 16, 1942."

6. Kichikov, dissertation, p. 92.

7. *Ibid.*

8. *Ibid.*, pp. 92–93.

9. Patrik von zur Mühlen, *Zwischen Hakenkreuz and Sowjetstern: Der Nationalsozialismus der sowjetischen Orientvölker im zweiten Weltkrieg* (Dusseldorf, 1971), p. 188.

10. *Kalmykia during the War*, document no. 94, p. 151.

11. *Ibid.*, document no. 140, p. 226 (from a memorandum of the Kalmyk regional committee of the party to the party Central Committee summarizing the results of partisan activity in Kalmykia, April 2, 1943).

12. *Ibid.*, p. 143.

13. Kichikov, dissertation, p. 217.

14. *Ibid.*, p. 218.

15. *Kalmykia during the War*, document no. 94, pp. 149–50.

16. Kichikov, dissertation, p. 222.

17. J. Hoffman, *Deutsche und Kalmuken, 1942 bis 1945* (Freiburg, 1974), p. 104.

18. Mühlen, p. 126.

19. *Kalmykia during the War*, document no. 94, p. 151.

20. Hoffman, p. 76.

21. Hoffman, pp. 27–28; Mühlen, p. 122.

22. Kichikov, dissertation, p. 234.

23. Hoffman, p. 122.

24. Kichikov, dissertation, p. 233.

25. Hoffman, p. 180.

26. *Ibid.*, p. 179.

27. A January 12, 1943, memorandum from the Kalmyk regional committee to the Central Committee of the party states that "the demagogic policies of the fascists in the city and the rural areas were quite unique." See M. L. Kichikov, "O nekotorykh voprosakh istorii Kalmykii v gody Velikoi Otechestvennoi voiny" [Certain problems of the history of Kalmykia during the Great Patriotic War], in the *Uchenye zapiski* [Proceedings] of the Kalmyk Scientific Research Institute of Language, Literature, and History, History Series No. 6 (Elista, 1968), p. 174. Hereafter cited as Kichikov (1968).

28. *Ibid.*, pp. 174–75.

29. *Kalmykia during the War*, document no. 94, p. 150.

30. *Ibid.*, document no. 140, p. 226.

31. M. L. Kichikov, *Vo imia pobedy nad fashizmom. Ocherki istorii Kalmytskoi ASSR v gody Velikoi Otechestvennoi voiny* [For victory over fascism: essays in the history of the Kalmyk ASSR during the Great

Patriotic War] (Elista, 1970), p. 121. Hereafter cited as Kichikov (1970).

32. Hoffman, pp. 23, 28, 29.

33. Mühlen, pp. 188–89.

34. *Kalmykia during the War,* document no. 94, p. 150.

35. Hoffman, p. 62.

36. *Ibid.,* p. 65.

37. Kichikov (1970), p. 233.

38. Hoffman, pp. 130–34.

39. Kichikov (1968), p. 173.

40. *Kalmykia during the War,* document no. 94, p. 151 (from a memorandum of the Kalmyk regional committee to the Central Committee of the party on the military and political situation in the Kalmyk ASSR, dated Astrakhan, November 18, 1942).

41. Kichikov, dissertation, p. 241.

42. *Ibid.,*

43. Hoffman, p. 136.

44. *Ibid.,* pp. 187–88 (notes on an interview with Doll by Lieutenant General Shartov, Colonel Khan, and others on June 20, 1943, in Dniepropetrovsk, regarding the Kalmyk formation of Dr. Doll; dated July 21, 1943).

45. *Ibid.,* p. 136.

46. *Ibid.,* pp. 118, 121, 148, 153.

47. *Kalmykia during the War,* p. 227.

48. Hoffman, p. 168.

49. Kichikov, dissertation, p. 312.

50. Kichikov (1968), p. 177.

51. Kichikov, dissertation, p. 66.

52. *Ibid.,* pp. 319–20.

53. *Ibid.,* p. 320.

54. *Ibid.,* p. 190.

55. *Essays in the History of the Kalmyk ASSR,* p. 306.

56. *Kalmykia during the War,* document no. 94, p. 152.

57. Kichikov, dissertation, p. 324. (The archival references for this document are "regional party archive of the Kalmyk ASSR, collection 1, shelf 3, file 456, sheets 166–94." Kichikov summarizes this twenty-eight-page document in an extremely laconic way.)

58. *Ibid.,* pp. 324–25.

59. *Ibid.,* p. 325.

60. *Ibid.,* p. 326 (regional party archive of the Kalmyk ASSR, collection 1, shelf 3, file 456, sheet 274).

61. *Ibid.,* p. 333.

62. *Ibid.,* p. 334.

63. *Ibid.,* p. 74.

64. *Ibid.*, p. 90.
65. *Ibid.*, p. 152.
66. *Ibid.*, p. 335.
67. *Ibid.*, p. 334.
68. *Essays in the History of the Kalmyk ASSR*, p. 309.
69. S. Sulkevich, *Territoriia i naselenie SSSR* [The territory and population of the USSR] (Moscow, 1940), p. 16.
70. Dallin, p. 248.

CHAPTER IV

1. Georgy Gulia, *Dmitrii Gulia. Povest' o moem ottse* [Dmitry Gulia: The story of my father] (Moscow, 1962), pp. 214–15.
2. *Groznenskii rabochii*, February 25, 1944.
3. *Ibid.*, March 3, 1944.
4. *Ibid.*, March 4, 1944.
5. S. M. Shtemenko, *General'nyi shtab v gody voiny* [The general staff during the war years] (Moscow, 1968), pp. 221–22.
6. *Izvestia*, June 26, 1946.
7. Khutuyev, dissertation, p. 97.
8. Kulayev, p. 180.
9. *Vneshniaia politika Sovetskogo Soiuza v period Otechestvennoi voiny* [The foreign policy of the Soviet Union during the Patriotic War], vol. 2 (Moscow, 1946), p. 50.
10. "Privetstvie I. V. Stalina Piku i Grotevoliu po sluchaiu obrazovaniia GDR" ["Stalin's greetings to Pieck and Grotewohl on the formation of the German Democratic Republic, October 13, 1949"], in *Vneshniaia politika Sovetskogo Soiuza. 1949 god.* [Foreign policy of the Soviet Union: 1949] (Moscow, 1953), p. 28.
11. *Foreign Relations of the U.S.A.: The Conferences at Cairo and Teheran* (Washington, D.C., 1963), p. 583 (notes of Major Boettiger).
12. Robert Conquest, *The Soviet Deportation of Nationalities* (London, 1960), pp. 87–88.
13. J. V. Stalin, *Sochineniia* [Works], 13 vols. (Moscow, 1946–52), vol. 5, p. 272.
14. V. I. Lenin, "K voprosu o natsional'nostiakh ili ob 'avtonomizatsii'" [On the question of nationalities or "autonomization"], in *Polnoe sobranie sochinenii* [Collected works], 55 vols. (Moscow, 1958–65), vol. 45, pp. 356–62.
15. *Ibid.*, p. 359.
16. *Ibid.*
17. *Ibid.*, p. 362.
18. Stalin, *Sochineniia*, vol. 5, p. 282.
19. USSR Academy of Sciences, Institute of History, *Kolokol* [The

bell], 4th reprint ed. (Moscow, 1962). For the issue of *Kolokol* cited here, No. 117 (1861), see pp. 976–77 of this reprint.

20. Ye. Markov, *Ocherki Kryma* [Crimean essays] (St. Petersburg and Moscow, 1902), pp. 103–4.

21. N. A. Smirnov, *Politika Rossii na Kavkaze v XVI–XIX vekakh.* [Russian policy in the Caucasus from the 16th to 19th centuries] (Moscow, 1958).

22. From the "Appeal of the Crimean Tatar People to the Twenty-Third Congress of the Communist Party of the Soviet Union," in Muzafarov, p. 105. The appeal was addressed to the Presidium of the Central Committee.

23. *Ibid.*

24. From the October 14, 1944, memorandum from First Secretary Tiulayev of the Crimean regional committee to the Central Committee, in Muzafarov, p. 67.

25. *Khronika tekushchikh sobytii* (New York, 1974), p. 146.

26. Khutuyev, dissertation, p. 106.

27. *Essays in the History of the Kalmyk ASSR*, pp. 317–18.

28. Khutuyev, dissertation, pp. 106–7.

29. *Ibid.*, p. 103.

30. Kulayev, p. 181.

31. Khutuyev, dissertation, p. 103.

32. Kh. I. Khutuyev, "Balkarskii narod v gody Velikoi Otechestvennoi voiny i poslevoennyi period" [The Balkar people during the Great Patriotic War and postwar period] (author's abstract, Rostov-on-Don, 1965), p. 12. Hereafter cited as Khutuyev, author's abstract.

33. Muzafarov, pp. 104–5.

34. *Ibid.*, p. 105.

35. Khutuyev, dissertation, p. 103.

36. A. Kh. Dudayev, "Vozniknovenie i osnovnye etapy stanovleniia Checheno-Ingushskoi natsional'noi sovetskoi gosudarstvennosti" [The origin and main formative stages of the Chechen-Ingush national Soviet state structure] (dissertation, Moscow University, Faculty of Law, 1964), p. 186.

37. *Ibid.*

38. *Ibid.*

39. *Ibid.*

40. Khutuyev, dissertation, p. 102.

41. *Ibid.*

42. *Ibid.*, p. 112.

43. *Ibid.*, p. 102.

44. *Ibid.*

45. *Ibid.*, p. 105.

46. *Ibid.*, p. 103.
47. *Ibid.*, p. 107.
48. *Ibid.*
49. *Ibid.*, p. 108.
50. *Ibid.*, pp. 106–7.
51. *Ibid.*, p. 134.
52. *Ibid.*, p. 144.
53. Muzafarov, p. 107.
54. *Ibid.*
55. Khutuyev, dissertation, p. 198.
56. *Ibid.*, p. 110.
57. *Ibid.*, p. 118.
58. *Ibid.*, p. 124.
59. *Ibid.*, p. 132.
60. *Ibid.*, p. 138.
61. *Ibid.*, p. 113.
62. D.-Ts. D. Nominkhanov, "Kul'turnoe stroitel'stvo v sovetskoi Kalmykii (1917–1967 gg.)" [Cultural work in Soviet Kalymkia (1917–1967)] (dissertation, Academy of Social Sciences under the CPSU Central Committee, Department of the History of Soviet Society, Moscow, 1967), p. 177. Hereafter cited as Nominkhanov, dissertation.
63. *Ibid.*
64. Khutuyev, dissertation, pp. 114–15.
65. Nominkhanov, dissertation, p. 184.
66. *Ibid.*, p. 190.
67. *Essays in the History of the Kalmyk ASSR,* pp. 330–31.
68. Nominkhanov, dissertation, p. 191.
69. *Ibid.*, p. 164.
70. *Istoriia Kabardino-Balkarskoi ASSR s Velikoi Oktiabr'skoi sotsialisticheskoi revoliutsii do nashikh dnei* [The history of the Kabardino-Balkar ASSR from the Great October Socialist Revolution to the present], vol. 2 (Moscow, 1967), p. 287.
71. *Essays in the History of the Kabardino-Balkar Organization of the CPSU,* p. 242.
72. Khutuyev, dissertation, p. 163.
73. *Ibid.*, pp. 164–68.
74. *Khrushchev Remembers,* pp. 346–49.
75. Khutuyev, dissertation, p. 168.
76. *Ibid.*, p. 170.
77. *Ibid.*, p. 171.
78. *Khrushchev Remembers,* pp. 596–7.
79. Khutuyev, dissertation, p. 171.
80. *Ibid.*, p. 175.

81. *Ibid.*, p. 178.

82. *Vedomosti Verkhovnogo Soveta SSSR* [Bulletin of the USSR Supreme Soviet], February 24, 1957, no. 4 (871), p. 134.

CHAPTER V

1. *Stavropol'skaia pravda*, March 22, 1957.

2. See Korkmasova, p. 498.

3. *Stavropol'skaia pravda*, March 27, 1957.

4. M. M. Bekizhev, "Partiinoe rukovodstvo kul'turnym stroitel'stvom v Karachaevo-Cherkesii (1920–1967 gg.)" [Party direction of cultural work in Karachai-Cherkessia (1920–1967)] (dissertation, Piatigorsk State Pedagogical Institute of Foreign Languages, Department of CPSU History, 1969), p. 164.

5. *Ibid.*, p. 166.

6. *Zasedaniia Verkhovnogo Soveta Kabardino-Balkarskoi ASSR chetvertogo sozyva (piataia sessiia), 28–29 marta 1957 g. Stenograficheskii otchet* [Proceedings of the Fourth Supreme Soviet of the Kabardino-Balkar ASSR (fifth session), March 20–28, 1957: stenographic record], (Nalchik, 1957), pp. 4–5.

7. *Kabardino-Balkarskaia pravda*, April 10, 1957.

8. *Ibid.*, May 21, 1957.

9. Khutuyev, dissertation, p. 237.

10. *Kabardino-Balkarskaia pravda*, August 24, 1957.

11. *Ibid.*, September 24, 1957.

12. Khutuyev, dissertation, p. 306.

13. *Narodnoe khoziaistvo Kabardino-Balkarskoi ASSR statisticheskii sbornik* [The national economy of the Kabardino-Balkar ASSR: a handbook] (Nalchik, 1964), p. 131.

14. *Ibid.*

15. *Bulletin of the USSR Supreme Soviet*, February 24, 1957, no. 4 (871), p. 134.

16. *Ibid.*, August 7, 1958, no. 17 (912), p. 694.

17. *Zasedaniia Verkhovnogo Soveta Kalmytskoi ASSR vtorogo sozyva, pervaia sessiia (28 oktiabria 1958 goda). Stenograficheskii otchet* [Proceedings of the Second Supreme Soviet of the Kalmyk ASSR, first session (October 28, 1958): stenographic record] (Elista, 1958), p. 31. Hereafter cited as *Proceedings of the Supreme Soviet of the Kalmyk ASSR* (1958). The present quotation is from the report by E. A. Satayev, chairman of the Council of Ministers of the Kalmyk ASSR.

18. *Essays in the History of the Kalmyk ASSR*, p. 353.

19. *Ibid.*

20. *Proceedings of the Supreme Soviet of the Kalmyk ASSR* (1958), p. 78.

21. *Ibid.*, p. 73.

22. *Ibid.*, p. 31.

23. *Essays in the History of the Kalmyk ASSR*, p. 366.

24. *Ibid.*, p. 329.

25. *Chetvertaia iubileinaia sessiia Verkhovnogo Soveta Kalmytskoi ASSR, 2. XI. 1940 g. Stenograficheskii otchet* [Fourth anniversary session of the Supreme Soviet of the Kalmyk ASSR, November 2, 1940: stenographic record] (Elista, 1941), p. 23. The quotation is from the speech by N. L. Garyaev, chairman of the Council of Ministers of the Kalmyk ASSR.

26. *Narodnoe khoziaistvo Kalmytskoi ASSR. Statisticheskii sbornik* [National economy of the Kalmyk ASSR: statistical handbook] (Elista, 1960), p. 117.

27. D.-Ts. D. Nominkhanov, *V edinoi sem'e* [All one family] (Elista, 1967), p. 67.

28. *Essays in the History of the Kalmyk ASSR*, pp. 330–31.

29. *Iubileinaia sessiia Verkhovnogo Soveta Kalmytskoi ASSR, posviashchennaia 40-letiiu ustanovleniia Sovetskoi vlasti, 29 oktiabria 1960 g. Stenograficheskii otchet* [Anniversary session of the Supreme Soviet of the Kalmyk ASSR celebrating forty years since the establishment of Soviet power, October 29, 1960: stenographic record] (Elista, 1961), pp. 57–58.

30. *Groznenskii rabochii*, December 24, 1957.

31. *Ibid.*

32. *Ibid.*, December 7, 1957.

33. *Ibid.*

34. *Ibid.*, June 15, 1957.

35. *Ibid.*, July 12, 1957.

36. Dzhuguryants, dissertation, p. 60.

37. *Groznenskii rabochii*, August 18, 1957.

38. See Dzhuguryants, dissertation.

39. *Ibid.*, p. 66.

40. *Ibid.*, p. 91.

41. *Ibid.*, p. 93.

42. *Ibid.*, p. 92.

43. *Ibid.*, p. 278.

44. *Ibid.*, p. 93.

45. *Groznenskii rabochii*, March 23, 1958.

46. *Ibid.*, August 25, 1957.

47. Dzhuguryants, dissertation, p. 278.

48. *Ibid.*, p. 96.

49. *Narodnoe khoziaistvo Checheno-Ingushskoi ASSR* [National economy of the Chechen-Ingush ASSR] (Grozny, 1963), p. 249.

50. *Zasedaniia Verkhovnogo Soveta Checheno-Ingushskoi ASSR, vtorogo sozyva* . . . [Proceedings of the Second Supreme Soviet of the Chechen-Ingush ASSR . . .] (Grozny, 1958), p. 61.

51. *Ibid.*, p. 151.

52. *Ibid.*, p. 161.

53. Dzhuguryants, dissertation, p. 193.

54. *Ibid.*, p. 189.

55. *Itogi vsesoiuznoi perepisi naseleniia 1959 g. SSSR. Svodnyi tom* [Results of the All-Union census of 1959 for the USSR: summary volume] (Moscow, 1962), p. 205.

56. Dzhuguryants, dissertation, p. 61.

57. *Groznenskii rabochii,* March 23, 1958.

58. Dzhuguryants, dissertation, p. 84.

59. *Groznenskii rabochii,* June 29, 1973.

60. *Ibid.,* April 3, 1973.

61. *Ibid.*

62. *Ibid.*

63. *Ibid.*

64. *Ibid.,* July 3, 1973.

65. *Ibid.,* April 3, 1973.

66. *Ibid.,* April 11, 1973.

67. *Ibid.*

68. *Ibid.*

69. *Ibid.,* June 27, 1973.

70. *Ibid.,* August 3, 1973.

71. *Ibid.,* April 3, 1973.

72. *Ibid.*

73. *Ibid.,* June 30, 1974.

74. *Ibid.,* March 18, 1975. Professor K. Yefanov holds a doctorate in history and is head of the department of CPSU history at the Chechen-Ingush State University.

75. *Ibid.,* June 27, June 28, and August 4, 1973.

76. *Ibid.,* May 19, 1975.

77. *Ibid.,* October 27, 1973.

78. *Ibid.,* March 27, 1973.

79. *Naselenie SSSR. Spravochnik* [The population of the USSR: a handbook] (Moscow, 1974), pp. 92–93.

80. *Groznenskii rabochii,* June 28, 1973.

81. *Ibid.,* November 30, 1973.

82. *Ibid.*

83. *Ibid.,* June 30, 1974.

CHAPTER VI

1. *Krasnyi Krym,* February 18, 1944 (an article by P. Chursin entitled "Volki v ovech'ei shkure" [Wolves in sheep's clothing]).

2. *Voprosy istorii* [Problems of history], 1948, No. 12, pp. 179–84. (A report on the conference mentions Chursin's statement in general terms.)

3. P. Nadinsky, *Ocherki po istorii Kryma* [Essays in the history of the Crimea], part 1 (Simferopol, 1951), p. 98.

4. *Ibid.*

5. *Krym v period Velikoi Otechestvennoi voiny 1941–1945 gg.* [The Crimea during the Great Patriotic War, 1941–1945] (Simferopol, 1973). (Compiled by I. Kondranov, curator of the Crimean region party archive, and A. Stepanova, research fellow.)

6. G. Babichev, *Komsomol'tsy Kryma—aktivnye pomoshchniki partii v Velikoi Otechestvennoi voine (1941–1944)* [Komsomols of the Crimea—active helpers of the party during the Great Patriotic War (1941–1944)], author's abstract of a dissertation in history (Kiev, 1959), p. 21.

7. *Sbornik Zakonov SSSR i Ukazov Presidiuma Verkhovnogo Soveta SSSR, 1938–1967* [Collection of Laws of the USSR and Decrees of the Presidium of the USSR Supreme Soviet, 1938–1967], (Moscow, 1968), p. 165.

8. *Ibid.,* pp. 166–67.

9. *Khronika tekushchikh sobytii,* p. 133.

10. *Iubileinai sessiia Verkhovnogo Soveta Krymskoi ASSR. 6 noiabria 1940 g. Stenograficheskii otchet* [Anniversary session of the Supreme Soviet of the Crimean ASSR, November 6, 1940: stenographic record] (Simferopol, 1941), pp. 19–21.

11. V. I. Lenin, *Polnoe sobranie sochinenii* [Collected works], vol. 30, p. 36.

NOTE ON SOURCES

1. A. Kh. Dudayev, "Vozniknovenie i osnovnye etapy stanovleniia Checheno-Ingushskoi natsional'noi sovetskoi gosudarstvennosti" [The origin and main formative stages of the Chechen-Ingush national Soviet state structure] (dissertation, Moscow University, Faculty of Law, 1964).

2. Kh. I. Khutuyev, "Balkarskii narod v gody Velikoi Otechestvennoi voiny i poslevoennyi period (Vosstanovlenie avtonomii balkarskogo naroda)" [The Balkar people during the Great Patriotic War and the postwar period (the restoration of the autonomy of the Balkar people)] (dissertation, Rostov State University, 1965).

3. Kh. I. Khutuyev, "Balkarskii narod v gody Velikoi Otechestvennoi

218 NOTES (pages 196–197)

voiny i poslevoennyi period'' [The Balkar people during the Great Patriotic War and postwar period] (author's abstract, Rostov-on-Don, 1965).

4. D.-Ts. D. Nominkhanov, ''Kul'turnoe stroitel'stvo v sovetskoi Kalmykii (1917–1967 gg.)'' [Cultural work in Soviet Kalymkia (1917–1967)] (dissertation, Academy of Social Sciences under the CPSU Central Committee, Department of the History of Soviet Society, Moscow, 1967).

5. D.-Ts. D. Nominkhanov, *V edinoi sem'e* [All one family] (Elista, 1967). Also *Ocherki po istorii kul'tury kalmytskogo naroda* [Essays in the history of the culture of the Kalmyk people] (Elista, 1969).

6. S. N. Dzhuguryants, ''Deiatel'nost' Checheno-Ingushskoi partiinoi organizatsii po osushchestvleniiu leninskoi natsional'noi politiki na osnove reshenii XX i XXII s''ezdov KPSS (1956–1965)'' [The activity of the Chechen-Ingush party organization in implementing Leninist national policy on the basis of the decisions of the 20th and 22nd CPSU congresses (1956–1965)] (dissertation, Dagestan State University, Makhachkala, 1966).

7. S. N. Dzhuguryants, *Osushchestvlenie leninskoi natsional'noi politiki v Checheno-Ingushetii na osnove reshenii XX s''ezda KPSS.* [The implementation of Leninist national policy in Checheno-Ingushetia on the basis of the decisions of the 20th CPSU congress] (Grozny, 1965).

8. Ch. S. Kulayev, ''Partiinye organizatsii Karachaia i Cherkesii v period Velikoi Otechestvennoi voiny Sovetskogo Soiuza (1941–1945 gg.)'' [The party organizations of Karachai and Cherkessia during the Great Patriotic War in the Soviet Union (1941–45)] (dissertation, Voronezh State University, 1968).

9. M. M. Bekizhev, ''Partiinoe rukovodstvo kul'turnym stroitel'stvom v Karachaevo-Cherkesii (1920–1967 gg.)'' [Party direction of cultural work in Karachai-Cherkessia (1920–1967)] (dissertation, Piatigorsk State Pedagogical Institute of Foreign Languages, Department of CPSU History, 1969).

10. M. L. Kichikov, ''Sovetskaia Kalmykia v Velikoi Otechestvennoi voine 1941–1945 godov'' [Soviet Kalmykia during the Great Patriotic War] (dissertation, Leningrad State University imeni A. A. Zhdanov, 1972), p. 14.

11. *Kalmykiia v Velikoi Otechestvennoi voine, 1941–1945. Dokumenty i materialy* [Kalmykia during the Great Patriotic War, 1941–1945: documents and materials] (Elista, 1966).

12. *V boiakh za Don. Vospominaniia voinov 110 Otdel'noi Kalmytskoi kavaleriiskoi divizii* [Fighting for the Don: memoirs of soldiers of the 110th Special Kalmyk Cavalry Division], compiled and edited by M. L. Kichikov (Elista, 1969); *V boiakh za Severnyi Kavkaz. Vospominaniia voinov 110 Otdel'noi Kalmytskoi kavaleriiskoi divizii* [Fighting for the

Northern Caucasus: memoirs of soldiers of the 110th Special Kalmyk Cavalry Division], compiled and edited by M. L. Kichikov (Elista, 1973).

13. M. L. Kichikov, *Vo imia pobedy nad fashizmom. Ocherki istorii Kalmytskoi ASSR v gody Velikoi Otechestvennoi voiny* [For victory over fascism: essays in the history of the Kalmyk ASSR during the Great Patriotic War] (Elista, 1970).

14. K. D. Korkmasova, "Natsional'naia gosudarstvennost' v SSSR (osnovnye gosudarstvenno-pravovye problemy)" [National statehood in the USSR (fundamental problems of public law)] (dissertation, Rostov State University, Rostov-on-Don, 1971).

15. *Ocherki istorii Kalmytskoi ASSR. Epokha sotsializma* [Essays in the history of the Kalmyk ASSR: the epoch of socialism] (Moscow, 1970); *Ocherki istorii Checheno-Ingushskoi ASSR, 1917–1970 gody* [Essays in the history of the Chechen-Ingush ASSR, 1917–1970], vol. 2 (Grozny, 1972); *Istoriia Kabardino-Balkarskoi ASSR s Velikoi Oktiabr'skoi sotsialisticheskoi revoliutsii do nashikh dnei* [The history of the Kabardino-Balkar ASSR from the Great October Socialist Revolution to the present], vol. 2 (Moscow, 1967), *Ocherki istorii Kabardino-Balkarskoi organizatsii KPSS* [Essays in the history of the Kabardino-Balkar organization of the CPSU] (Nalchik, 1971); *Ocherki istorii Stavropol'skoi organizatsii KPSS* [Essays in the history of the Stavropol organization of the CPSU] (Stavropol, 1970).

16. *Narodnoe khoziaistvo Kabardino-Balkarskoi ASSR. Statisticheskii sbornik* [National economy of the Kabardino-Balkar ASSR: statistical handbook] (Nalchik, 1975); *Narodnoe khoziaistvo Kabardino-Balkarskoi ASSR* [National economy of the Kabardino-Balkar ASSR] (Nalchik, 1964); *50 let Kabardino-Balkarskoi ASSR. Statisticheskii sbornik* [Fifty years of the Kabardino-Balkar ASSR: statistical handbook] (Nalchik, 1971); *Spravochnik po narodnomu khoziaistvu i kul'ture Karachaevskoi avtonomnoi oblasti* [Guide to the economy and culture of the Karachai Autonomous Region] (Piatigorsk, 1939); *Sovetskii Karachai, 1920–1940* [Soviet Karachai, 1920–1940] (Mikoyan-Shakhar, 1940); *Narodnoe khoziaistvo Checheno-Ingushskoi ASSR. Statisticheskii sbornik* [National economy of the Chechen-Ingush ASSR: statistical handbook] (Grozny, 1957, 1963); *Narodnoe khoziaistvo Kalmytskoi ASSR. Statisticheskii sbornik* [National economy of the Kalmyk ASSR: statistical handbook] (Elista, 1960); *Kalmytskaia ASSR za 50 let sovetskoi vlasti. Statisticheskii sbornik* [The Kalmyk ASSR over the fifty years of Soviet power: statistical handbook] (Elista, 1967); S. Sulkevich, *Territoriia i naselenie SSSR* [Territory and population of the USSR] (Moscow, 1940); *Itogi vsesoiuznoi perepisi naseleniia 1959 g. SSSR. Svodnyi tom* [Results of the All-Union census of 1959 for the USSR: summary volume] (Moscow,

1962); *Itogi vsesoiuznoi perepisi naseleniia 1959 g Kirgizskaia SSSR* [Results of the 1959 census for the Kirgiz SSSR] (Moscow, 1963); *Itogi vsesoiuznoi perepisi naseleniia 1959 g. Kazakhskaia SSSR* [Results of the 1959 census for the Kazakh SSSR] (Moscow, 1962); *Itogi vsesoiuznoi perepisi naseleniia 1959 g. Uzbekskaia SSSR* [Results of the 1959 census for the Uzbek SSSR] (Moscow, 1962); *Itogi vsesoiuznoi perepisi naseleniia 1959 g. RSFSR* [Results of the 1959 census for the RSFSR] (Moscow, 1963); *Naselenie SSSR. Spravochnik* [The population of the USSR: a handbook] (Moscow, 1974).

17. V. I. Fiklin, *Partiinaia organizatsiia Checheno-Ingushetii v gody bor'by za uprochenie i razvitie sotsialisticheskogo obshchestva (1937–iun' 1941 gg.)* [The party organization in Checheno-Ingushetia during the struggle for the consolidation and development of socialist society (1937–June 1941)] (Grozny, 1961); V. I. Filkin, *Checheno-Ingushskaia partiinaia organizatsiia v gody Velikoi Otechestvennoi voiny Sovetskogo Soiuza* [The Chechen-Ingush party organization during the Great Patriotic War of the Soviet Union] (Grozny, 1960).

18. R. I. Muzafarov, "Vdali ot krymskikh gor. Anatomiia deportatsii" [Far from the Crimean hills: anatomy of a deportation], manuscript (Moscow, 1974).

19. *XX s''ezd Kommunisticheskoi partii Sovetskogo Soiuza. Stenograficheskii otchet* [20th Congress of the Communist Party of the Soviet Union: stenographic record], vols. 1–3 (Moscow, 1956); *XXII s''ezd Kommunisticheskoi partii Sovetskogo Soiuza. Stenograficheskii otchet* [22nd Congress of the Communist Party of the Soviet Union: stenographic record], vols. 1–3 (Moscow, 1962).

20. *Khrushchev Remembers* (Boston, 1970).

21. *Zasedaniia Verkhovnogo Soveta Kabardino-Balkarskoi ASSR chetvertogo sozyva (piataia sessiia), 28–29 marta 1957 g. Stenograficheskii otchet* [Proceedings of the Fourth Supreme Soviet of the Kabardino-Balkar ASSR (fifth session), March 20–28, 1957: stenographic record], (Nalchik, 1957); *Iubileinaia sessiia Verkhovnogo Soveta Checheno-Ingushskoi ASSR, posviashchennaia 40-letiiu okonchatelnogo utverzhdeniia sovetskoi vlasti v Checheno-Ingushskoi ASSR* [Anniversary session of the Supreme Soviet of the Chechen-Ingush ASSR, celebrating forty years since final consolidation of Soviet power in Checheno-Ingushetia] (Grozny, 1960); *Zasedaniia Verkhovnogo Soveta Checheno-Ingushskoi ASSR vtorogo sozyva (pervaia sessiia), 15–16 aprelia 1958 g. Stenograficheskii otchet* [Proceedings of the Second Supreme Soviet of the Chechen-Ingush ASSR (first session), April 15–16, 1958: stenographic record] (Grozny, 1958); *Chetvertaia iubileinaia sessiia Verkhovnogo Soveta Kalmytskoi ASSR, 2. XI. 1940 g. Stenograficheskii otchet* [Fourth anniversary session of the Supreme

Soviet of the Kalmyk ASSR, November 2, 1940: stenographic record]
(Elista, 1941); *Zasedaniia Verkhovnogo Soveta Kalmytskoi ASSR vtorogo sozyva, pervaia sessiia (28 oktiabria 1958 goda)*. *Stenograficheskii
otchet* [Proceedings of the Second Supreme Soviet of the Kalmyk ASSR,
first session (October 28, 1958): stenographic record] (Elista, 1958).
*Iubileinaia sessiia Verkhovnogo Soveta Kalmytskoi ASSR,
posviashchennaia 40-letiiu ustanovleniia Sovetskoi vlasti, 29 oktiabria
1960 g. Stenograficheskii otchet* [Anniversary session of the Supreme
Soviet of the Kalmyk ASSR celebrating forty years since the establishment of Soviet power, October 29, 1960: stenographic record] (Elista,
1961).

22. *Krym v period Velikoi Otechestvennoi voiny 1941 1945 gg.* [The
Crimea during the Great Patriotic War, 1941–1945] (Simferopol, 1973).

23. A. Dallin, *German Rule in Russia, 1941–1945: A Study of Occupation Policies* (London, 1957).

24. Robert Conquest, *The Soviet Deportation of Nationalities* (London, 1960).

25. M. Luther, *Die Krim unter deutscher Besatzung im zweiten
Weltkrieg*, in *Forschungen zur Osteuropäischen Geschichte*
(Berlin,1956), vol. 3, pp. 28–98; Patrik von zur Mühlen, *Zwischen
Hakenkreuz and Sowjetstern: Der Nationalsozialismus der sowjetischen
Orientvölker im zweiten Weltkrieg* (Dusseldorf, 1971); D. Littlejohn, *The
Patriotic Traitors;* J. Hoffman, *Deutsche und Kalmuken, 1942 bis 1945*
(Freiburg, 1974); R. Gehlen, *Der Dienst: Erinnerungen, 1942–1971*
(Mainz, 1971; E. Kirimal, *Der nationale Kampf der Krimtürken* (Ems-
detten, 1952).

26. *Dokumenty ministerstva inostrannykh del Germanii. Vypusk II:
Germanskaia politika v Turtsii (1941–1943 gg.)* [Documents of the
Foreign Ministry of Germany. Issue II: German policy in Turkey
(1941–1943)] (Moscow, 1946).

27. *Trial of the Major War Criminals before the International Military
Tribunal*, vol. XXXVIII (Nuremberg, 1949).

28. *Trials of War Criminals before the Nuremberg Military Tribunals
under Control Council Law No. 10*, vol. IV (Ohlendorf) (Washington,
D.C., 1952).

29. *Akten zur Deutschen auswärtigen Politik, 1918–1945*. Series E:
1941–1945, vols. 1–2 (Göttingen, 1964–1972).

Index

Abdakhanova, Alime, 171
Abkhazians, deportation of, 105
Abliakim, Kandar, 27
Adzhimambetova, Adzhigulsum, 117
Aedinov, Abliaz, 34
Agayev, Seidali, 171
Aidayev, Yu., 162
Akhokhov (party official), 64–65
Akhriyev, D., 162
Aliadin, Shamil, 28, 111, 117
Aliyev, A., 33
Alkhastov (Caucasian bandit), 53
Alkhoyev (nationalist), 161
All-Union Conference of Historians, 194–95
Altai region, *see* special settlements and deportations
Andizhan uprising, 102
Andreyev, Andrei Andreevich, 97
Andreyevna, Yelena, 86–87
Andzheyevsky (collaborator), 32
Apriatkin, S. S., 160, 161, 162, 163, 166

Arksamakov (nationalist), 161
Armenia, Armenians, 26, 37
  in Chechen-Ingush ASSR, 43
  deportation of, 11, 105, 105n, 133
  legions and battalions, 9
  in partisan units, 33, 172
Asanova, Elmas, 170
Asmanov, Nuri, 28
AUCP(B) (All Union Communist Party
  [Bolsheviks])
  Central Committee, 50, 54, 80
  Central Committee Orgburo, 65
  Crimean regional committee, 30
  Grozny regional committee, 88
  Kabardinian regional committee, 63, 65
  "On Measures to Protect Socialized Lands from Being Sold Off," 51
  "Short Course of the History of the AUCP(B)," 55
  see also CPSU
Avars, 60, 149